Hometown Inequality

Local governments play a central role in American democracy, providing essential services such as policing, water, and sanitation. Moreover, Americans express great confidence in their municipal governments. But is this confidence warranted?

Using big data and a representative sample of American communities, this book provides the first systematic examination of racial and class inequalities in local politics. We find that nonwhites and less affluent residents are consistent losers in local democracy. Residents of color and those with lower incomes receive less representation from local elected officials than do whites and the affluent. Additionally, they are much less likely than privileged community members to have their preferences reflected in local government policy. Contrary to the popular assumption that governments that are "closest" govern best, we find that inequalities in representation are most severe in suburbs and small towns. Typical reforms do not seem to improve the situation, and we recommend new approaches.

BRIAN F. SCHAFFNER is Newhouse Professor of Civic Studies at Tufts University. He is coauthor of *Campaign Finance and Political Polarization: When Purists Prevail*, which was the winner of the 2016 Virginia Gray Best Book Award. He is also coeditor of *Winning with Words: The Origins and Impact of Political Framing* and coauthor of *Understanding Political Science Research Methods: The Challenge of Inference*. His research has appeared in more than forty peer-reviewed journal articles and has received over $2 million in external grant funding.

JESSE H. RHODES is Professor of Political Science and Department Chair at the University of Massachusetts Amherst and Associate Director of the UMass Poll. His research focuses on struggles over policy development and the consequences of these battles for politics and citizenship. He is the author of *An Education in Politics: The Origin and Development of No Child Left Behind* and *Ballot Blocked: The Political Erosion of the Voting Rights Act*, along with more than twenty peer-reviewed journal articles.

RAYMOND J. LA RAJA is Professor of Political Science and Associate Dean of the College of Social and Behavioral Sciences at the University of Massachusetts Amherst and Associate Director of the UMass Poll. His research focuses on political parties, political participation, and campaign finance. He is coauthor of *Campaign Finance and Political Polarization: When Purists Prevail*, which was the winner of the 2016 Virginia Gray Best Book Award. He is also a coauthor on policy reports from the Brookings Institution. He is founding editor of *The Forum*, a journal on American politics, and past president of the Political Organizations and Parties section of the American Political Science Association.

Hometown Inequality

Race, Class, and Representation in American Local Politics

BRIAN F. SCHAFFNER

Tufts University

JESSE H. RHODES

University of Massachusetts Amherst

RAYMOND J. LA RAJA

University of Massachusetts Amherst

CAMBRIDGE
UNIVERSITY PRESS

CAMBRIDGE
UNIVERSITY PRESS

University Printing House, Cambridge CB2 8BS, United Kingdom

One Liberty Plaza, 20th Floor, New York, NY 10006, USA

477 Williamstown Road, Port Melbourne, VIC 3207, Australia

314–321, 3rd Floor, Plot 3, Splendor Forum, Jasola District Centre, New Delhi – 110025, India

79 Anson Road, #06–04/06, Singapore 079906

Cambridge University Press is part of the University of Cambridge.

It furthers the University's mission by disseminating knowledge in the pursuit of education, learning, and research at the highest international levels of excellence.

www.cambridge.org
Information on this title: www.cambridge.org/9781108485944
DOI: 10.1017/9781108662550

First published 2020

A catalogue record for this publication is available from the British Library.

ISBN 978-1-108-48594-4 Hardback
ISBN 978-1-108-72537-8 Paperback

To every American who has struggled to make their
local government more responsive, just,
and equitable.

Contents

Figures

Tables

Acknowledgments

Throughout our careers as political scientists, we have each had a strong interest in studying local government. But the endeavor always seemed too challenging, particularly because it was often so difficult to get even the most basic data about communities and their elected officials. (One of us can even remember driving hours through cornfields just to photocopy precinct-level data on local elections from two communities.) Today, the data landscape in our discipline has been completely transformed. The past decade has witnessed a surge in scholarship seeking to understand inequalities in representation at the national and state level, but much less has been done to extend that work to local government. We saw an opportunity with the detailed voter file data that has recently become available to researchers and began developing the idea for this book.

This book was five years in the making. Even though data on local communities and elected officials is easier to collect than it once was, it is still not simple or straightforward. And much of the work was tedious and time-consuming. Catalist provided the core data on constituents and elected officials that we rely on in this book, and we are appreciative for their help along the way in helping us make sense of that data. In particular, Bob Blaemire and Jonathan Robinson have been helpful at various points in terms of answering our questions (or pointing us to those who have the answers). Of course, the fact that the Catalist data was available to us at all is due in large part to the pioneering efforts of Eitan Hersh to encourage Catalist to make their data available to the academic community. Eitan, Steve Ansolabehere, and Bernard Fraga have all been particularly influential by producing pathbreaking research using Catalist data. To the extent that this book succeeds in its implementation of this data, it is only because we were able to build on their work. Eitan and Bernard also patiently answered countless queries about best practices for using Catalist data and we cannot thank them enough for this help.

Compiling the data was itself an enormous task, and we benefited from the assistance of a large team of research assistants. In particular, we thank Jacob Edel, Cobi Frangillo, Stephen Ganley, Nicholas Hill, Josh Melton, Kim Phan, Nate Reynolds, and Noah Scott for helping to collect data on communities and elected officials. We especially thank Victoria Brandley and Ellie Davis who both did tremendous work on nearly every aspect of the data collection for the book. Finally, Saige Calkins and Greg Wall helped us finalize the book manuscript.

It also took time (and a lot of false starts) to figure out how to best tell the story that unfolded from our data. Thankfully, we had a lot of help along the way. We were extremely fortunate to have two top-notch discussants – Martin Gilens and Peter Enns – during one of our first presentations of this work. The following year we were again lucky to get abundant and insightful feedback from Adam Bonica. Chris Warshaw also provided very useful guidance when we shared an early version of our work with him. We are grateful to have had the opportunity to present this work at the University of North Carolina's American Politics Research Group and at Princeton's Center for the Study of Democratic Politics. The scholars at both venues provided valuable input at a particularly important time during the development of the book. We received further strong encouragement from APSA Class and Inequality Section members Tali Mendelberg and Eleanor Neff Powell, who (along with section chair Nick Carnes) awarded us the Section's "Best Paper Award" in 2017 for research from this book. And, of course, our editor, Sara Doskow, and the anonymous reviewers provided us with excellent guidance to help bring this book to completion.

Of course, our colleagues at the University of Massachusetts Amherst (UMass) were especially crucial for the success of this project. It is impossible to recall how many times we presented or discussed this work with the American Politics Research Group at UMass, but we could not have completed the book without their guidance along the way. We are especially grateful to Scott Blinder, Paul Collins, Justin Gross, Rebecca Hamlin, Paul Musgrave, Tatishe Nteta, Doug Rice, Meredith Rolfe, and Elizabeth Sharrow. This book also would not have been possible without significant research support provided by the College of Social and

Behavioral Sciences at UMass. We especially thank Dean John Hird and Associate Dean Jen Lundquist for their support.

Finally, and most importantly, our families provided the consistent emotional support and encouragement necessary to sustain this five-year effort. We especially thank our wives, Mia, Megan, and Taryn.

Race, Class, and Representation in Local Government

Houston, Texas is a city of roughly 2.3 million people, located in the southeastern portion of the state, near Galveston Bay and the Gulf of Mexico. It has a dynamic economy, with two dozen Fortune 500 companies, the nation's second-most-active port, and significant energy, technology, aerospace, medical, and manufacturing sectors.[1] Although the city has a white-plurality population (37.3 percent of residents identify as white), it is very racially diverse, with 36.5 percent of residents identifying as Hispanic/Latino; 16.6 percent identifying as African American; 7.5 percent identifying as Asian; and 2 percent identifying as "Other."[2] Compared with many cities of similar size, Houston boasts an attractive combination of abundant jobs, affordable housing, and exciting cultural amenities.[3]

At least at first blush, Houston's economic dynamism and multiracial demographics make it seem like a modern-day success story – a place where "it's still possible to attain the American Dream."[4] Indeed, the city has experienced a dramatic transformation over the past four decades,

[1] "Business Overview," About Houston, City of Houston, www.houstontx.gov/abouthouston/business.html.

[2] "Facts and Figures," About Houston, Visit Houston, www.visithoustontexas.com/about-houston/facts-and-figures.

[3] Nona Willis Aronowitz, "I Wanted to Be Successful, and I Could Do That in Houston," *CityLab*, November 12, 2013, www.citylab.com/life/2013/11/i-wanted-be-successful-and-i-could-do-houston/7534.

[4] Tom Dart, "After Harvey, It's Clear the Secret of Houston's Success Has Also Been Its Downfall," *The Guardian*, September 4, 2017, www.theguardian.com/us-news/2017/sep/04/after-harvey-its-clear-the-secret-of-houstons-success-has-also-been-its-downfall.

more than doubling in size, diversifying rapidly, and transforming its economy from almost total dependence on oil to reliance on a wide array of industries and services.[5] Yet Houston is also a city with a difficult racial past – a past it still struggles to escape. Although it made a somewhat more graceful transition from the Jim Crow era than did many other southern cities, Houston remains heavily segregated on the basis of race, and economic and racial inequality have increased in recent decades.[6]

Indeed, in 2017 Houston was rocked by allegations of serious violations of federal housing rules by the city's mayor and city council members. In a memorandum dated January 11, 2017, the US Department of Housing and Urban Development (HUD) found that the city's elected officials violated the Civil Rights Act of 1964 by blocking a proposal to build a large affordable housing complex (known as "Fountain View") in the affluent Galleria neighborhood. HUD concluded that the decision by the mayor and city council was in significant part taken in response to opposition from white residents to the prospect of increasing racial and income diversity in the area. More generally, HUD found that the city's procedures for approving applications for tax credits to support development of low-income housing were "influenced by racially motivated opposition to affordable housing and perpetuate discrimination." Ultimately, HUD concluded, "the city's complete deference to local opposition perpetuates segregation by deterring developers from proposing projects in areas where they are likely to face opposition."[7] At the time of HUD's intervention, fully 97 percent of the city's Low-Income Housing Tax Credit developments were located in majority–minority census tracts.[8]

Rather than take decisive steps to address the concerns about residential segregation and lack of access to affordable housing raised in the HUD letter, the city's elected officials seemed eager to avoid disturbing the

---

[5] Tony Perrottet, "What Makes Houston the Next Great American City?" *Smithsonian Magazine*, July 2013, www.smithsonianmag.com/travel/what-makes-houston-the-next-great-american-city-4870584.

[6] Aaron Williams and Armand Emamdjomeh, "America Is More Diverse than Ever – but Still Segregated," *The Washington Post*, May 10, 2018, www.washingtonpost.com/graphics/2018/national/segregation-us-cities/?utm_term=.8235083dae7d; Jonathan Silver, "Houston's Income Inequality Spiked Higher than Anywhere Else in Texas," *CultureMap Houston*, May 2, 2019, http://houston.culturemap.com/news/city-life/04-30-19-houston-income-gap-inequality-growing-fastest-in-texas.

[7] Quoted in Megan Flynn, "Feds Find Houston's Housing Policies Perpetuate Segregation," *Houston Press*, January 16, 2017, www.houstonpress.com/news/feds-find-houstons-housing-policies-perpetuate-segregation-9111804.

[8] Flynn, "Feds Say Houston's Housing Policies Violate Civil Rights Act."

status quo. The city's mayor, Sylvester Turner – who is African American – insisted that his and the council's opposition to the project was based on its high projected cost rather than on white resistance to anticipated demographic changes.[9] More significantly, city officials lobbied incoming HUD Secretary Ben Carson – a Donald Trump appointee and staunch critic of federal fair housing rules – to drop the housing discrimination case against the city.[10] Carson was happy to comply. As a first step, Carson directed HUD to release Houston's federal housing funds, and certified that the city was acting in compliance with federal law.[11] Then, in March 2018, Carson announced a "voluntary compliance agreement" with the city that putatively "resolve[d]" the civil rights violations identified in the January 2017 HUD letter.[12]

The voluntary compliance agreement committed the city to encourage landlords in areas with good schools to rent to families with housing vouchers; set clearer policies to govern the city council's consideration of tax credit housing applications; and seek support from HUD to develop a comprehensive affordable housing plan.[13] However, the agreement did not require Houston officials to take decisive steps to establish affordable housing units in higher-income neighborhoods. Consequently, both Houston–area housing activists and former HUD officials savaged the agreement, claiming that it effectively amounted to an endorsement of racially discriminatory housing practices by Houston city officials and HUD. "Having concluded that Houston's generic policies keep that kind of [affordable] housing from being put in affluent, predominantly white, high-opportunity areas, the [voluntary compliance agreement] offers

[9] Alvaro "Al" Ortiz, "Turner Announces Agreement Resolving HUD's Investigation That Found Improprieties on Procedures for Low Income Housing Projects," *Houston Public Media*, March 9, 2018, www.houstonpublicmedia.org/articles/news/2018/03/09/272519/turner-announces-agreement-resolving-huds-investigation-that-found-improprieties-on-procedures-for-low-income-housing-projects.
[10] Rebecca Elliott, "City Asks HUD to Drop Housing Discrimination Case," *Houston Chronicle*, April 10, 2017, www.houstonchronicle.com/news/politics/houston/article/City-asks-HUD-to-drop-housing-discrimination-case-11064134.php.
[11] Kriston Capps, "In Houston, HUD Assailed for 'Government-Sponsored Segregation,'" *CityLab*, March 22, 2018, www.citylab.com/equity/2018/03/in-houston-hud-assailed-for-government-sponsored-segregation/556100.
[12] U.S. Department of Housing and Urban Development, *Voluntary Compliance Agreement between the U.S. Department of Housing and Urban Development Office of Fair and Equal Opportunity and the City of Houston, Texas*, 06-16-R001–6, 2018.
[13] Mike Morris, "HUD, Houston Come to Agreement on City's Affordable Housing Efforts," *Houston Chronicle*, March 9, 2018, www.houstonchronicle.com/news/houston-texas/houston/article/HUD-Houston-come-to-agreement-on-city-s-12742434.php.

nothing to undo the segregationist effect of Houston's policies," argued Michael Allen, counsel for Texas Housers, a local advocacy group. "Fundamentally, it does nothing to provide another Fountain View development. It does not provide any actual relief in the form of affordable housing in these high-quality neighborhoods."[14] Betsy Julian, a former HUD assistant secretary for fair housing, argued that the voluntary compliance agreement was "outrageous" because it failed to remediate in a serious way the problems identified in the original HUD report.[15] As Julian concluded, "I'm a little appalled that the government would enter into a compliance agreement that doesn't address those issues at all." Angered by the agreement, Texas Housers have sued HUD for failing to enforce existing civil rights laws.

The struggle over access to affordable housing in Houston raises fundamental questions about the quality of local democracy in the United States. How well (or poorly) are people of color and those with lower incomes represented by the local governments in their communities? What factors – institutional, social, and economic – influence the degree to which municipalities are responsive to the preferences of these disadvantaged groups? Why do historically disadvantaged groups receive considerable representation in some communities, while in others their preferences are largely ignored? And what, if anything, can citizens do to ensure that local governments better represent people of color and the less affluent?

In a "compound republic" like the United States – where responsibility for governing is shared among a national government, fifty state governments, and thousands of local governments – these are foundational questions.[16] Indeed, it is worth emphasizing the centrality of local governments in shaping Americans' general understanding of politics and democracy in the United States. Americans typically view local governments as "closest to the people" and thus most deserving of veneration and trust.[17] Local politics have also historically been viewed as above the fray of the ideological and partisan polarization that mar national and state politics, enabling more reasoned and informed deliberation of the

---

[14] Capps, "HUD Assailed."
[15] Morris, "Housing Efforts."
[16] Martha Derthick. *Keeping the Compound Republic: Essays on American Federalism.* Washington, DC: Brookings Institution Press, 2004.
[17] Justin McCarthy, "Americans Still More Trusting of Local than State Government, *Gallup*, October 8, 2018, https://news.gallup.com/poll/243563/americans-trusting-local-state-government.aspx.

merits of policy proposals.[18] Finally, the country's robust tradition of decentralization and local control means that local governments have traditionally served as a focal point of civic education, where citizens learn and practice the skills of self-government and obtain lessons about what government means in their lives.[19] If local government responsiveness – or lack thereof – affects citizens' interest in political participation or informs their beliefs about the performance of "government" in general, it is crucial that we better understand whether and to what extent local governments represent their constituents, and particularly less advantaged groups.[20]

Indeed, local governments play a central role in serving the needs of Americans. The United States has nearly 90,000 local governments, with hundreds of thousands of local elected officials. These governments employ more than 11 million workers, collect roughly 25 percent of the nation's tax revenues, and distribute many of the public goods that citizens use every day.[21] In many communities, they perform vital tasks that many citizens depend on but often take for granted, such as policing, trash disposal, water and sanitation services, and road maintenance. In short, local governments are the "frontline" governments that citizens interact with day in and day out. Given their central importance in Americans' daily experience of democracy, we need to know whether municipalities provide equitable representation to all their residents.

In fact, determining whether and to what extent local governments represent their residents is especially pressing today. The United States, like many advanced industrialized democracies in the Western world, is becoming both more racially and ethnically diverse and more economically unequal, creating a range of new and complex demands on municipalities.[22] At the same time, the impact of local government activity on the lives of citizens is growing markedly due to a paradoxical increase in *both*

---

[18] J. Eric Oliver, Shang E. Ha, and Zachary Callen. *Local Elections and the Politics of Small-Scale Democracy.* Princeton, NJ: Princeton University Press, 2012.

[19] Alexis de Tocqueville. *Democracy in America.* New York: Regnery Publishing, 2003.

[20] Jesse H. Rhodes. "Learning Citizenship? How State Education Reforms Affect Parents' Political Attitudes and Behavior." *Political Behavior* 37, no. 1 (2015): 181–220.

[21] Christopher Warshaw. "Local Elections and Representation in the United States." *Annual Review of Political Science* (2019), https://doi.org/10.1146/annurev-polisci-050317-071108.

[22] Robert D Putnam. "E Pluribus Unum: Diversity and Community in the Twenty-First Century: The 2006 Johan Skytte Prize Lecture." *Scandinavian Political Studies* 30, no. 2 (2007): 137–174; Larry M. Bartels. *Unequal Democracy: The Political Economy of the New Gilded Age.* Princeton, NJ: Princeton University Press, 2018.

the mandates issued by, and the devolution of significant responsibilities from, the federal government and the states.[23] The collision of increasing diversity and inequality, on one hand, and increasing local government responsibility, on the other, has drastically increased the range and complexity of tasks facing local governments today. This makes understanding whether and to what extent municipalities represent disadvantaged residents more important now than ever.

Finally, studying how well (or poorly) local governments serve the demands of less advantaged residents provides a powerful lens for examining questions about unequal representation in general.[24] Many scholars have expressed concern that American democracy fails to equitably represent the preferences of historically disadvantaged citizens – particularly people of color and the less affluent.[25] However, data limitations and

[23] Jessica Trounstine. "Representation and Accountability in Cities." *Annual Review of Political Science* 13 (2010): 407–423; Zoltan Hajnal and Jessica Trounstine. "Identifying and Understanding Perceived Inequities in Local Politics." *Political Research Quarterly* 67, no. 1 (2014): 56–70; Zoltan Hajnal and Jessica Trounstine. "What Underlies Urban Politics? Race, Class, Ideology, Partisanship, and the Urban Vote." *Urban Affairs Review* 50, no. 1 (2014): 63–99; Chris Tausanovitch and Christopher Warshaw. "Representation in Municipal Government." *American Political Science Review* 108, no. 3 (2014): 605–641; Linda Lobao. "The Rising Importance of Local Government in the United States: Recent Research and Challenges for Sociology." *Sociology Compass* 10, no. 10 (2016): 893–905.

[24] Patrick Flavin has made the similar point that studying cross-*state* variation in inequality in representation can help scholars better understand and explain unequal democracy in the United States. See Patrick Flavin. "Income Inequality and Policy Representation in the American States." *American Politics Research* 40, no. 1 (2012): 29–59.

[25] Bartels, *Unequal Democracy*; Martin Gilens. "Inequality and Democratic Responsiveness." *Public Opinion Quarterly* 69, no. 5 (2005): 778–796; Martin Gilens. *Affluence and Influence: Economic Inequality and Political Power in America*. Princeton, NJ: Princeton University Press, 2012; Christopher Ellis. "Social Context and Economic Biases in Representation." *The Journal of Politics* 75, no. 3 (2013): 773–786; Elizabeth Rigby and Gerald C. Wright. "Political Parties and Representation of the Poor in the American States." *American Journal of Political Science* 57, no. 3 (2013): 552–565; Martin Gilens and Benjamin I. Page. "Testing Theories of American Politics: Elites, Interest Groups, and Average Citizens." *Perspectives on Politics* 12, no. 3 (2014): 564–581; John D. Griffin and Brian Newman. "The Unequal Representation of Latinos and Whites." *The Journal of Politics* 69, no. 4 (2007): 1032–1046; John D. Griffin and Brian Newman. *Minority Report: Evaluating Political Equality in America*. Chicago: University of Chicago Press, 2008; Butler and Broockman, "Do Politicians"; James M. Avery and Jeffrey A. Fine. "Racial Composition, White Racial Attitudes, and Black Representation: Testing the Racial Threat Hypothesis in the United States Senate." *Political Behavior* 34, no. 3 (2012): 391–410; Daniel Q. Gillion. "Protest and Congressional Behavior: Assessing Racial and Ethnic Minority Protests in the District." *The Journal of Politics* 74, no. 4 (2012): 950–962; David E. Broockman. "Black Politicians Are More Intrinsically Motivated to Advance Blacks' Interests: A Field Experiment Manipulating Political

research design choices have, to date, largely prevented them from studying both racial and class biases in representation at the same time. And the relatively limited variation in social and institutional contexts at the federal and state levels has circumscribed understanding of how such factors may moderate, or exacerbate, biases in representation.[26] As we explain, our research design allows us to simultaneously examine both racial and class biases in representation, in a large sample of communities with very diverse social and institutional characteristics. This approach allows us to make direct comparisons of the respective scales of racial and class biases in representation at the local level, while also permitting new insights on how community characteristics can either reduce or increase these inequalities. As such, we are in an especially good position to assess how race and class influence responsiveness in American politics, and to identify practical courses of action for addressing inequities we observe.

Of course, many scholars have sought to understand how well local governments serve disadvantaged communities. Some have examined racial or class patterns of support for political candidates in an effort to assess who wins and who loses in municipal electoral democracy.[27] Others have investigated how racial diversity, economic inequality, or both, influence access to public jobs and spending on "public goods" like education or anti-poverty programs.[28] Still others have polled residents of different racial or class backgrounds to obtain their opinions of how well

Incentives." *American Journal of Political Science* 57, no. 3 (2013): 521–536; Zoltan L. Hajnal and Jeremy D. Horowitz. "Racial Winners and Losers in American Party Politics." *Perspectives on Politics* 12, no. 1 (2014): 100–118.

[26] These limitations in existing research on political inequalities in the United States are discussed at length in John Griffin, Zoltan Hajnal, Brian Newman, and David Searle. "Political Inequality in America: Who Loses on Spending Policy? When Is Policy Less Biased?" *Politics, Groups, and Identities* 7, no. 2 (2017): 367–385.

[27] Zoltan Hajnal and Jessica Trounstine. "Where Turnout Matters: The Consequences of Uneven Turnout in City Politics." *The Journal of Politics* 67, no. 2 (2005): 515–535; Zoltan Hajnal. *America's Uneven Democracy: Race, Turnout, and Representation in City Politics.* Cambridge: Cambridge University Press, 2009; Zoltan Hajnal and Jessica Trounstine. "Race and Class Inequality in Local Politics." In *The Double Bind: The Politics of Racial and Class Inequalities in the Americas*, eds. Rodney Hero, Juliet Hooker, and Alvin B. Tillery, Jr. Washington, DC: American Political Science Association, 2016.

[28] Peter K. Eisinger. *The Politics of Displacement: Racial and Ethnic Transition in Three American Cities.* New York: Academic Press, 1980; Kenneth R. Mladenka. "Blacks and Hispanics in Urban Politics." *American Political Science Review* 83, no. 1 (1989): 165–191; James M. Poterba. "Demographic Structure and the Political Economy of Public Education." *Journal of Policy Analysis and Management* 16, no. 1 (1997): 48–66; Claudia Goldin and Lawrence F. Katz. "The Origins of State-Level Differences

local governments serve the needs of diverse constituents.[29] And another group of scholars has used so-called audit experiments to investigate potential biases in the responsiveness of representatives to different groups of constituents.[30]

While each of these studies has, in its own way, advanced understanding of how local governments (fail to) represent their constituents, our goal is different. In this book, we seek to determine how well the *underlying preferences* of (different groups of) residents are reflected on municipal councils and in local government policy. As we argue throughout the book, focusing on the preferences of (groups of) residents – and how well or poorly they are represented on municipal councils and in local government policy – provides an intuitive and powerful lens for observing both the overall quality and the fairness of representative democracy at the local level.

Since our goal is to probe how well residents' preferences get represented at the municipal level, we need a direct measure of these preferences. This is not as straightforward a task as it might seem. In principle,

in the Public Provision of Higher Education: 1890–1940." *The American Economic Review* 88, no. 2 (1998): 303–308; Alberto Alesina, Reza Baqir, and William Easterly. "Public Goods and Ethnic Divisions." *The Quarterly Journal of Economics* 114, no. 4 (1999): 1243–1284; Erso F.P. Luttmer. "Group Loyalty and the Taste of Redistribution." *Journal of Political Economy* 109, no. 5 (2001): 500–528; Tim R. Sass and Stephen L. Mehay. "Minority Representation, Election Method, and Policy Influence." *Economics & Politics* 15, no. 3 (2003): 323–339; Sean Corcoran and William N. Evans. *Income Inequality, the Median Voter, and the Support for Public Education*, no. w16097, National Bureau of Economic Research, 2010; Leah Boustan, Fernando Ferreira, Hernan Winkler, and Eric M. Zolt. "The Effect of Rising Income Inequality on Taxation and Public Expenditures: Evidence from US Municipalities and School Districts, 1970–2000." *Review of Economics and Statistics* 95, no. 4 (2013): 1291–1302; Jessica Trounstine. "Segregation and Inequality in Public Goods." *American Journal of Political Science* 60, no. 3 (2016): 709–725.

[29] Ruth Hoogland DeHoog, David Lowery, and William E. Lyons. "Citizen Satisfaction with Local Governance: A Test of Individual, Jurisdictional, and City-Specific Explanations." *The Journal of Politics* 52, no. 3 (1990): 807–837; Gregg G. Van Ryzin, Douglas Muzzio, and Stephen Immerwahr. "Explaining the Race Gap in Satisfaction with Urban Services." *Urban Affairs Review* 39, no. 5 (2004): 613–632; Wendy M. Rahn and Thomas J. Rudolph. "A Tale of Political Trust in American Cities." *Public Opinion Quarterly* 69, no. 4 (2005): 530–560; Melissa J. Marschall and Anirudh V. S. Ruhil. "Substantive Symbols: The Attitudinal Dimension of Black Political Incorporation in Local Government." *American Journal of Political Science* 51, no. 1 (2007): 17–33; Hajnal and Trounstine, "Identifying and Understanding Perceived Inequities."

[30] Butler and Broockman, "Do Politicians"; Daniel M. Butler and Adam M. Dynes. "How Politicians Discount the Opinions of Constituents with Whom They Disagree." *American Journal of Political Science* 60, no. 4 (2016): 975–989.

we could ask residents in a survey about their voting decisions and policy preferences and then observe who gets elected and what policies they pursue. The fundamental challenge with that approach, however, is the overwhelming cost of surveying so many residents and elected officials across hundreds of communities. Moreover, residents may not necessarily be familiar with all the candidates and specific policies, even if they have latent preferences about both. Finally, comparisons across communities would be exceedingly difficult because candidates and policies can be so different across far-flung communities within the United States.

What we need, then, is a concept that taps into individuals' desires and preferences that might tell us something about the *kinds* of candidates and *kinds* of policies residents might prefer across a range of choices. The concept of *ideology* is well suited for this. Political scientists see ideology as a set of interconnected and stable beliefs that compose an individual's worldview.[31] This ideology can predict more specific attitudes and behaviors in politics, such as preferences in certain policy areas or predilections for particular candidates. To be sure, the concept of ideology is an imperfect distillation of individuals' preferences. People are complicated, and the world is even more complex. But research shows that individuals draw on ideologies in predictable ways to make sense of the world and their place in it.[32] Whether used consciously or (more likely) unconsciously, ideology is a powerful organizing device used every day by individuals to make shortcut judgments about politics. It can help individuals choose among political alternatives, explain the way things are, or make claims about how politics should be.

Of course, few individuals are consistent ideologues. They may be "liberals" on one issue and "conservatives" on another. This is especially true of ordinary individuals, who are not always as consistent in their beliefs as political elites.[33] For instance, in a world comprising individuals of complete ideological consistency, a person who supports additional government spending on education would also support additional spending on health care. Clearly, this is not always the case, and scholars have arrived at more nuanced understandings of how Americans sort into

[31] Angus Campbell, Philip E. Converse, Warren E. Miller, and Donald E. Stokes. *The American Voter*. Ann Arbor: University of Michigan Press, 1960.

[32] John T. Jost, Christopher M. Federico, and Jaime L. Napier. "Political Ideology: Its Structure, Functions, and Elective Affinities." *Annual Review of Psychology* 60 (2009): 307–337.

[33] Philip E. Converse. "The Nature of Belief Systems in Mass Publics." In *Ideology and Discontent*, ed. David E. Aptor. New York: Free Press of Glencoe, 1964.

different clusters of political reasoning.[34] But despite these complexities, ideology is among the strongest and most consistent predictors of political preferences.[35] For example, simply knowing somebody's ideology – in the way we measure it for this book – would allow us to correctly predict their 2016 presidential vote choice with greater than 80 percent accuracy. Our ideology measure is also a strong predictor of peoples' positions on issues that often confront local governments, such as support for increasing funding for education, law enforcement, and infrastructure. Accordingly, we use ideology as a simple heuristic for tapping into underlying preferences about politics. In the next chapter we explain how we measure ideology among both municipal residents and among elected officials; for now, though, we focus on why we center attention on *ideological representation* as our key measure of the health of local democracy.

Ideological representation is central to contemporary understandings of democracy. As a first observation, Michael MacKuen, Robert Erikson, James Stimson, and Kathleen Knight suggest that

[t]he nature of democratic government depends in large part on citizens' and politicians' ability to communicate with each other about their preferences and actions. In the contemporary United States ... the shorthand language of "ideology" facilitates such conversation. Here by ideology, we mean the notions of liberalism and conservatism or left and right that are used in everyday political discourse.[36]

In short, ideology is essential for representation because it is a simple and direct way to facilitate meaningful communication between constituents and elected officials.

More pointedly, the idea of ideological representation – by elected officials of constituents – undergirds the core normative principle of democracy that the people are ultimately sovereign, and therefore should exercise "control" over their elected representatives.[37] When we assess

---

[34] Edward G. Carmines, Michael J. Ensley, and Michael W. Wagner. "Political Ideology in American Politics: One, Two, or None?" *The Forum* 10, no. 3 (2012): https://doi.org/10.1515/1540-8884.1526.

[35] William G. Jacoby. "Ideological Identification and Issue Attitudes." *American Journal of Political Science* 35, no. 1 (1991): 178–205. John T. Jost. "The End of the End of Ideology." *American Psychologist* 61, no. 7 (2006): 651–670.

[36] Michael B. MacKuen, Robert S. Erikson, James A. Stimson, and Kathleen Knight. "Elections and the Dynamics of Ideological Representation." In *Electoral Democracy*, eds. Michael B. MacKuen and George Rabinowitz. Ann Arbor: University of Michigan Press, 2003. 200.

[37] John Stuart Mill. *On Liberty: Collected Works of John Stuart Mill*, ed. J. Robson. Toronto: University of Toronto Press, 1965.

elected officials' representation of their constituents, we typically want to know "how close" representatives are to their constituents' political views, as well as "how responsive" they are to their constituents' demands.[38] All things being equal, representatives who are "closer" and "more responsive" to their constituents better conform to the principle of popular sovereignty than do those who are more distant and autonomous. In short, ideological representation captures both a key feature of how democracies operate in practice and a core normative principle of how elected officials should behave, thus making it a valuable lens for assessing representation at the local level.

While previous research on (un)equal representation at the municipal level has enriched our understanding of how local governments serve – or fail to serve – residents of color and the less well-to-do, none of these studies directly assesses how well the ideologies of disadvantaged groups are reflected in the *ideologies of local government officials* or the *overall ideological orientation of local government policy*. As Zoltan Hajnal and Jessica Trounstine, two preeminent scholars of local politics, note, evaluating the representation of group ideologies at the municipal level is typically bedeviled by two problems: Scholars "rarely have data on group preferences and government actions apart from a specific policy area or across a large number of communities"; and they typically want for measures that account for the "lack of unanimity [of opinion] within each group" being studied.[39] As we have noted, conventional sources of information about individuals' preferences – typically, surveys of public opinion – simply are not expansive enough to provide detailed measures of group ideologies across a wide array of diverse communities. Even studies that pool multiple surveys and use sophisticated methods such as multilevel regression and post-stratification to estimate resident ideologies in municipalities have, to date, lacked a sufficient number of observations to estimate racial and class group ideologies in most communities across the United States.[40]

---

[38] Warren E. Miller and Donald E. Stokes. "Constituency Influence in Congress." *American Political Science Review* 57, no. 1 (1963): 45–56; Larry M. Bartels. "Constituency Opinion and Congressional Policy Making: The Reagan Defense Buildup." *American Political Science Review* 85, no. 2 (1991): 457–474; Christopher H. Achen. "Measuring Representation." *American Journal of Political Science* 22, no. 3 (1978): 475–510; James A. Stimson, Michael B. MacKuen, and Robert S. Erikson. "Dynamic Representation." *American Political Science Review* 89, no. 3 (1995): 543–565.
[39] Hajnal and Trounstine, "Identifying and Understanding Perceived Inequalities," at 57–58.
[40] Warshaw, "Elections and Representation."

Focusing on ideological representation, this book provides a more rigorous and detailed assessment of the quality of representative democracy in local governments in the United States. We use advances in "big data" – specifically, data drawn from the Catalist database, a national database of demographic, political, and marketing information on over 240 million adults – to estimate the ideologies of various racial and class groups in hundreds of diverse communities from around the United States.[41] Using Catalist, we also estimate the ideologies of thousands of municipal councilors in the same communities. To measure the ideological orientation of local policy, we draw on surveys of municipal policy adoptions developed by the International City Managers Association (ICMA). These data allow us to evaluate directly how well or poorly the ideologies of different racial and class groups are represented in both the ideology of municipal councils (Catalist) and the ideology of local government policy (ICMA).

We combine these data with comprehensive information about the characteristics of local electoral and governing institutions to determine whether and how (1) the openness of local political institutions and (2) the "overlap" in ideologies – that is, shared ideological leanings – between various racial and class groups affect the representation received by less advantaged groups. We also incorporate data from the US Census to investigate how (3) patterns of economic and racial inequality within local communities affect the prospects for representation of the ideologies of disadvantaged groups.

Our research reveals several striking insights about the character of local democracy in the United States:

1   While some scholars and pundits have portrayed local politics as relatively nonideological (especially outside large cities), our research suggests just the opposite.[42] **We find remarkable variation**

[41] The characteristics of Catalist data are described at length in Stephen Ansolabehere and Eitan Hersh. "Validation: What Big Data Reveal about Survey Misreporting and the Real Electorate." *Political Analysis* 20, no. 4 (2012): 437–459; Eitan D. Hersh. *Hacking the Electorate: How Campaigns Perceive Voters*. Cambridge: Cambridge University Press, 2015; and Bernard L. Fraga. *The Turnout Gap: Race, Ethnicity, and Political Inequality in a Diversifying America*. Cambridge: Cambridge University Press, 2018.

[42] Oliver, Ha, and Callen, *Local Elections and the Politics of Small Scale Democracy*; Douglas W. Rae. *City: Urbanism and Its End*. New Haven, CT: Yale University Press, 2003; Fernando Ferreira and Joseph Gyourko. "Do Political Parties Matter? Evidence from US Cities." *The Quarterly Journal of Economics* 124, no. 1 (2009): 399–422; Michael A. Bailey and Mark Carl Rom. "A Wider Race? Interstate Competition across

in the ideologies of different racial and class groups within and across local communities. The United States is characterized by an extremely rich diversity of perspectives among whites and non-whites and among rich and poor, and this diversity is in evidence within many municipalities, including suburban communities and small towns. While this plurality of perspectives is a major source of national pride and strength, it also greatly increases the complexity of the task of representation facing local governments. Because many localities are quite diverse ideologically, providing equitable representation of diverse views is no easy task, even for the most conscientious elected officials. Furthermore, the presence of significant ideological diversity that falls along racial and/or class lines creates the potential for tensions between groups within communities.

2   Indeed, the challenges involved in representing a wide diversity of perspectives is plainly illustrated in our findings about how different groups are represented in their local communities. In a departure from recent studies that emphasize the responsiveness of local governments to the *average* resident, our research reveals systematic racial and class *biases* in representation in local government.[43] Whites and wealthier people receive substantially more ideological representation both from local government officials and from municipal policy outputs than do nonwhites and less wealthy individuals. The inequities in representation we identify are frequently shocking in their magnitude. For example, we find that it is only when blacks make up 80–100 percent of the community population that they receive the same amount of ideological representation from elected officials on municipal councils that whites attain when

Health and Welfare Programs." *The Journal of Politics* 66, no. 2 (2004): 326–347; Amalie Jensen, William Marble, Kenneth Scheve, and Mathew J. Slaughter, "City Limits to Partisan Polarization in the American Public," working paper, March 2019, https://williammarble.co/docs/CityLimits-Mar2019.pdf.

[43] Sang Ok Choi, Sang-Seok Bae, Sung-Wook Kwon, and Richard Feiock. "County Limits: Policy Types and Expenditure Priorities." *The American Review of Public Administration* 40, no. 1 (2010): 29–45; Christine Kelleher Palus. "Responsiveness in American Local Governments." *State and Local Government Review* 42, no. 2 (2010): 133–150; Tausanovitch and Warshaw, "Municipal Government"; Katherine Levine Einstein and Vladimir Kogan. "Pushing the City Limits: Policy Responsiveness in Municipal Government." *Urban Affairs Review* 52, no. 1 (2016): 3–32; Michael W. Sances, "When Voters Matter: The Growth and Limits of Local Government Responsiveness," working paper, August 2, 2017, https://astro.temple.edu/~tul67793/papers/polarization.pdf.

they represent only 20–40 percent of the population. Such findings –
which appear again and again in the pages that follow – raise
profound and difficult questions about the capacity of municipalities to represent the interests of less advantaged residents. Our
results suggest that the current trend toward political decentralization and reduced federal government authority in the United
States – itself part of a broader global drive toward government
decentralization – will likely hurt already vulnerable Americans
the most.[44]

3   **Of great importance to studies of inequality in American democracy, we find that racial biases in representation in local politics are
much larger and more pervasive than are economic biases.** In an era
of rising economic inequality, many scholars have understandably
focused attention on the relationship between affluence and influence in American politics. Yet, as we show in this book, at the local
level the magnitude and pervasiveness of racial biases in representation far exceed those based on wealth. These findings are consistent with an emergent literature on biases in representation in
national politics that directly compares inequities in representation
on the basis of race and class, respectively, which also finds that
racial biases are much more serious.[45] In highlighting the greater
severity of racial inequalities in representation, we hope to encourage scholars, activists, and ordinary citizens to face head-on the
deep-seated racial divides that pose such a difficult challenge to
American democracy.

4   Our work also suggests important – and quite troubling – conclusions about the respective roles of local political institutions, racial
inequality, and economic inequality in conditioning the representation received by less advantaged groups within communities. **We
find that while specific local political institutions that make local
politics more open and accessible – such as holding local elections
concurrently with federal ones – modestly reduce inequalities in
representation, the formal structure of local institutions plays a
very limited role in determining how much (or how little)**

---

[44] Roberto Ezcurra and Andrés Rodríguez-Pose. "Can the Economic Impact of Political
Decentralisation Be Measured?" *Centre for Economic Policy Research* (2011): https://
ideas.repec.org/p/imd/wpaper/wp2011–02.html.

[45] Griffin and Newman, "The Unequal Representation of Latinos and Whites"; Griffin and
Flavin, "Racial Differences in Information, Expectations, and Accountability"; Griffin,
Hajnal, Newman, and Searle, "Political Inequality in America."

representation nonwhite and less affluent people receive from local government. Of course, we encourage efforts by residents, activists, and local officials to institute reforms and experiment with novel institutions as ways to enliven the practice of local democracy. But our findings caution against excessive confidence in the efficacy of such institutional "fixes" to reduce racial and class biases in representation in local politics.

5   **Our research strongly suggests that the degree of "overlap" between the ideologies of less advantaged groups and the ideologies of advantaged groups plays a very important role in determining the amount of ideological representation enjoyed by the less fortunate.** When nonwhite groups (or less affluent groups) have similar ideologies to white groups (or wealthier residents), they receive considerable ideological representation from municipal councils and local government outputs. But when the ideologies of nonwhites (or less affluent residents) are distant from those of whites (or affluent residents), they receive little representation. This finding suggests that, due to the happy coincidence of overlapping ideologies between disadvantaged and advantaged groups, opportunities for substantial representation of the ideologies of nonwhite/less affluent residents in local politics and policy do exist.[46]

6   **However, such opportunities for "coincidental representation" are more available for some disadvantaged groups than for others.** For example, the ideologies of Latinos are on average much closer to the ideologies of whites than are the ideologies of African Americans, suggesting much greater opportunities for the coincidental representation of the ideologies of Latinos than of African Americans.[47] Of equal concern, the prospects for coincidental representation vary considerably – and in systematic ways – across communities. Indeed, we find that communities with the greatest racial inequities on socioeconomic benchmarks are also those with the worst prospects for coincidental representation, because these

[46] Peter K. Enns. "Relative Policy Support and Coincidental Representation." *Perspectives on Politics* 13, no. 4 (2015): 1053–1064; J. Alexander Branham, Stuart N. Soroka, and Christopher Wlezien. "When Do the Rich Win?" *Political Science Quarterly* 132, no. 1 (2017): 43–62.

[47] Jesse H. Rhodes, Brian F. Schaffner, and Sean McElwee. "Is America More Divided By Race or Class? Race, Income, and Attitudes among Whites, African Americans, and Latinos." *The Forum* 15, no. 1 (2017): www.degruyter.com/view/j/for.2017.15.issue-1/for-2017-0005/for-2017-0005.xml.

are the communities where more and less advantaged residents disagree the most. Finally, we need to keep in mind that coincidental representation will always be a poor substitute for genuine responsiveness to the ideologies of less advantaged groups. After all, if residents of color and those with low incomes must depend on their agreement with the relatively powerful in order to obtain representation in local government, they will always be "in a politically tentative and precarious position."[48]

7 **Patterns of racial and economic inequality within communities have important consequences for inequality in representation.** When there are more racially disparate social and economic outcomes within communities, African Americans and whites tend to have more distinctive ideologies. Because African Americans are highly dependent on coincidental representation with whites for ideological representation on municipal councils, greater racial inequality within communities reduces the likelihood that African Americans will be well represented. Greater economic inequality within communities has cross-cutting effects for representation in local government. In communities with more economic inequality, the ideologies of the least affluent are more distant from those of the wealthy; but they are closer to those of the middle class. Ironically, higher levels of economic inequality within communities may help poorer residents find common cause with more politically powerful middle class residents.

Together, our findings present a sobering portrait of the state of local democracy in the twenty-first century. Our work suggests that many local governments fail a central test of democracy, falling well short of their responsibility to provide equitable representation to their residents without regard to race or class. Of course, representation is a complex task, and this is especially true in today's increasingly diverse communities. Nonetheless, in failing to equitably represent the demands of residents of color and those with lower incomes, municipalities are arguably complicit in the entrenchment of racial and class disparities that are the primary obstacles to the full realization of the promise of American life.

There are no easy solutions to the severe shortcomings of local democracy that we identify in the pages that follow. Rather than being a

---

[48] Martin Gilens. "The Insufficiency of 'Democracy by Coincidence': A Response to Peter K. Enns." *Perspectives on Politics* 13, no. 4 (2015): 1065–1071.

surrender to despair, however, this book is a call to action. All Americans – but particularly the relatively advantaged (including, we suspect, many of those who are reading this book) – have the responsibility to contribute to the advancement of democracy and to the fuller extension of its benefits to their fellow citizens. Faced with serious threats to the practice of local democracy, we must ask ourselves, and each other, hard questions. What *can* we do to make local governments more responsive to the demands of their less advantaged residents? What *should* we do? And, perhaps most importantly, do we have the *determination* to do it? Ultimately, whether the promise of local democracy withers, or is reborn, is up to us. We hope that, by exposing the limitations of local democracy as it is currently practiced, we will inspire scholars, activists, and ordinary citizens to remake municipalities so that they express the highest ideals of American democracy and meet the needs of all their residents.

DO LOCAL GOVERNMENTS PROVIDE LESS IDEOLOGICAL REPRESENTATION TO DISADVANTAGED GROUPS?

Do local governments provide less ideological representation to disadvantaged groups than they do to privileged residents? While the question appears straightforward, there is as yet no consensus on the answer. Rather, working in a variety of research traditions, scholars have developed theories and provided empirical evidence that suggest – without demonstrating conclusively – divergent views on this question.

A large and diverse body of research suggests reasons for skepticism about the presence of systematic biases in ideological representation by local governments. As a first observation, recent empirical research reveals that local governments are responsive to the policy preferences of the average resident, with more liberal communities enacting more liberal policies and more conservative municipalities adopting more conservative initiatives.[49] By demonstrating the "robust role for citizen policy preferences in determining municipal policy outcomes," this work provides initial reasons for optimism about the responsiveness of local governments to the demands of groups of residents within communities.[50]

---

[49] Choi et al., "County Limits"; Palus, "Responsiveness"; Chris Tausanovitch and Christopher Warshaw. "Measuring Constituent Policy Preferences in Congress, State Legislatures, and Cities." *The Journal of Politics* 75, no. 2 (2013): 330–342; Tausanovitch and Warshaw, "Municipal Government"; Einstein and Kogan, "Pushing the City Limits."

[50] Tausanovitch and Warshaw, "Municipal Government." Notably, influential research on state politics similarly suggests a close correspondence between public preferences and

Furthermore, there are reasons to suspect that, due to constraints on the scope of ideological conflict at the municipal level, racial or economic biases in representation in local politics are likely to be muted.[51] The fact that individuals have the freedom to migrate to communities that better reflect their preferences for taxation and spending on social services may serve as a natural limit on the representational biases of local governments.[52] Second, the substantial legal and fiscal dependence of local governments on state governments and the federal government may reduce the range of ideological conflict in local politics.[53] State governments and the federal government frequently restrict local government activity, as, for example, when state governments prohibit local sales taxes. They also circumscribe local government discretion through their involvement in areas of policy where responsibility is shared, as through legal conditions on grants in aid to municipalities.[54] Such constraints on the autonomy of local government might, by handcuffing local government discretion, limit the degree to which local governments can favor some residents over others.

Finally, the rigors of economic competition among municipalities may constrict local government decision-making and thereby curtail biases in municipal representation.[55] Because local governments must

policy outputs, e.g. Robert S. Erikson, Gerald C. Wright, and John P. McIver. *Statehouse Democracy: Public Opinion and Policy in the American States*. Cambridge: Cambridge University Press, 1993.

[51] Paul E. Peterson. *City Limits*. Chicago: University of Chicago Press, 1981; Helen F. Ladd and John Yinger. *Ailing Cities: Fiscal Health and the Design of Urban Policy*. Baltimore: Johns Hopkins University Press, 1989; Bailey and Rom, "A Wider Race"; Elisabeth R. Gerber and Daniel J. Hopkins. "When Mayors Matter: Estimating the Impact of Mayoral Partisanship on City Policy." *American Journal of Political Science* 55, no. 2 (2011): 326–339; Oliver, Ha, and Callen, *Local Elections and the Politics of Small Scale Democracy*.

[52] Charles M. Tiebout. "A Pure Theory of Local Expenditures." *Journal of Political Economy* 64, no. 5 (1956): 416–424; Keith Dowding, Peter John, and Stephen Biggs. "Tiebout: A Survey of the Empirical Literature." *Urban Studies* 31, no. 4–5 (1994): 767–797; Oliver, Ha, and Callen, *Local Elections and the Politics of Small Scale Democracy*.

[53] Ladd and Yinger, *Ailing Cities*.

[54] Paul E. Peterson. *The Price of Federalism*. Washington, DC: Brookings Institution Press, 1995; Pietro S. Nivola. *Tense Commandments: Federal Prescriptions and City Problems*. Washington, DC: Brookings Institution Press, 2002; David R. Berman. *Local Government and the States: Autonomy, Politics, and Policy*. Armonk, NY: ME Sharp Incorporated, 2003; Michael Craw. "Overcoming City Limits: Vertical and Horizontal Models of Local Redistributive Policy Making." *Social Science Quarterly* 87, no. 2 (2006): 361–379.

[55] Peterson, *City Limits*; Bailey and Rom, "A Wider Race"; Ladd and Yinger, *Ailing Cities*; Berman, *Local Government and the States*; Rae, *City*.

compete for investment capital, employers, and skilled labor, they all
face pressures to enact similar bundles of growth-friendly policies, such
as relatively low corporate taxes, good schools, well-maintained roads,
and high-quality industrial and retail parks. According to this view,
economic competition among municipalities hinders communities' ability to enact the redistributive policies that are commonly the focus of
traditional left–right ideological conflict. If the struggle for economic
survival curbs local government discretion, municipalities may lack the
leeway to substantially overrepresent or underrepresent particular
groups of residents.

   At the same time, though, there are reasons to suspect that local
governments may fail to represent the ideologies of residents of color
and the less affluent as well as they represent those of white and well-off
residents.[56] A large body of empirical research demonstrating that the
ideologies and policy preferences of nonwhites and the poor are less well
represented by elected officials and in government policy at the federal
and state levels suggests that similar patterns may also prevail in municipal governments.[57] While some proponents of local self-government tout
the superior representative capacities of governments that are "close to
the people," empirical research on the racial and class biases of actual
governments suggests a more chastened view of how democracy works –
and fails to work.

   Furthermore, the fact that less advantaged residents seem to "lose"
when it comes to other forms of representation at the municipal level
provides a reasonable basis for expecting that they also receive less
ideological representation in local government. After all, if nonwhite
and less affluent residents are less likely to elect preferred candidates to

[56] DeHoog, Lowery, and Lyons, "Citizen Satisfaction"; Van Ryzin, Muzzio, and Immer-
wahr, "Explaining the Race Gap"; Rahn and Rudolph, "A Tale of Political Trust";
Marschall and Ruhil, "Substantive Symbols"; Hajnal and Trounstine, "Identifying and
Understanding."

[57] Bartels, *Unequal Democracy*; Gilens, "Inequality and Democratic Responsiveness";
Gilens, *Affluence and Influence*; Ellis, "Social Context and Economic Biases in Represen-
tation"; Rigby and Wright. "Political Parties and Representation of the Poor"; Gilens and
Page, "Testing Theories of American Politics"; Griffin and Newman, "The Unequal
Representation of Latinos and Whites"; Griffin and Newman, *Minority Report*; Butler
and Broockman, "Do Politicians"; Avery and Fine, "Racial Composition, White Racial
Attitudes, and Black Representation"; Gillion, "Protest and Congressional Behavior";
Broockman, "Black Politicians"; Hajnal and Horowitz, "Racial Winners and Losers in
American Party Politics."

local office and are less likely to perceive that municipal services meet their needs, we might also anticipate that they are less likely to enjoy ideological representation on par with that of whites and the well-to-do.[58]

Finally, indications that racial diversity, racial segregation, and economic inequality are all associated both with reduced provision of "public goods" and with increased use of exploitative revenue sources such as fines and court fees imply that less advantaged residents may receive less ideological representation from local governments than do the more advantaged.[59] Indeed, scholars have hypothesized that increased racial and/or economic diversity impedes the provision of public goods both by increasing ideological diversity (which makes consensus building around redistributive spending more difficult) and by depressing support for public goods provision among advantaged groups. If advantaged groups often oppose the extension of government opportunities and benefits to others who are not of their group, it seems quite likely that less advantaged groups will often be on the losing side of local democracy.[60]

In short, whether disadvantaged racial and class groups actually receive less ideological representation in municipal politics remains the subject of considerable disagreement. In the following chapters, we aim to provide a more definitive empirical resolution to this important debate.

[58] Hajnal, *America's Uneven Democracy*; Hajnal and Trounstine, "Race and Class Inequality in Local Politics"; Hajnal and Trounstine, "Identifying and Understanding"; DeHoog, Lowery, and Lyons, "Citizen Satisfaction with Local Governance"; Van Ryzin, Muzzio, and Immerwahr, "Explaining the Race Gap"; Marschall and Shah, "The Attitudinal Effects of Minority Incorporation."

[59] Steven N. Durlauf. "A Theory of Persistent Income Inequality." *Journal of Economic Growth* 1, no. 1 (1996): 75–93; Roland Benabou. "Inequality and Growth." *NBER Macroeconomics Annual* 11 (1996): 11–74; Poterba, "Demographic Structure"; Alesina, Baqir, and Easterly, "Ethnic Divisions"; Luttmer, "Group Loyalty"; Lisa R. Anderson, Jennifer M. Mellor, and Jeffrey Milyo. "Inequality and Public Good Provision: An Experimental Analysis." *The Journal of Socio-Economics* 37, no. 3 (2008): 1010–1028; Trounstine, "Segregation"; Brian Beach and Daniel B. Jones. "Gridlock: Ethnic Diversity in Government and the Provision of Public Goods." *American Economic Journal: Economic Policy* 9, no. 1 (2017): 112–136; Brian An, Morris Levy, and Rodney Hero. "It's Not Just Welfare: Racial Inequality and the Local Provision of Public Goods in the United States." *Urban Affairs Review* 54, no. 5 (2018): 833–865; Michael W. Sances and Hye Young You. "Who Pays for Government? Descriptive Representation and Exploitative Revenue Sources." *The Journal of Politics* 79, no. 3 (2017): 1090–1094; Noli Brazil. "The Unequal Spatial Distribution of City Government Fines: The Case of Parking Tickets in Los Angeles." *Urban Affairs Review* (2018): DOI: 1078087418783609.

[60] Luttmer, "Group Loyalty."

WHAT AFFECTS THE IDEOLOGICAL REPRESENTATION RECEIVED BY DISADVANTAGED RESIDENTS? THREE THEORETICAL LENSES

In addition to assessing *whether* and *to what extent* racially or economically disadvantaged residents receive (in)equitable ideological representation from local governments, we also seek to shed light on the factors that explain the *degree* of (in)equality in representation within communities. Building on the most recent research on political inequalities in American democracy at other levels of government, we investigate why disadvantaged groups receive considerable ideological representation from their local governments in some communities, even as they receive little if any from local governments in other communities.[61]

We draw inspiration from three distinctive theoretical lenses relating to the representation of groups in American politics: the *institutional lens*; the *coincidental representation* lens; and the *racial and economic inequality* lens. We believe that this approach synthesizes various strands of research on the contextual moderators of inequalities in American democracy, providing a useful model for future research on biases in representation at the local, state, and national levels.

The Institutional Lens

Scholars of local politics have long suggested that the design of municipal institutions affects the opportunities available to historically disadvantaged groups. Building on previous research we develop and test hypotheses about how the characteristics of local electoral institutions influence race- and class-based inequalities in local representation.[62] We make a

---

[61] Griffin, Hajnal, Newman, and Searle, "Political Inequality in America"; Griffin and Newman, *Minority Report*; Gilens, *Affluence and Influence*; Ellis, "Social Contexts and Economic Biases in Representation"; Patrick Flavin. "Campaign Finance Laws, Policy Outcomes, and Political Equality in the American States." *Political Research Quarterly* 68, no. 1 (2015): 77–88; Patrick Flavin. "Lobbying Regulations and Political Equality in the American States." *American Politics Research* 43, no. 2 (2015): 304–326.

[62] Zoltan L. Hajnal and Paul G. Lewis. "Municipal Institutions and Voter Turnout in Local Elections." *Urban Affairs Review* 38, no. 5 (2003): 645–668; Hajnal and Trounstine, "Where Turnout Matters"; Sarah F. Anzia. *Timing and Turnout: How Off-Cycle Elections Favor Organized Groups*. Chicago: University of Chicago Press, 2013; J. Eric Oliver. *Democracy in Suburbia*. Princeton, NJ: Princeton University Press, 2001; Kim Quaile Hill and Tetsuya Matsubayashi. "Civic Engagement and Mass–Elite Policy Agenda Agreement in American Communities." *American Political Science Review* 99,

key distinction between institutional designs oriented toward wide participation in elections – what we call a Political Model – and those that
prioritize government effectiveness – what we call a Professional Model.

The Political Model is rooted in the mass politics of the nineteenth
century, which challenged the elite status quo. The extension of the
franchise to propertyless white men encouraged the formation of local
parties that mobilized voters around candidates and issues framed by a
party ticket. Intense partisan rivalries and electoral competition stimu-
lated an environment of political bargaining in which disadvantaged
groups won a share of decision-making power and economic resources.
During this era, municipal elections were often highly partisan and frequently contested at the same time as state and federal races in order to
maximize the ability of party organizations to mobilize their supporters.

The Professional Model, in contrast, emerged from a reform movement
in the late nineteenth and early twentieth centuries to challenge the
Political Model.[63] Progressive reformers sought to thwart the allegedly
"corrupt" politics of party machines and create efficient managerial-style
government, arguing that municipal policies and services should not
reflect partisan loyalties but professional administration. By changing
electoral and governing institutions, reformers aimed to professionalize
government and insulate it from partisan politics. As Schaffner, Streb, and
Wright explain, "The Progressives' normative view of the good citizen
was that of the interested and involved individual, who with other well-
meaning and public regarding citizens use the electoral process to select
the most competent leaders who will then work for the common good."[64]
These changes included shifting to nonpartisan ballots, having an

no. 2 (2005): 215–224; Susan E. Howell and Huey L. Perry. "Black Mayors/White
Mayors: Explaining Their Approval." *Public Opinion Quarterly* 68, no. 1 (2004):
32–56; Kevin Arceneaux. "Does Federalism Weaken Democratic Representation in the
United States?" *Publius: The Journal of Federalism* 35, no. 2 (2005): 297–311; Peggy
Heilig and Robert J. Mundt. *Your Voice at City Hall*. New York: SUNY Press, 1984;
Susan Welch and Timothy Bledsoe. *Urban Reform and Its Consequences: A Study in
Representation*. Chicago: University of Chicago Press, 1988; Robert L. Lineberry and
Edmund P. Fowler. "Reformism and Public Policies in American Cities." *American
Political Science Review* 61, no. 3 (1967): 701–716; Albert K. Karnig. "Black Represen-
tation on City Councils: The Impact of District Elections and Socioeconomic
Factors." *Urban Affairs Quarterly* 12, no. 2 (1976): 223–242.
[63] Amy Bridges. "Textbook Municipal Reform." *Urban Affairs Review* 33, no. 1 (1997):
97–119.
[64] Brian F. Schaffner, Matthew Streb, and Gerald Wright. "Teams without Uniforms: The
Nonpartisan Ballot in State and Local Elections." *Political Research Quarterly* 54, no. 1
(2001): 7–30, at 9.

appointed executive, using at-large elections, and holding elections off-cycle to insulate them from state and federal campaigns.

The institutions of the Political Model tend to make politics easier to understand and less costly to engage in, and to strengthen elected officials' incentives to respond to constituent demands.[65] In contrast, the institutions of the Professional Model insulate policy decisions from factional politics in order to promote efficient and effective municipal services for the community as a whole. This depoliticized model, though often more efficient, makes politics less accessible to ordinary residents.[66]

In the Political Model, elections tend to be organized so that they are likely to maximize voters' interest and information. They feature elections that are concurrent with (high-profile, and often more exciting) federal contests; partisan in organization, thus providing voters with information-rich cues about candidates' ideologies and policy positions; and organized by specific geographic districts, which provide concentrated interests and communities with their own representatives in local government. By contrast, in the Professional Model elections are organized in ways that are less exciting and less informative to the average voter. Thus, for example, Professional Model elections are typically held off-cycle, organized in a nonpartisan fashion, and controlled by at-large, rather than district-based, forms of representation.

The research indicates that some of these institutions matter quite significantly for participation in politics. For example, nonpartisan elections have been shown to depress turnout and make government policy less responsive to the positions of citizens.[67] Off-cycle elections appear to have an even stronger negative effect on turnout, thus leading to less

---

[65] Robert A. Dahl. *Who Governs? Democracy and Power in an American City.* New Haven, CT: Yale University Press, 2005.

[66] Welch and Bledsoe, *Urban Reform and Its Consequences*; Lineberry and Fowler, "Reformism and Public Policies in American Cities"; Karnig, "Black Representation on City Councils"; Jessica Trounstine and Melody E. Valdini. "The Context Matters: The Effects of Single-Member versus At-Large Districts on City Council Diversity." *American Journal of Political Science* 52, no. 3 (2008): 554–569; Trounstine, "Representation and Accountability in Cities"; Albert K. Karnig, and B. Oliver Walter. "Decline in Municipal Voter Turnout: A Function of Changing Structure." *American Politics Quarterly* 11, no. 4 (1983): 491–505.

[67] Schaffner, Streb, and Wright, "Teams without Uniforms"; Brian F. Schaffner and Matthew J. Streb. "The Partisan Heuristic in Low-Information Elections." *Public Opinion Quarterly* 66, no. 4 (2002): 559–581; Gerald C. Wright and Brian F. Schaffner. "The Influence of Party: Evidence from the State Legislatures." *American Political Science Review* 96, no. 2 (2002): 367–379.

responsiveness.[68] People of color and the less affluent are disproportionately likely to possess fewer of the social, economic, and educational resources associated with robust participation in politics.[69] Accordingly, it is natural to expect that when local institutions produce lower turnout, it is among the disadvantaged that turnout (and representation) will suffer the most.

Consider, for example, the case of Ferguson, Missouri, where two-thirds of the population is African American. In the November 2012 presidential election, 76 percent of registered voters in Ferguson came out to vote – and among those voters, 71 percent were black. This helped Barack Obama win 85 percent of the vote in Ferguson in that election. But the Ferguson municipal elections were not held at that time; instead, they were contested on nonpartisan ballots the following April (2013). In that election, just 12 percent of registered voters turned out to vote and African Americans accounted for less than half of those voters. This experience is fairly typical – when turnout drops, it is typically whites and those with higher socioeconomic status who are left in the electorate, as we illustrate in Chapter 4. And, of course, politicians are likely to be most responsive to those who vote. Accordingly, we expect that the Political Model – which favors institutions that facilitate more participation – will promote more equal representation of disadvantaged groups; while the Professional Model – which depresses turnout – will be biased toward more advantaged community members.

The Coincidental Representation Lens

Scholars of group inequalities in representation have repeatedly found that – despite important differences in life experiences and access to opportunities – distinctive groups may have similar preferences on important political issues.[70] Indeed, a striking finding of research on

[68] Anzia, *Timing and Turnout*; Hajnal and Lewis, "Municipal Institutions."

[69] Sidney Verba, Kay Lehman Schlozman, and Henry E. Brady. *Voice and Equality: Civic Voluntarism in American Politics.* Cambridge, MA: Harvard University Press, 1995; Kay Lehman Schlozman, Sidney Verba, and Henry E. Brady. *The Unheavenly Chorus: Unequal Political Voice and the Broken Promise of American Democracy.* Princeton, NJ: Princeton University Press, 2013; Eduardo Bonilla-Silva. *Racism without Racists: Color-Blind Racism and the Persistence of Racial Inequality in the United States.* New York: Rowman & Littlefield Publishers, 2006.

[70] Enns, "Relative Policy"; Joseph Daniel Ura and Christopher R. Ellis. "Income, Preferences, and the Dynamics of Policy Responsiveness." *PS: Political Science & Politics* 41,

economic inequality in representation, for example, is that there is considerable agreement among low-, middle-, and high-income groups in many areas of public policymaking, though there are also areas of substantial disagreement.[71]

Commonality in preferences across distinctive groups creates opportunities for what researchers call "coincidental representation" of the desires of disadvantaged groups by elected officials.[72] To the degree that the preferences of a disadvantaged group overlap with the preferences of an advantaged group, the disadvantaged group will receive representation from elected officials *even if elected officials intended to be responsive only to the advantaged group.* As J. Alexander Branham, Stuart N. Soroka, and Christopher Wlezien note in relation to ideological policy representation,

"In these instances [in which disadvantaged and advantaged groups agree], it does not matter whether public policy is more responsive to one group – policy will end up in the same place. This is not to say that it does not matter theoretically, of course – we ideally would want policy to respond to all citizens ... [But] it does not matter practically, as there will be no substantive difference in policy outputs."[73]

Due to the logic of coincidental representation, democracy may fortuitously work quite well for some disadvantaged groups even in the absence of intentional responsiveness on the part of elected officials.

Notably, however, the prospects for coincidental representation of less advantaged groups vary. For example, they likely differ across geographic space. Indeed, looking at economic gaps in policy preferences at the state level, Flavin found substantial variation across states in the magnitude of differences in preferences between low-, medium-, and high-income groups.[74] Flavin's descriptive findings suggest that there is also likely variation in the degree of overlap in preferences between disadvantaged and advantaged groups at the local level. More generally, this observation highlights the fortuitous – and ultimately arbitrary – nature of coincidental representation and underscores the inevitability of inequities in access to coincidental representation across different local communities.

---

no. 4 (2008): 785–794; Stuart N. Soroka and Christopher Wlezien. "On the Limits to Inequality in Representation." *PS: Political Science & Politics* 41, no. 2 (2008): 319–327.
[71] Enns, "Relative Policy"; Gilens, *Affluence and Influence.*
[72] Enns, "Relative Policy."
[73] Branham, Soroka, and Wlezien, "When Do the Rich Win?" 45.
[74] Patrick Flavin. "Income Inequality and Policy Representation in the American States." *American Politics Research* 40, no. 1 (2012): 29–59.

By the same token, some groups may be more likely on average to enjoy coincidental representation than others, simply because their preferences tend to be closer to those of the advantaged group than do the preferences of other groups. Thus, for example, a commonplace finding in research on economic inequality is that the preferences of the middle class are typically closer to those of the wealthy (the favored group) than are the preferences of the poor, a tendency that tends to create greater opportunities for coincidental representation for the middle class than for the poor. In the same way, the preferences of Latinos are typically closer to those of whites than are the preferences of African Americans, thus implying that Latinos may enjoy greater opportunities for coincidental representation than do African Americans.[75]

For example, we began this chapter by discussing the case of Houston, a racially diverse city that also seems to struggle to effectively represent its diverse citizens. One reason for this may be the fact that Houston's racial and ethnic groups differ quite a bit in terms of their political preferences. Surveys of Houston over the years have found that white residents are significantly less likely to back government programs that support child care, job availability, a higher minimum wage, or health care than their African American and Latino neighbors.[76] African Americans are also much more likely than whites to say that Houston does not do enough to meet the needs of the hungry and homeless. On most of these items, the opinions of the Latino population of Houston generally lie somewhere between those of whites and Blacks. Accordingly, if the Houston city government is responsive to the demands of white residents, then the views of Latinos (often) and African Americans (especially) will suffer as a result. Furthermore, the fact that African Americans and whites in Houston disagree so much on the issues means that African Americans are particularly unlikely to receive coincidental representation.

By contrast, a city like Boston, Massachusetts may be riper for coincidental representation, largely due to the fact that whites living in Boston are more liberal than whites living in Houston. Because whites in Boston are more liberal, their views are more likely to coincide with those of nonwhites living in the city (as we show in subsequent chapters,

---

[75] Rhodes, Schaffner, and McElwee, "Is America More Divided by Race or Class?"

[76] Stephen L. Klineberg, "Public Perceptions in Remarkable Times: Tracking Change through 24 Years of Houston Surveys," Rice University Kinder Institute for Urban Research, March 1, 2005, https://kinder.rice.edu/research/public-perceptions-remarkable-times-tracking-change-through-24-years-houston-surveys.

nonwhites are on average noticeably more liberal than whites). In fact, in a poll conducted in conjunction with the 2013 Mayoral Election in Boston, 43 percent of white Bostonians identified their ideological point of view as liberal, which was precisely the same percentage of nonwhites who identified as liberals.[77] Perhaps as a result, the preferences of whites in that mayoral election were quite similar to those of nonwhites, with both groups demonstrating strong support for the eventual winner, Marty Walsh. Unlike Houston, Boston is a city where the views of white and nonwhite citizens tend to coincide to a considerable degree, a pattern that means the conditions are good for racial and ethnic minorities to benefit from coincidental representation. This is not to say that racial minorities do not experience significant problems in getting represented in Boston – they most certainly do – but that the overlapping preferences between them and white residents make the prospects for decent representation much more likely than in cities like Houston where the two populations diverge to a greater extent.

Of course, the specific patterns evident in other geographic or political contexts may or may not be present in the communities we study in this book. Even so, we anticipate that the ideological representation received by less advantaged groups from local governments is likely to be influenced by the degree to which the ideologies of less advantaged groups overlap with those of more advantaged groups. When the ideologies of less advantaged groups overlap to a greater degree with the ideologies of more advantaged groups, less advantaged groups will receive more ideological representation by virtue of the logic of coincidental representation. But when the ideologies of less advantaged groups overlap to a lesser degree with the ideologies of more advantaged groups, they will receive less representation.

The Racial and Economic Inequality Lens

Local patterns of racial and economic inequality may also shape prospects for the representation of disadvantaged communities within municipalities. Indeed, one of the key insights of the most recent research on inequalities in American democracy is that context – and, in particular, the prevalence of race- or class-based disparities in economic and social outcomes – can have important consequences for the severity of racial or

---

[77] UMass Poll. "2013 October UMass Phone Poll of Boston Registered Voters," Harvard Dataverse (2014), V1.

class biases in representation.[78] In this book, we build on this important insight to investigate how local patterns of racial and economic inequality are associated with the degree of representational inequality experienced by less advantaged residents.

The concept of economic inequality is relatively familiar - by this we simply mean the degree to which economic resources are distributed unequally among members of a community. But the idea of racial inequality requires additional explanation. By racial inequality, we mean the unequal distribution of economic and social resources between different racial groups within the same community. As Rodney Hero and Morris Levy, two prominent scholars of racial inequality, explain, it is important to differentiate between these two concepts, because "two societies with the same total amount of ... inequality between individuals may differ greatly in the degree to which resources are unequally distributed across salient social groups."[79] For example, given two societies that are each composed of equal proportions of two racial groups, it is mathematically possible for the two societies to have an identical overall level of economic inequality, even if in one society the percentages of high- and low-income earners are equal across racial groups, while in the other society most members of one racial group are low earners while most members of the other racial group are high earners. In order to obtain a full picture of the structure of inequality within and across communities, therefore, it is essential to evaluate both the overall degree of inequality and the extent to which resources are equitably distributed across racial groups.[80] Racial inequality indicates systematic biases in the allocation of social and economic resources in the community based on group traits, above and beyond such economic categories as "working class."

Extensive research has documented the serious adverse consequences of both economic inequality and racial inequality for the well-being of societies. Greater inequities are associated with a range of social ills, including weaker social ties, higher crime rates, worse health outcomes,

---

[78] Ellis, "Social Context and Economic Biases in Representation."

[79] Hero and Levy, "The Racial Structure of Economic Inequality," 493.

[80] Rodney E. Hero and Morris E. Levy. "The Racial Structure of Inequality: Consequences for Welfare Policy in the United States." *Social Science Quarterly* 99, no. 2 (2018): 459–472; Brian An, Morris E. Levy, and Rodney E. Hero. "It's Not Just Welfare: Racial Inequality and the Local Provision of Public Goods in the United States." *Urban Affairs Review* 54, no. 5 (2018): 833–865.

lower educational achievement, and slower economic growth.[81] Racial and economic inequalities are also associated with specifically political dysfunctions, including lower provision of public goods and increased corruption by both citizens and government officials.[82]

Finally, where greater economic and/or racial inequality exists, the advantages in political influence enjoyed by privileged social groups are generally compounded, with important implications for inequality in ideological representation.[83] Clearly, "political resources" such as wealth and education provide a foundation for superior political influence via greater participation in elections, increased access to elected officials, more expertise and funds for interest group organizing and advocacy, and higher capacity to convey messages to the mass public.[84] Since this is

---

[81] Ichiro Kawachi and Bruce P. Kennedy. "Socioeconomic Determinants of Health: Health and Social Cohesion: Why Care about Income Inequality?" *British Medical Journal* 314, no. 7086 (1997): 1037; Richard G. Wilkinson and Kate E. Pickett. "Income Inequality and Population Health: A Review and Explanation of the Evidence." *Social Science & Medicine* 62, no. 7 (2006): 1768–1784; Pablo Fajnzylber, Daniel Lederman, and Norman Loayza. "What Causes Violent Crime?" *European Economic Review* 46, no. 7 (2002): 1323–1357; Hero and Levy, "The Racial Structure of Inequality"; Alberto Alesina and Eliana La Ferrara. "Participation in Heterogeneous Communities." *The Quarterly Journal of Economics* 115, no. 3 (2000): 847–904; Arline T. Geronimus and J. Phillip Thompson. "To Denigrate, Ignore, or Disrupt: Racial Inequality in Health and the Impact of a Policy-Induced Breakdown of African American Communities." *Du Bois Review: Social Science Research on Race* 1, no. 2 (2004): 247–279; James Y. Nazroo. "The Structuring of Ethnic Inequalities in Health: Economic Position, Racial Discrimination, and Racism." *American Journal of Public Health* 93, no. 2 (2003): 277–284; Federico Cingano, "Trends in Income Inequality and Its Impact on Economic Growth," OECD Social, Employment, and Migration Working Papers, no. 163, OEC Publishing: http://englishbulletin.adapt.it/wp-content/uploads/2014/12/oecd_9_12_2014.pdf; Joseph E. Stiglitz. "Inequality and Economic Growth." In *Rethinking Capitalism*, eds. Michael Jacobs and Mariana Mazzucato. Wiley, 2016. 134–155.

[82] Alesina, Baqir, and Easterly, "Ethnic Divisions"; An, Levy, and Hero, "Not Just Welfare"; Lyle Scruggs and Thomas J. Hayes. "The Influence of Inequality on Welfare Generosity: Evidence from the US States." *Politics & Society* 45, no. 1 (2017): 35–66; You Jong-Sung and Sanjeev Khagram. "A Comparative Study of Inequality and Corruption." *American Sociological Review* 70, no. 1 (2005): 136–157; Alberto Chong and Mark Gradstein. "Inequality and Institutions." *The Review of Economics and Statistics* 89, no. 3 (2007): 454–465; Nicholas Apergis, Oguzhan C. Dincer, and James E. Payne. "The Relationship between Corruption and Income Inequality in US States: Evidence from a Panel Cointegration and Error Correction Model." *Public Choice* 145, no. 1–2 (2010): 125–135; Eric M. Uslaner and Bo Rothstein. "The Historical Roots of Corruption: State Building, Economic Inequality, and Mass Education." *Comparative Politics* 48, no. 2 (2016): 227–248.

[83] Schlozman, Brady, and Verba, *The Unheavenly Chorus*; Gilens and Page, "Testing Theories of American Politics."

[84] Steven J. Rosenstone and John Mark Hansen. *Mobilization, Participation, and Democracy in America*. New York: Macmillan Publishing Company, 1993; Verba, Brady, and

so, greater inequities in access to such political resources across economic and racial groups are highly likely to yield similarly inequitable outcomes in all of these areas – and, in turn, even more unequal representation in politics.[85] Increasing economic and racial inequality can become self-reinforcing, as more privileged groups use their superior resources to further extend their advantages through the political process.

In fact, there is growing evidence for important links in this causal chain. Research at the national, state, and local levels indicates that increased economic inequality is associated with reduced rates of voting and other forms of civic participation.[86] And studies of economic inequality in representation in Congress indicate that inequality in representation is greatest in congressional districts with higher levels of economic inequality.[87] More worrisome, higher levels of inequality may lead to increased levels of partisan polarization, which can stymie changes to the political system that might reduce inequalities and enhance representation.[88]

Together, these observations suggest that patterns of social inequality likely moderate the severity of biases in representation. Inequality in ideological representation will likely be higher in communities where the socioeconomic disparities are greatest, and should be less in political units in which racial inequality and/or economic inequality are lower.

Schlozman, *Voice and Equality*; Schlozman, Brady, and Verba, *The Unheavenly Chorus*; Adam Bonica, Nolan McCarty, Keith T. Poole, and Howard Rosenthal. "Why Hasn't Democracy Slowed Rising Inequality?" *Journal of Economic Perspectives* 27, no. 3 (2013): 103–124; Jan E. Leighley and Jonathan Nagler. *Who Votes Now? Demographics, Issues, Inequality, and Turnout in the United States*. Princeton, NJ: Princeton University Press, 2013.

[85] Jacob S. Hacker and Paul Pierson. *Winner-Take-All Politics: How Washington Made the Rich Richer – and Turned Its Back on the Middle Class*. New York: Simon and Schuster, 2010.

[86] Frederick Solt. "Economic Inequality and Democratic Political Engagement." *American Journal of Political Science* 52, no. 1 (2008): 48–60; Frederick Solt. "Does Economic Inequality Depress Electoral Participation? Testing the Schattschneider Hypothesis." *Political Behavior* 32, no. 2 (2010): 285–301; Eric Joseph van Holm. "Unequal Cities, Unequal Participation: The Effect of Income Inequality on Civic Engagement." *The American Review of Public Administration* 49, no. 2 (2019): 135–144.

[87] In a similar vein, Rigby and Wright, "Political Parties and the Representation of the Poor," find that, at the state level, inattention to the political opinions of low-income residents is particularly flagrant in states with below average median income.

[88] John Voorheis, Nolan McCarty, and Boris Shor, "Unequal Incomes, Ideology and Gridlock: How Rising Inequality Increases Political Polarization," SSRN paper, August 21, 2015, https://papers.ssrn.com/sol3/papers.cfm?abstract_id=2649215.

PLAN FOR THE BOOK

Our argument, and its associated evidence, unfolds in a series of steps. In Chapter 2, we discuss our unique approach to studying inequalities in representation at the local level. We introduce our various sources of data and explain how we use them to measure representation of racial and class groups in a representative sample of communities from across the United States.

Chapter 3 exploits the unique characteristics of our data to provide a detailed examination of ideological diversity among racial and class groups both between and within local communities throughout the United States. Contrary to the conventional view that local politics are largely nonideological, we find strong evidence of ideological diversity within local communities, as well as clear indications that ideological differences map onto racial and class cleavages in predictable ways. Generally speaking, significant ideological differences between advantaged and disadvantaged groups exist within many communities, with privileged residents typically adopting more conservative views than their less advantaged neighbors.

Because those who participate in politics tend to enjoy much greater representation in government than those who do not, in Chapter 4 we investigate patterns in participation in local politics. We find that whites, wealthy people, and those with more extreme attitudes are more likely to vote in local elections and contact local elected officials. We also provide evidence that these biases in local political participation seem to translate to racial and class biases in the composition of municipal elected officials. These findings provide strong reasons to suspect systematic racial and class biases in representation in local government.

Chapters 5 and 6 focus on racial inequality in representation. In Chapter 5, we explore various forms of representation – descriptive representation, ideological congruence representation between constituents and members of municipal councils, and policy responsiveness by governments to the ideologies of residents – and investigate the effectiveness of municipalities in providing each of these forms of representation to whites, African Americans, and Latinos, respectively. Having demonstrated systematic biases in representation by local governments against African Americans and Latinos, we turn in Chapter 6 to an investigation of factors that may moderate these biases. Troublingly, our results suggest that residents of color are heavily dependent on the logic of coincidental representation for representation in local government; and that the availability of coincidental representation for African Americans is contingent on the presence of a relatively high degree of racial equality within communities. In contrast, the characteristics of local institutions play a limited role in determining the representation accorded to residents of color.

Starting with Chapter 7, we begin an in-depth investigation of economic inequality in representation at the municipal level. Chapter 7 examines how well local governments provide various forms of representation to residents of different levels of wealth. Again, we find systematic biases in representation. Local governments are quite representative of middle- and upper-class residents, but they are typically indifferent to the concerns of the least affluent. In Chapter 8, we evaluate how local political institutions, the dynamics of conditional representation, and patterns of economic inequality shape the prospects for representation of residents of different economic means. We find that coincidental representation is very important for less affluent residents (though not for the wealthy); and that the scheduling of elections on-cycle with federal elections or off-cycle in November increases representation in local government for all residents without regard to economic circumstances. Surprisingly, we find that economic inequality has cross-cutting implications for the representation of low-wealth residents. Increased inequality leads to a larger ideological gap between the least affluent and the well-to-do, raising obstacles to coincidental representation. But it simultaneously narrows the ideological gap between the poor and the middle class, potentially granting the least affluent a powerful ally in local government.

In the conclusion, we bring together our findings to discuss the broader implications for our understanding of the practice of local democracy in the United States. Our findings suggest the need both for sober reflection about the dismal state of municipal politics in the contemporary United States and for concerted efforts to rejuvenate local democracy. Our analysis raises numerous complex and difficult questions, which readers should keep in mind as they examine the pages that follow. Many, if not most, Americans cherish municipalities as embodiments of the principle of local autonomy and self-government. Yet, as we demonstrate conclusively in this book, local governments – especially in small towns – have great difficulty equitably representing the diverse views of their constituents. Particularly disturbing, local governments consistently favor the "haves" (whites and the well-to-do) over the "have-nots" (residents of color and the less affluent). How can the understandable preference of many Americans for a strong measure of local self-government be reconciled with the moral imperative that governments treat their residents equitably?

Our research also suggests the need for further consideration of the difficult trade-offs between the merits of geographic diversity and the normative demands of political equality. In the United States, diversity in local government institutions, processes, and outputs has long been celebrated, both as a reflection of distinctive local preferences and as a mechanism for the testing and dissemination of innovations (i.e. the description of local governments as "laboratories of democracy"). However, as we illustrate in this book, geographic variation in local government activity goes hand in hand with stark geographic differences in local government responsiveness to the preferences of the most vulnerable Americans. Some local governments are relatively responsive to the demands of residents of color and those with lower incomes and wealth; but many, indeed most, are not. Given these patterns, how can the virtues of the "laboratories of democracy" be squared with the responsibility of all governments to provide equitable representation to their constituents without regard to race or class?

In the pages that follow, we urge readers to keep in mind the implications of our findings for the politics of municipal reform today. As we demonstrate in the following pages, there are no easy solutions to the problems of inequitable representation in local government. But we do not have the luxury of inaction. The stark evidence of systematic biases against residents of color and less affluent residents that we uncover in this book calls us to grapple with the difficult, but essential, task of making local government live up to its democratic responsibilities.

Although we do not provide a comprehensive plan for reform, we do point to possible avenues for improving the performance of local government. Building on recent research, we highlight that a major challenge for local democracy is a serious dearth of information about the activities of local officials and the performance of local governments. Due to the severe erosion of local media, and in particular local coverage of politics, many residents likely lack adequate information to evaluate how well local elected officials are fulfilling their promises and serving the public interest.[89] Indeed, recent research suggests that the loss of local political

---

[89] Christopher R. Berry and William G. Howell. "Accountability and Local Elections: Rethinking Retrospective Voting." *The Journal of Politics* 69, no. 3 (2007): 844–858; Lee Shaker. "Dead Newspapers and Citizens' Civic Engagement." *Political*

news coverage is associated with reductions in citizens' political know-ledge and participation.[90] The impact of the decline of local news is likely to be felt most severely among less advantaged residents, who already face the steepest challenges to obtaining equitable representation from govern-ment officials. We suggest that activists, scholars, and citizens must find ways to make information about the workings of local government more available and accessible to all residents, especially those already facing disadvantages.

We also argue that those interested in rejuvenating municipal democ-racy must find novel and effective ways of communicating to local elected officials accurate information about what constituents want. Existing evidence strongly suggests that several forms of bias – the particular content of elected officials' beliefs and opinions, the characteristics of the groups they tend to listen to, and the tendency of elected officials to ignore constituents with differing views – lead elected officials to provide limited representation to many of their constituents, and especially non-whites and the less affluent.[91] However, elected officials are motivated to represent their constituents, and they change their behavior when they

Communication 31, no. 1 (2014): 131–148; Danny Hayes and Jennifer L. Lawless. "As Local News Goes, So Goes Citizen Engagement: Media, Knowledge, and Participation in US House Elections." *The Journal of Politics* 77, no. 2 (2015): 447–462; Danny Hayes and Jennifer L. Lawless. "The Decline of Local News and Its Effects: New Evidence from Longitudinal Data." *The Journal of Politics* 80, no. 1 (2018): 332–336; Daniel J. Hopkins and Lindsay M. Pettingill. "Retrospective Voting in Big-City US Mayoral Elections." *Political Science Research and Methods* 6, no. 4 (2018): 697–714; Gregory J. Martin and Joshua McCrain. "Local News and National Politics." *American Political Science Review* 113, no. 2 (2019): 372–384.

[90] Sam Schulhofer-Wohl and Miguel Garrido. "Do Newspapers Matter? Short-Run and Long-Run Evidence from the Closure of The Cincinnati Post." *Journal of Media Economics* 26, no. 2 (2013): 60–81; Hayes and Lawless, "Decline of Local News"; Meghan E. Rubado and Jay T. Jennings. "Political Consequences of the Endangered Local Watchdog: Newspaper Decline and Mayoral Elections in the United States." *Urban Affairs Review* (2019), https://doi.org/10.1177/1078087419838058.

[91] Daniel M. Butler and Adam M. Dynes. "How Politicians Discount the Opinions of Constituents with Whom They Disagree." *American Journal of Political Science* 60, no. 4 (2016): 975–989; Butler and Broockman, "Do Politicians"; David E. Broockman, "Black Politicians"; Daniel M. Butler. *Representing the Advantaged: How Politicians Reinforce Inequality.* Cambridge: Cambridge University Press, 2014; David E. Broockman and Timothy J. Ryan. "Preaching to the Choir: Americans Prefer Communicating to Copartisan Elected Officials." *American Journal of Political Science* 60, no. 4 (2016): 1093–1107; Nicholas Carnes. "Does the Numerical Underrepresentation of the Working Class in Congress Matter?" *Legislative Studies Quarterly* 37, no. 1 (2012): 5–34; Nicholas Carnes. *White-Collar Government: The Hidden Role of Class in Economic Policy Making.* Chicago: University of Chicago Press, 2013.

learn more about what their constituents want.[92] Thus, we suggest, it is imperative that we develop new and effective ways of conveying clear, detailed information about what constituents want to local leaders. We also argue that state governments, nonprofits, and advocacy organizations need to take clear steps to lower the costs of running for and holding elective office for nonwhite and less affluent residents. If less advantaged residents held a larger share of local elective offices, it is likely that the concerns and needs of nonwhites and less affluent residents would be better represented in local government.

Finally, we suggest that state governments must get more involved in monitoring the quality of local democracy, and possibly intervening in communities with serious and intractable biases in representation. Since municipalities are creatures of state governments, it is ultimately the responsibility of states to take meaningful steps to ensure that localities are providing equitable representation to all their residents.

In the end, our book raises more questions than answers about how to make local governments more responsive to the demands of residents of color and the less economically advantaged. Yet, we hope, these questions will spur scholars, activists, and elected officials to renewed efforts to invigorate the promise of local democracy in the United States. In the end, clearly identifying the problems and raising pointed questions about their causes are the necessary, if painful, first steps in remedying current political injustices. The next steps are up to us all.

---

[92] Daniel E. Bergan. "Does Grassroots Lobbying Work? A Field Experiment Measuring the Effects of an E-mail Lobbying Campaign on Legislative Behavior." *American Politics Research* 37, no. 2 (2009): 327–352; Daniel M. Butler and David W. Nickerson. "Can Learning Constituency Opinion Affect How Legislators Vote? Results from a Field Experiment." *Quarterly Journal of Political Science* 6, no. 1 (2011): 55–83.

2

Studying Inequality in Representation in Local Government

A New Approach

An impressive body of research has expanded our understanding of how American democracy works, as well as when and why it fails to do so. Important studies have focused on inequalities in representation based on race, generally finding that nonwhites receive less representation from government than do white constituents.[1] Meanwhile, a growing body of research examining the relationship between income and representation suggests that "the wealthiest Americans exert more political influence than their less fortunate fellow citizens do."[2]

This research is compelling. But much remains to be learned about the relationship between race, income, and representation in American

---

[1] Avery and Fine, "Racial Composition, White Racial Attitudes, and Black Representation"; David E. Broockman. "Distorted Communication, Unequal Representation: Constituents Communicate Less to Representatives Not of Their Race." *American Journal of Political Science* 58, no. 2 (2014): 307–321; Butler and Broockman, "Do Politicians Racially Discriminate against Constituents?": 463–477; Gillion, "Protest and Congressional Behavior"; Griffin and Newman, *Minority Report*; Griffin and Newman, "The Unequal Representation of Latinos and Whites"; Hajnal and Horowitz, "Racial Winners and Losers in American Party Politics."

[2] Benjamin I. Page, Larry M. Bartels, and Jason Seawright. "Democracy and the Policy Preferences of Wealthy Americans." *Perspectives on Politics* 11, no. 1 (2013): 51–73; Bartels, *Unequal Democracy*; Ellis, "Social Context and Economic Biases in Representation"; Gilens, "Inequality and Democratic Responsiveness"; Gilens, *Affluence and Influence*; Gilens and Page, "Testing Theories of American Politics"; Hacker and Pierson, *Winner-Take-All Politics*; Rigby and Wright, "Political Parties and Representation of the Poor in the American States"; Jeffrey A. Winters and Benjamin I. Page. "Oligarchy in the United States?" *Perspectives on Politics* 7, no. 4 (2009): 731–751; Lawrence R. Jacobs and Benjamin I. Page. "Who Influences US Foreign Policy?" *American Political Science Review* 99, no. 1 (2005): 107–123.

politics. Studies of racial inequality in representation and analyses of economic inequality in representation have made the greatest progress in analyzing these dynamics in Congress and in state governments; we know much less about the scope of racial or class inequalities in representation at the local level.[3]

Of course, scholars of local politics have investigated inequalities in descriptive representation (i.e. the degree of similarity between elected officials and local residents with respect to relevant descriptive characteristics, such as race, ethnicity, gender, and so forth) on municipal councils and in access to particular government resources.[4] They have also examined racial and class differences in who wins and loses in local electoral democracy, and studied racial and class differences in perceptions of local government performance.[5]

This is vitally important work that points to real biases in the operation of local governments. Yet, to date, scholars have made less headway in evaluating racial and class inequalities in two critical forms of representation that are the main focus of research on national and state politics: *ideological congruence representation* (that is, the closeness between the ideologies of constituents and those of elected officials); and *policy responsiveness* (i.e. the relationship between the ideologies of constituents and the overall liberal or conservative direction of policy outputs).

Assessing inequality in these two forms of representation is essential for understanding whether and to what extent the promise of local democracy is being fulfilled. Some examples from our research illustrating the complex relationship between descriptive representation and ideological congruence representation point to the importance of looking at the forms of representation that are the focus of this book. Here, briefly,

[3] Warshaw, "Local Elections and Representation in the United States."
[4] Rufus Browning, Dale R. Marshall, and David Tabb. *Protest Is Not Enough: The Struggle of Blacks and Hispanics for Equality in Urban Politics.* Los Angeles: University of California Press, 1984; Gerber and Hopkins, "When Mayors Matter"; Karnig and Welch, *Black Representation and Urban Policy*; Hajnal, *America's Uneven Democracy*; Hajnal and Trounstine, "Where Turnout Matters"; Mladenka, "Blacks and Hispanics in Urban Politics"; Sass and Mehay, "Minority Representation, Election Method, and Policy Influence"; Paru R. Shah, Melissa J. Marschall, and Anirudh V. S. Ruhil. "Are We There Yet? The Voting Rights Act and Black Representation on City Councils, 1981–2006." *Journal of Politics* 75, no. 4 (2013): 993–1008; Trounstine and Valdini, "The Context Matters."
[5] DeHoog, Lowery, and Lyons, "Citizen Satisfaction with Local Governance"; Hajnal and Trounstine, "What Underlies Urban Politics?"; Marschall and Shah, "The Attitudinal Effects of Minority Incorporation"; Rahn and Rudolph, "A Tale of Political Trust in American Cities"; Van Ryzin, Muzzio, and Immerwahr, "Explaining the Race Gap in Satisfaction with Urban Services."

are two. Newberry, South Carolina, is a community of about 14,600 residents, 42 percent of whom are African American. Half of the Newberry city councilors are black. From the perspective of descriptive representation, African Americans are *well represented* on the council relative to their share of the community population. However, based on the research we will describe, we estimate that the average African American Newberry resident is, ideologically, nearly 24 points distant (on a 100-point scale, which is described in greater detail later in this chapter) from the average municipal councilor in the city – a far greater disparity than the average distance of 12 points among similar communities in our sample. This means that, from the perspective of ideological congruence representation, African American residents of that community are relatively *poorly represented* on the council. The situation in Opelika, Alabama, a community of 33,100 residents – 35 percent of whom are African American – is similar. Forty percent of the city's councilors are African American – quite good from the perspective of descriptive representation given African Americans' share of the municipal population. But, using the 100-point scale described shortly, the council is 26 points distant ideologically from the average African American resident – poor from the perspective of ideological congruence representation. As we demonstrate throughout this book, examples like these abound. Consequently, failing to take account of ideological congruence representation and policy responsiveness results in a distorted picture of how well or badly local governments actually serve their residents. By focusing on ideological congruence representation and policy responsiveness rather than merely descriptive representation, we bring to light inequalities in representation in municipal politics that have previously been unstudied.

Towns like Newberry and Opelika illustrate that inequities in ideological congruence representation and policy responsiveness are very real in municipal politics. Documenting them requires clearly defining these concepts and developing rigorous measures that allow us to observe them in real communities throughout the United States. To understand the first concept – ideological congruence representation – we must know (1) the likely ideological viewpoints of those who are elected to office and (2) the ideologies of different groups within the community. With this measure, a group would be better represented when the ideologies of the elected officials in their town or city are closer to those of the group. But when this distance grows, representation for that group suffers. For the second measure – policy responsiveness – we must again know the ideological viewpoints of different constituent groups in a community: That is, we must be able to capture the extent to which the local government generally produces policies that are in line with each group's ideological viewpoint. Specifically, we want to know whether, as the "liberalism" of a group within a community becomes stronger, policy also tends to move in a more liberal direction (and whether, as the "conservatism" of a group increases, policy also tends to become more conservative).

One reason, and perhaps the most important reason, that there is a dearth of research examining inequalities in ideological congruence representation and policy responsiveness in municipalities is that we generally lack information about the ideologies of particular racial and class groups at the local level. While estimates of the ideologies of distinctive racial and class groups aggregated at the national or state level are relatively common, ideology estimates aggregated at the level of the municipality are hard to come by, particularly for smaller communities. This difficulty arises because social scientists typically rely on surveys to collect information on the ideologies of citizens; yet, existing surveys have inadequate sample sizes to estimate the ideologies of groups even within large cities, much less in smaller cities and towns.[6] The pooling of multiple large surveys and the use of a technique called *multilevel regression and poststratification* (MRP) permits estimation of the ideology of the average adult in medium-to-large municipalities.[7] But, to our knowledge, no one has yet attempted to estimate the ideologies of racial or class groups within both large and small communities using MRP, most likely due to the absence of a sufficiently large data set to make this feasible.[8]

---

[6] Tausanovitch and Warshaw, "Measuring Constituent Policy Preferences in Congress, State Legislatures, and Cities"; Tausanovitch and Warshaw, "Representation in Municipal Government"; Trounstine, "Representation and Accountability in Cities."

[7] Tausanovitch and Warshaw, "Measuring Constituent Policy Preferences in Congress, State Legislatures, and Cities"; Devin Caughey and Christopher Warshaw. "Public Opinion in Subnational Politics." *The Journal of Politics* 81, no. 1 (2019): 352–363.

[8] Some scholars have relied on other approaches to estimating the ideology of smaller towns and cities, such as demographic indicators and presidential vote shares (see, e.g., Choi, Bae, Kwon, and Feiock, "County Limits"; Michael Craw. "Deciding to Provide: Local Decisions on Providing Social Welfare." *American Journal of Political Science* 54, no. 4 (2010): 906–920; and Einstein and Kogan, "Pushing the City Limits"). However, these alternative measures generally cannot be used to estimate the ideologies of racial or class sub-constituencies, which means that they cannot be used to study racial and class inequalities in representation in local politics.

This conversation also points to another, more general limitation of studies of inequality in representation in local government, and at the state and federal levels as well – a tendency of research to focus *either* on racial inequalities, *or* on economic inequalities, but not both at the same time.[9] Of course, such work is of vital importance, but it also leaves essential questions unanswered. As prominent political scientists John Griffin, Zoltan Hajnal, Brian Newman, and David Searle argue,

> Whites and the wealthy garner most of the government's attention, but is class or race really driving responsiveness in American politics? Since existing studies tend to employ research designs that only allow them to look at one demographic characteristic in isolation, we do not know which factor is really behind differential responsiveness. More than just an academic question, this is also practically important as efforts currently directed toward decreasing income-based disparities in political influence may be ineffectual unless they also attend to racial disparities.[10]

The limitations of existing data sources and research designs for studying ideological congruence representation and policy responsiveness in municipal government suggest that a new approach is needed. In this book we draw on recent advances in "big data," using voter file records to generate estimates of the ideological preferences of both racial and class groups within large metropolises, midsize cities, and small towns. Because our data sources, measures, and methods may be unfamiliar, we discuss them here in considerable detail, and we document our efforts as a way to strengthen readers' confidence in their validity.

Ultimately, the virtue of our approach is that we are able to draw on hundreds of millions of records, enabling us to estimate the ideologies of various demographic groups even in very small towns. Whereas most previous research on local politics has tended to focus on larger municipalities, where the data are most plentiful,[11] our approach allows us to study both racial and class inequalities in representation in communities ranging in population from 1.5 million to just 400 individuals. As a result, we are able to make with confidence much broader generalizations about the state of representative democracy in local government than was

---

[9] There are, of course, exceptions to this general trend. See, e.g., Griffin and Newman, "Racial Differences in Information, Expectations, and Accountability"; Griffin and Newman, "The Unequal Representation of Latinos and Whites"; Griffin, Hajnal, Newman, and Searle, "Political Inequality in America"; and Hajnal and Trounstine, "Identifying and Understanding Perceived Inequities."

[10] Griffin, Hajnal, Newman, and Searle, "Political Inequality in America."

[11] Warshaw, "Elections and Representation."

previously possible. This turns out to be significant, because as we show in Chapter 9, the greatest inequalities in how the poor and especially racial minorities are represented tend to be found in America's medium and small-sized towns. Yet, until now, these communities have rarely, if ever, been the focus of a systematic analysis of representation.

HOW WE USE VOTER FILE DATA

Our effort to understand *who* gets represented in local politics requires ideological estimates for groups within communities – including in jurisdictions that are sparsely populated. This means that what we really need are population-level data. For this reason, we turn to the voter file firm Catalist, a private political data vendor that sells detailed voter information to candidates, interest groups, and academics. The full Catalist database comprises detailed records of more than 240 million American adults. The Catalist database begins with voter registration data from all states and counties, which are cleaned and standardized. Then, Catalist appends hundreds of variables to each record. Using registration addresses, Catalist appends census data describing the characteristics of the neighborhood in which each individual resides. Catalist also contracts with other data vendors to incorporate data on the consumer habits of each household. Finally, Catalist generates an array of imputed variables from the other variables it has gathered, validating its imputation models against survey data that have been merged into its database and matched with relevant records. Hersh provides a detailed explanation of the Catalist data;[12] the essential insight is that the Catalist database provides the closest possible approximation of full population-level data available today.

While Catalist was originally designed for electioneering purposes, academic researchers are increasingly using Catalist data to study representation, voter turnout, campaign finance, and many other political and social issues.[13] Catalist datasets have several features that make them especially useful for understanding how sub-constituencies are represented at the local level. First, Catalist includes an estimate of each

[12] Hersh, *Hacking the Electorate*.

[13] See, e.g., Fraga, *The Turnout Gap*; Raymond La Raja and Brian F. Schaffner. *Campaign Finance and Political Polarization: When Purists Prevail*. Ann Arbor: University of Michigan Press, 2015; Jesse H. Rhodes and Brian F. Schaffner. "Testing Models of Unequal Representation: Democratic Populists and Republican Oligarchs?" *Quarterly Journal of Political Science* 12, no. 2 (2017): 185–204.

individual's household wealth. This estimate comes from a model that predicts household wealth and places each adult into one of six distinct wealth brackets (under $30,000; $30,001–$60,000; $60,001–$100,000; $100,001–$300,000; $300,001–$1 million; and greater than $1 million). The prediction model was produced by InfoUSA using a combination of consumer variables for each household as well as census block data. In the next section, we describe a test we conducted to assess the validity of this measure.

Second, Catalist also includes an estimate of each individual's racial and ethnic identity.[14] Catalist uses a combination of information based on names and local racial/ethnic context to make a prediction about the individual's race or ethnicity. Fraga finds that Catalist correctly coded the race/ethnicity of survey respondents 91.4 percent of the time.[15] We also present the results of our own validation test of this model in this chapter.

Third, Catalist includes an estimate of each individual's ideology. While the details of the model used to estimate individual ideology are proprietary, we know that the model is built as a series of linear regressions using variables from the database to predict the values of a liberal/conservative ideology index, with the index based on a wide range of questions selected from national polls and merged into the database. Catalist's individual ideology scores have a value between 0 and 100, with 0 being the most conservative and 100 being the most liberal. (This is the 100-point scale referred to earlier in this chapter.) To provide a sense of what different scores on this scale mean, Figure 2.1 plots the issue positions of respondents to the 2016 Cooperative Congressional Election Study survey based on their ideological score on Catalist's scale. Specifically, the figure plots the percentage of respondents at each level of ideology who said they supported increasing funding in each of the different policy areas. For example, only about 40 percent of people who receive a 20 on the ideology scale support increasing funding for education, but that increases to nearly 80 percent among those with a score of 60. Indeed, higher values on the ideology scale are associated with support for increasing spending in each of the policy areas except for law enforcement, where the pattern is reversed.

---

[14] In several southern states individuals actually report this information when registering to vote. Thus, in those states an individual's race is not an estimate but rather a direct report from their registration form.

[15] Bernard L. Fraga. "Candidates or Districts? Reevaluating the Role of Race in Voter Turnout." *American Journal of Political Science* 60, no. 1 (2016): 97–122.

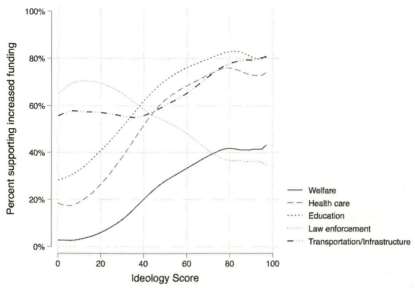

FIGURE 2.1 How Catalist's ideology scale relates to issue positions
Source: 2016 Cooperative Congressional Election Study survey

Catalist has performed a validation of its ideology model and found that it predicts actual issue positions taken by individuals with a reliability of .67. Given the centrality of this measure for our analysis, we have conducted several additional evaluations of our own to strengthen our confidence in its validity. As we discuss in detail in the next section, our validation exercises provide strong evidence that the Catalist ideology variable is a reasonable measure of ideology, both for subgroups within communities and for individual elected officials.

Importantly, the vast majority of Americans receive an ideological prediction, an estimate of their wealth, and an estimate of their race or ethnicity. Catalist has an ideology prediction for more than 99 percent of the 240 million adults in its database. Wealth predictions are somewhat less complete, but still, this information exists for 82.4 percent of individuals tracked by Catalist. A race prediction is made for 97 percent of individuals in the Catalist database. Because most individuals have records for ideology, income, and race, our findings are unlikely to be systematically biased by missing data.

Since this information exists at the population level, we can use tools available in Catalist to create estimates of ideology among different wealth groups, or among different racial and ethnic groups, at a variety of levels of aggregation, including at the municipal level. This is possible even for very small jurisdictions. Thus, for each community in our sample (the characteristics of which are described shortly), we have created ideology estimates for whites, African American, and Latinos, as well as for those with low, middle, and high wealth.[16] We have also extracted information from Catalist about the respective size of each racial and wealth group in each community, allowing us to account for group size in evaluating ideological congruence representation and policy responsiveness.

Thus, when combined with measures of the ideologies of municipal councils and the ideological direction of local government policy (the measures of which are described in detail shortly), the use of Catalist data enables us to provide an unprecedented examination of ideological congruence representation and policy responsiveness in local government regardless of community population size. For the first time, assessing the quality of local democracy is as feasible in modest cities and small towns as it is in large urban areas. This degree of granularity enables us to make a much more general and comprehensive assessment of the functioning of democracy at the local level than was previously possible.

VALIDATING THE CATALIST ESTIMATES

Catalist's population-level data provide us with much more extensive coverage than we could ever achieve with a survey. However, the trade-off we face is that the measures produced by Catalist are typically predictions or estimates of an individual's income, race/ethnicity, or ideology rather than direct measures of those characteristics. Catalist has, of course, conducted a significant amount of testing and refining of their models, and they report that the models are quite accurate. But, to increase readers' confidence in the Catalist estimates, we present the results of our own independent tests of these estimates to see how well they match up with data we obtained from surveys and other sources. In brief, our efforts to validate the Catalist measures have given us substantial confidence in using Catalist data to examine ideological congruence representation and policy responsiveness in a wide array of American municipalities.

---

[16] Approximately 96% of individuals in the Catalist database are identified as white, African American, or Hispanic/Latino. For this reason, we focus on these three racial groups in our analysis.

The Race Model

Catalist's race model has been used extensively in other work, such as Fraga's in-depth research into voting patterns among racial groups.[17] Following Fraga, we matched the 2016 Cooperative Congressional Election Study (CCES) survey to Catalist records. The 2016 CCES included interviews with a nationally representative sample of 64,600 American adults. Respondents were asked a variety of demographic questions as well as many questions about politics. Catalist was able to match 42,504 of the CCES respondents to a record in their database.[18]

Conducting this match allowed us to examine the extent to which Catalist successfully predicted the race/ethnicity of survey respondents. As researchers, we were interested in knowing what percentage of Catalist's predictions about individuals' race/ethnicity matched the individuals' actual responses to the question about race in the CCES survey. Fortunately for our purposes, the Catalist model proved to be quite accurate. For example, 88 percent of individuals classified as Caucasian by Catalist in fact self-identified as white (and not Hispanic) on the CCES survey. Similarly, 86 percent of individuals whom Catalist classified as black identified themselves as black. Finally, 88 percent of people classified by Catalist as Hispanic in fact identified themselves as Hispanic. Thus, Catalist appeared to perform quite well at predicting an individual's race/ethnicity, making a correct inference for nearly nine out of every ten American adults, and with minimal differences in accuracy across racial groups.

The Wealth Model

We were unable to match Catalist's wealth model with CCES survey data to support a validation study similar to that which we performed for race. However, we found another approach to validate the model. Taking advantage of the fact that the names, occupations, and salaries of many government employees are available through searchable online databases, we gathered publicly available data on the first names, surnames, occupations, and salaries of all municipal employees of the cities of Boston,

---

[17] Fraga, *The Turnout Gap.*

[18] The primary reason that Catalist is unable to find a match for an individual is because that person is not registered to vote. While Catalist does have records on unregistered individuals, those records are typically much less complete and are less likely to be up to date.

Massachusetts; Omaha, Nebraska; Nashville, Tennessee; Phoenix, Arizona; and San Jose, California. We took a random sample of 800 public employees from across these communities for closer analysis. Next, we developed a comprehensive search protocol to identify the home addresses of each of the individuals in this sample, using the information about first names, surnames, occupations, and salaries to help us identify correct home addresses. With this information in hand, we took advantage of another feature of a Catalist subscription: the ability to match lists of individuals to records in the Catalist database and extract Catalist variables about the individuals on the lists. We matched each of the individuals in our sample to their respective records in the Catalist database and extracted Catalist's household wealth prediction for each individual.

This process, though labor-intensive, enabled us to make a direct comparison of the relationship between individuals' salaries as reported by municipalities and the household wealth predictions for the same individuals generated by Catalist. Readers should keep in mind the important difference between "salary," meaning the income earned directly from the employer; and "household wealth," which refers to all assets (retirement savings, real estate holdings, other savings, and so forth) minus all liabilities (mortgage debt, consumer debt, college debt, etc.).

Although we postulated some slippage between individuals' salaries and their household wealth predictions as estimated by Catalist – not least because wealth is a complex concept, as we have noted – we hoped to find a strong enough relationship between these two quantities to support our intended reliance on the Catalist household wealth model to provide valid estimates.

Figure 2.2 shows the results of our validation exercise. The x-axis in the graph groups individuals according to the prediction that Catalist made about the household wealth category for those individuals. The y-axis shows the median salary that we found for individuals in each group from online databases. For example, the first bar in the figure indicates that for individuals whom Catalist classified as having wealth of less than $30,000, we found a median salary of $49,916. Although this may seem a fairly large discrepancy, the estimate accords with several key patterns that we observed in our results. First, the household wealth predictions made by Catalist were apparently incapable of making fine-grained distinctions. For example, people for whom Catalist predicted household wealth of less than $30,000 per year had very similar salaries as those for whom Catalist predicted wealth between $30,000 and $60,000. However, a second important pattern that we observed was

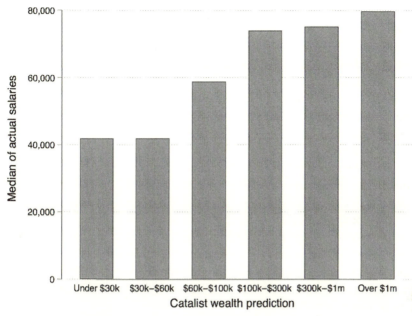

FIGURE 2.2 Validation of Catalist household wealth model
Note: Authors' comparison of municipal employees' salaries and the wealth prediction made by Catalist.

that the wealth model was generally fairly effective at separating individuals into broad household income groupings. For example, the bottom two categories on the Catalist household wealth model have significantly lower incomes than the next wealth group. And then the next three categories after that have even higher incomes.

Overall, then, the Catalist model performed fairly well at dividing the population into a few general wealth groupings that aligned with actual salary data, though it was better at creating broad wealth bins than making finer-grained distinctions. Fortunately, this worked well for our purposes, since (following much work on economic inequality in representation) we used the household wealth model to create three commonly recognized wealth groups within each community: households with low, medium, and high wealth.

The Ideology Model

Catalist's ideology measure is at the core of our study, because we rely on it to gauge an individual's general preference for liberal versus conservative policies. Accordingly, we took several different approaches to validating this measure. First, we matched the CCES survey data to the Catalist data to test the validity of the ideology model among individuals. In this validation test we found that Catalist's model correlated with a scale of issue attitudes at 0.67 – precisely the same reliability score that Catalist reports in its own documentation.[19] Thus, the ideology model does provide a useful (albeit somewhat noisy) measure of individuals' ideologies.

Importantly, we conjectured that much of the noise that might occur with individual-level predictions would be canceled out when we aggregated the scores at the community level. To explore this conjecture, our second validation task took advantage of the municipal ideological estimates created by Tausanovitch and Warshaw.[20] These ideological estimates were based on MRP and made use of several large-scale surveys with a combined sample of hundreds of thousands of Americans. For our validation exercise, we calculated the mean ideology from Catalist for 1,149 municipalities included in the Tausanovitch and Warshaw database, and then we calculated the extent to which the Catalist ideology measure was correlated with the ideology score Tausanovitch and Warshaw generated with MRP. The results of this validation appear in the left-hand panel of Figure 2.3. Note that the observations cluster close to the regression line, and that the two measures are correlated at 0.82. These observations suggest a very close correspondence between the two aggregated ideology measures. Additionally, this figure shows that, in contrast to individual-level predictions, aggregated ideology scores display a much less noisy signal. For our purposes, this is good news, as we rely in this book primarily on aggregated measures of ideology (at the community, racial group, and economic group levels) rather than on individual-level estimates.

The first two validation exercises were useful for demonstrating that the Catalist ideology measure provided an accurate estimate of constituent opinion aggregated at the level of the municipality. However, as we discuss in greater detail shortly, we also wanted to examine the power of

---

[19] The issue scale was created using a two-parameter logistic item response model on thirty-one issue questions from the 2016 CCES. These items covered topics such as gun control, immigration, abortion, the environment, crime, trade, highway funding, minimum wage, the Affordable Care Act, and spending on welfare, health care, and education. The correlation between the Catalist ideology score and the CCES scale was 0.30 among people identifying as Democrats and 0.39 for Republicans.

[20] Tausanovitch and Warshaw, "Measuring Constituent Policy Preferences."

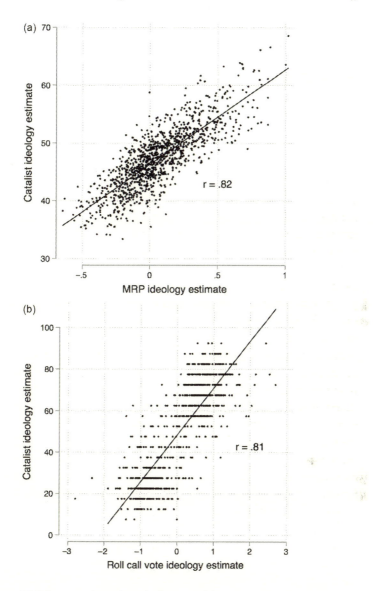

FIGURE 2.3 Validations of Catalist ideology model
Note: Authors' comparison of ideological estimates from external sources and ideology estimates produced by Catalist model.

the Catalist ideology estimate for predicting the ideologies of elected officials. Accordingly, for our third validation exercise, we again took advantage of the ability to match lists of individuals to records in the Catalist database. In many states, it is relatively easy to find the addresses of state legislators. We successfully matched 792 state legislators from across thirty-four states in the Catalist database and extracted Catalist's ideological estimate for each of those individuals. Then, to validate the Catalist-based ideology measure, we compared the Catalist ideology scores for the 792 state legislators against ideology scores derived from roll call votes for these same individuals created by McCarty and Shor.[21]

The results of this third validation exercise appear in the right-hand panel of Figure 2.3. Even among individual politicians, a strong relationship between the estimate of ideology generated by Catalist and the estimate of ideology created by McCarty and Shor is evident. Indeed, the measures are correlated at .81, suggesting that the Catalist ideology scores are a valid measure of the ideologies of elected officials.

Overall, the results from these validation tests indicate that the Catalist ideology measure is closely related to other, commonly used measures of ideology. Relying on this model provided much greater coverage than we could have achieved with any alternative measure of ideology, but it did come with the trade-off of some loss of precision. Fortunately, our usual practice in this study was to aggregate our estimates (as shown in the first panel of Figure 2.3), which removed much of this noise. Furthermore, the ideology measure was adept not only at estimating views among members of the public, but also at predicting how politicians would behave in office, as seen by the comparison of the model with roll call voting scores. Thus, these validation exercises gave us considerable confidence that this measure constituted a strong foundation for assessing racial and class inequalities in ideological congruence representation and in policy responsiveness.

MEASURING IDEOLOGICAL CONGRUENCE REPRESENTATION AND POLICY RESPONSIVENESS

Having described our methods for measuring the ideological viewpoints of different groups within each community, we will proceed to explain our methods for measuring the extent to which those ideologies are reflected both by who is elected to office and by the policies those officeholders enact.

[21] Boris Shor and Nolan McCarty. "The Ideological Mapping of American Legislatures." *American Political Science Review* 105, no. 3 (2011): 530–551.

Measuring Officeholder Ideology

Our measure of ideological congruence representation is the distance between the ideology of the average officeholder in a community and the ideology of the average member of a particular group. To calculate this measure, we need measures of the ideologies of both constituents *and* elected officials. As we've described, data from Catalist allow us to create valid measures of the ideologies of groups within municipalities. Importantly, we can also use Catalist to construct accurate measures of the ideologies of municipal elected officials.

To accomplish this, we matched lists of individual municipal councilors to the database and then extracted desired information about those individuals. We first developed a standardized search protocol to acquire identifying information (names, zip codes, and street addresses) for the councilors in each of the cities and towns in our sample, combining searches of local government websites, local property records, state campaign finance records, and internet "white pages." Using this procedure, we were able to recover at least the name and zip code for nearly every councilor in each of the cities and towns in our sample. For a majority of councilors in the cities and towns in our sample, we were also able to find street addresses. With this information in hand, we matched the councilors with Catalist information, ultimately matching 82 percent (or 4,033) of councilors across 583 towns and cities. Finally, for each of the matched councilors, we extracted a Catalist ideology score, and used this information to generate a mean ideology score for each municipal council.

Figure 2.4 shows examples from two communities to illustrate how we combined the ideology scores from the local elected officials with those for different racial groups to determine which groups enjoyed greater ideological congruence with the local government council. In the left-hand panel of the figure, we plotted the distribution of whites (the solid line) and African Americans (the dashed line) in Easton, Pennsylvania. The diamonds on the plot show the location of each elected official in Easton on the ideology scale. The axis labels the mean ideologies for each of these three groups. Notably, the elected officials in Easton have a mean ideology of 53.6, while white adults have a mean ideology of 54 and black adults a mean ideology of 55.3. Overall, then, the mean elected official in Easton is quite close to both the average white citizen and the average black citizen, indicating a high degree of ideological congruence. That is, both whites and African Americans in Easton appear to have elected officials who are likely to hold similar views about politics.

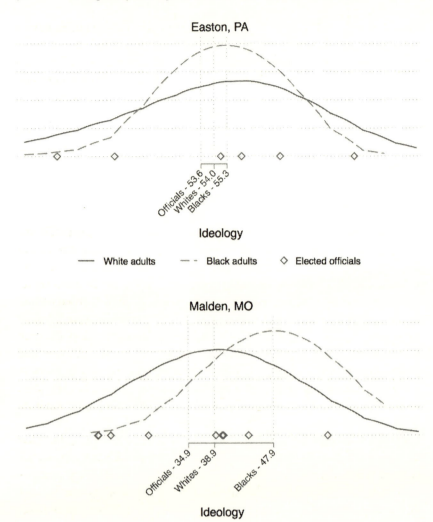

FIGURE 2.4 Illustration of ideological congruence representation of racial groups
Note: Authors' analysis of Catalist data.

The right-hand panel in Figure 2.4 presents the same information, but this time for Malden, Missouri. Here, we see a decreased amount of ideological congruence. The mean elected official in Malden has an ideological score of 34.9, which is relatively close to that of the average white citizen, who has an ideology of 38.9. But the black community is not nearly as well represented. In fact, African Americans in Malden have a mean ideology of 47.9, which means that elected officials are thirteen points more conservative than are African American residents. This suggests a substantial discrepancy between the degree to which whites and African Americans are represented by the ideological composition of the town's elected officials. In a following chapter, we show how much ideological congruence representation different racial groups receive across all of the communities in our study. But for now we simply note that the experience in Malden is hardly unique.

Measuring Policy Ideology

Of course, whether the elected officials in a community and their residents are likely to hold similar views is just one aspect of representation. After all, it may be that many individuals elected to office do not share the views of their constituents – but these officials could still provide good representation to their constituents if they tend to ignore their own views and implement policies that their constituents prefer. Accordingly, it is crucial to measure policy responsiveness – that is, the relationship between constituent ideology and the overall ideological orientation of municipal policy. Our work in this area builds on existing research on inequities in local government responsiveness by constructing a measure of the degree to which a community prioritizes the needs of underserved communities in its policymaking.

For our measure of local government policy responsiveness, we draw on data from three surveys fielded by the ICMA: (1) the 2015 Survey of Government Sustainability, (2) the 2010 Survey of Government Sustainability, and (3) the 2014 Survey of Economic Development. The surveys of Government Sustainability have been used in recent studies of municipal policy responsiveness.[22] In the surveys, city officials were asked questions about policies enacted by city government. The sustainability surveys emphasize environmental policies, but they also inquire about other policy areas and, importantly for our purposes, ask several questions about whether local governments implement policies that are designed to help those in need. The same is true of the 2014 Economic Development survey, which focuses on steps that communities are taking to encourage economic development, but also addresses whether those communities are focused on the needs of underserved populations.

[22] Tausanovitch and Warshaw, "Representation in Municipal Government."

The appendix for this chapter provides a full list of the policy items we took from each of the three surveys. There are twenty-six items in total, all of which address steps that the community has or has not taken to assist disadvantaged residents. This includes items asking whether social justice is a goal when the community engages in policymaking; whether the community provides incentives for affordable housing; whether the community has energy conservation programs targeted to low-income families; and the extent to which economic development plans are motivated by income inequality, to name just a few. Again, we focused specifically on identifying items that captured the real focus of this book – *the extent to which communities represent the needs of disadvantaged populations.*

Using this information, we created a scaled measure of municipal policy liberalism, which provided a sense of the overall "liberalism" or "conservatism" of a municipality's policies on these redistributive issues.[23] The scaling approach we used provided a score for a community even if it responded to just one of the three surveys. This allowed us to maximize the number of communities for which we could analyze policy liberalism. Ultimately, we generated a policy liberalism score for nearly half of our sample of communities.

Figure 2.5 presents the distribution of communities in our study on this measure of policy liberalism. The policy liberalism scale is standardized, which means that a value of 1 on this scale indicates that the community is one standard deviation above the mean in terms of the liberalism of the policies it has enacted, and a value of −1 suggests that the community is one standard deviation below the mean on the scale. Table 2.1 shows the ten communities that score the highest on policy liberalism (that, is the communities with the most liberal policies) as well as the ten communities that score the lowest (or those with the most conservative policies). One notable pattern that stands out in the figure is that many communities appear to do very little to address the needs of low-income citizens, whereas relatively few towns and cities do quite a bit.

OUR SAMPLE OF LOCAL COMMUNITIES

So far, we have described how we used unique data sources to measure inequality in representation in towns and cities across America. However,

---

[23] We created this scale by using a two-parameter logistic item response theory model. After estimating the model we extracted a prediction of the latent variable (which we term "policy liberalism") for each community.

TABLE 2.1 *Communities scoring highest and lowest on policy liberalism scale*

Communities with most liberal policy score		Communities with most conservative policy score	
Community	Score	Community	Score
Waco, TX	2.64	Bethany, OK	−1.38
Lakewood, WA	2.05	Green River, WY	−1.25
Hopewell, VA	2.02	Avon, IN	−1.22
Salem, OR	1.96	Wheaton, IL	−1.22
Riverside, CA	1.93	El Campo, TX	−1.18
Gloversville, NY	1.88	Brookings, OR	−1.08
Hayward, CA	1.79	Manheim, PA	−1.02
Rockford, IL	1.76	Pleasanton, TX	−1.02
Eugene, OR	1.67	Delafield, WI	−1.02
Bell Gardens, CA	1.63	Perkasie, PA	−1.02

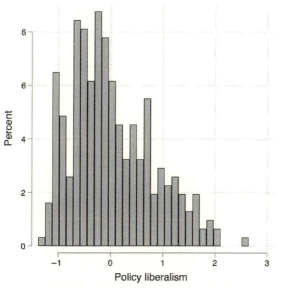

FIGURE 2.5 Distribution of policy liberalism in our sample of communities
Note: Authors' analysis of policy scales created from ICMA municipal surveys.

even with the large amount of data available to us through Catalist, we could not study these dynamics in every single town and city in the United States. Instead, our analysis focused on a sample of hundreds of munici-palities across the country. In selecting the communities for our sample, our aim was to understand not just whether ideological congruence representation and policy responsiveness occur at an aggregate level (that is, on average), but how institutional arrangements, the dynamics of coincidental representation, and patterns of economic and racial inequality affect *who* (i.e. which groups within communities) gets representation. We also aimed to make this assessment not only for a relatively small number of large urban centers, but for a much wider array of large, midsize, and small communities. Indeed, as we show later in this book, it is in the small towns and rural communities of America that we see the highest degree of inequality in representation – a pattern suggesting that much greater attention to the state of democracy in small communities is needed among scholars, activists, and lawyers.

Because we had access to population-level data on large, medium, and small communities, as described shortly, we were not constrained to sampling from large communities with readily available information about the ideologies of constituents.[24] Instead, we cast a wide net, drawing a very diverse sample of cities and towns from the International City Managers Association (ICMA)'s Form of Government Survey, a survey used frequently in recent research on local government politics in the United States.[25] We used the 2011 Form of Government Survey, the most recent iteration of the survey.

This survey is distributed to the city or town clerk in all municipalities with a population over 2,500 and to all towns with populations under 2,500 that are included in the ICMA database.[26] In total, the ICMA database includes 3,566 towns and cities ranging in population from 105 to 1.3 million. Figure 2.6 shows the distribution of towns and cities according to their population. The figure includes a vertical reference line at 25,000, which is the cutoff used in the Warshaw and Tausanovitch study of representation. Notably, 79 percent of municipalities have

---

[24] Tausanovitch and Warshaw, "Measuring Constituent Policy Preferences."

[25] Reza Baqir. "Districting and Government Overspending." *Journal of Political Economy* 110 (2002): 1318–1354; Victor DeSantis and Tari Renner. "Minority and Gender Representation in American County Legislatures: The Effect of Election Systems." In *United States Electoral Systems*, eds. Wilma Rule and Joseph F. Zimmerman. New York: Greenwood Press, 1992; Tim R. Sass and Bobby J. Pittman. "The Changing Impact of Electoral Structure on Black Representation in the South, 1970–1996." *Public Choice* 104, no. 3–4 (2000): 369–388; Tausanovitch and Warshaw, "Measuring Constituent Policy Preferences"; Tausanovitch and Warshaw, "Representation in Municipal Government"; Francesco Trebbi, Philippe Aghion, and Alberto Alesina. "Electoral Rules and Minority Representation in US Cities." *The Quarterly Journal of Economics* 123, no. 1 (2008): 325–357.

[26] The response rate for the 2011 ICMA survey was 41%.

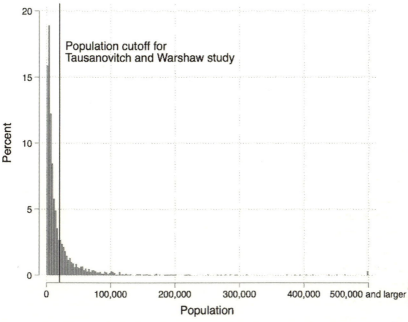

FIGURE 2.6 Distribution of population of communities in ICMA database
Note: Authors' analysis of 2011 ICMA Form of Government survey data.

populations below 25,000. This means that while the innovative work of Warshaw and Tausanovitch studied many more communities than previously possible, it still left out about four of every five municipal governments. By contrast, our study had no population threshold: We were able to study communities with just a few hundred residents as easily as those with hundreds of thousands.

Table 2.2 provides summary statistics about the towns and cities in the ICMA database. In this book, one objective is to understand the effects of different types of electoral and governing laws and characteristics on responsiveness in local government. It is important to note, however, that many governance characteristics overlap with others. For example, municipalities with council-manager forms of government also tend to have nonpartisan elections and at-large districts. In fact, that configuration accounts for 39 percent of all municipalities.

If we had simply randomly selected municipalities from the ICMA database, we might have had a difficult time studying the effects of individual institutions. For example, if nearly all of the communities we selected that had a council-manager form of government also had nonpartisan

TABLE 2.2 *Description of towns and cities in the ICMA database*

Type of Institution	Percentage/Average
Mayor-Council	36%
Council-Manager	64%
Nonpartisan elections	80%
Council elected by districts	17%
Council elected at-large	64%
Mixed at-large and districts	19%
Median size of council	6

Note: Excluded from these descriptive statistics are towns and cities using town meeting forms of government.

elections, then we would not be able to differentiate the effects of the form of government from the effects of the type of ballot used in elections. Fortunately, a specific sampling approach called stratified sampling provides an effective way to deal with this issue. Stratified sampling entails dividing the population into groups (called strata), each with combinations of particular characteristics about which we want to make inferences, and then sampling randomly from within each stratum. For example, we might create a stratum of municipalities that have both council-manager governments and partisan elections to ensure the selection of enough communities that fit that relatively rare combination of institutions.

To draw the sample for our study, we first stratified by the form of government (Mayor-Council or Council-Manager), the type of ballot (partisan or nonpartisan), and the type of jurisdictions (at-large, districts, or both). Because our research is focused on understanding racial and ethnic inequalities in representation, we also wanted to ensure that we had enough communities where minority groups constituted a significant proportion of the population. Thus, we also stratified on whether the municipality had a minority population that constituted at least 40 percent of the population. Ultimately, this produced twenty-four strata, ensuring sufficient coverage of each combination of governing institutions as well as sufficient coverage of communities with larger minority populations.

The total sample we drew for our study was 678 towns and cities. In some communities, we were not able to obtain complete information about the elected officials. This usually happened because the town government had posted insufficient information about elected officials on its website and did not respond to our attempts to contact them. In other communities, we could not gather sufficient information about the town's population. This occurred when the municipal boundaries did not match up well with geographic boundaries available to us in Catalist. These two issues reduced the effective sample size for our core analyses to 518.[27] These communities ranged in population from 415 (Morrison, CO) to 1.3 million (San Diego, CA). Notably, about three-quarters of the communities we analyzed had populations less than 25,000. To our knowledge, this is the first large-scale analysis of representation in America's towns and smaller cities, and the first large-scale investigation of racial and class inequalities in representation across communities of all sizes. As we discuss in the conclusion of this book, the inclusion of a large number of small towns in our analyses was crucial, because we found that it was in these communities that racial disparities in representation were most pronounced.

CONCLUSION

In this book we have pursued an ambitious objective: to assess both racial and class inequality in ideological congruence representation and policy responsiveness across a wide array of large cities, midsized communities, and small towns throughout the United States. To accomplish this goal, we drew on population-level data from the political marketing firm Catalist, which have rarely, if ever, been used in studies of representation in municipal politics. Because these data are novel, we have gone to great lengths to familiarize readers with their characteristics and establish their validity for our research purposes. We believe these data offer unprecedented insights into the quality – or lack thereof – of local democracy in the United States. For the first time, we have been able to examine racial and economic inequalities in both ideological congruence representation and policy responsiveness in communities ranging from very large cities to small towns from throughout the nation.

Now that we have provided readers with an overview of our data and methods, we turn to the tasks of assessing inequities in representation in local government and evaluating whether municipal institutions, coincidental representation, and socioeconomic context play any role in determining how well or poorly local governments represent groups of residents within communities.

---

[27] For analyses not involving elected officials, our effective sample size is 644.

Appendix: Issue Items Used in Policy Scaling

From 2010 Sustainability Survey:

- To what extent are the following a priority in your jurisdiction? Social justice
- To what extent are the following a priority in your jurisdiction? Housing for all income groups
- To what extent are the following a priority in your jurisdiction? Public transit
- Has your local government established any energy reduction programs targeted specifically to assist low-income residents?
- Please indicate which of the following programs your local government has: Provide financial support/incentives for affordable housing
- Please indicate which of the following programs your local government has: Provide supportive housing to people with disabilities
- Please indicate which of the following programs your local government has: Provide housing options to the elderly
- Please indicate which of the following programs your local government has: Provide housing within the community to homeless persons
- Please indicate which of the following programs your local government has: Provide access to information technology for persons without connection to the Internet
- Please indicate which of the following programs your local government has: Provide funding for preschool education
- Please indicate which of the following programs your local government has: Provide after-school programs for children

From 2014 Sustainability Survey:

- Indicate which of the following are a priority in your jurisdiction. Social equity
- Do you have a hazard mitigation plan or an emergency evacuation/ relocation plan? If yes, does either plan specifically address issues of at-risk (low income, seniors, etc.) residents?
- Please indicate if your local government has any energy conservation programs targeted to assist the following: low-income residents
- Which of the following actions has your government taken to reduce or manage water usage? Protect low-income households from water service shut off
- Which of the following programs does your local government provide? Financial support/incentives for affordable housing
- Which of the following programs does your local government provide? Supportive housing to people with disabilities
- Which of the following programs does your local government provide? Housing options for the elderly
- Which of the following programs does your local government provide? After-school programs for children
- Which of the following programs does your local government provide? Funding for early child care and education
- Which of the following programs does your local government provide? Housing options in community for homeless persons
- Has your government added or adopted any of the following in the past five years? Public transportation programs to assist low-income residents

2014 Economic Development survey:

- Indicate which of the following are economic development goals in your community: Social equity
- Please indicate the extent to which the considerations below motivated economic development priorities of your local government: Income inequality
- Please indicate your level of use of these economic development tools: Job training for low skill workers
- Please indicate your level of use of these economic development tools: Affordable workforce housing

3

Municipal Politics As Sites of Racial and Class Contention

Are local politics usually characterized by disagreement or consensus? While scholars of politics in major cities such as New York, Atlanta, and Los Angeles have long emphasized the centrality of racial and class cleavages in elections and governing, the conventional wisdom is that local politics *outside* such urban behemoths – that is, in the thousands of smaller cities and towns where nearly 3 in 4 Americans live – are relatively staid.[1] According to this view, local politics are distinctive from national or state politics because they typically revolve around relatively low-stakes issues and rely on elected officials who are characterized more by managerial acumen than ideological fervor. These characteristics, the argument goes, make local politics relatively placid in comparison with the pitched battles that frequently roil national politics.[2] As J. Eric Oliver, a major proponent of this perspective, argues,

Unlike national offices, the politics of local government are rarely fought along ideological lines. Whereas debates among "liberal" and "conservative" elites dominate national and state politics, most local governments are not amenable venues for contesting liberal, conservative, or any other ideological visions of social organization. Most American towns do not sustain the chronic political cleavages of states or the country, partly because losing sides to any political battle

---

[1] Hajnal and Trounstine, "Identifying and Understanding Perceived Inequities in Local Politics"; Hajnal and Trounstine, "What Underlies Urban Politics?"

[2] Ferreira and Gyourko. "Do Political Parties Matter?"; Oliver, Ha, and Callen, *Local Elections and the Politics of Small-Scale Democracy*; Charles R. Adrian. "Some General Characteristics of Nonpartisan Elections." *American Political Science Review* 46, no. 3 (1952): 766–776; Bailey and Rom, "A Wider Race?"; Jensen, Marble, Scheve, and Slaughter, *City Limits to Partisan Polarization in the American Public*; Rae, *City*.

can easily "exit". In other words, a conservative voter can easily move out of a liberal town, a disaffected community can seek to secede from a larger city, and so on. This is not to suggest that major political or ideological conflict will never emerge in all localities; rather, such struggles are likely to be more of an exception than the rule.[3]

In this view of local politics, political differences are not entirely absent, of course. However, disagreements, when they do arise, tend to be fleeting, and structured much more as personality conflicts or differing evaluations of managerial performance than as deep racial or class differences. As Oliver argues, "Unlike national elections, which are defined by long-standing political cleavages, local politics ... have fewer chronic issues that divide the citizenry ... The small size, limited scope, and low biases of most places greatly attenuate most of the political cleavages that fracture large, urban places."[4]

Scholars who emphasize the economic constraints facing cities similarly portray local politics as relatively nonideological, albeit for somewhat different reasons.[5] In this telling, municipalities tend to face similar imperatives to establish growth-friendly economic policies, limiting their capacity to indulge in redistribution through social spending. This dynamic takes most policies that are the focus of "left–right" ideological conflict off the table, yielding a managerial sort of politics that places growth-oriented proposals at the forefront of the agenda.[6] More recent research indicates that municipalities may provide more redistributive spending when that is supported by constituents, but this work, like the research it critiques, nonetheless highlights the importance of ideological agreement (as opposed to ideology-based differences) within communities in determining policy outcomes.[7]

---

[3] Oliver, Ha, and Callen, *Local Elections and the Politics of Small-Scale Democracy*, 7.

[4] Oliver, Ha, and Callen, *Local Elections and the Politics of Small-Scale Democracy*, 7–10.

[5] Peterson, *City Limits*; Peterson, *The Price of Federalism*.

[6] See also Jensen, Marble, Scheve, and Slaughter, *City Limits to Partisan Polarization in the American Public*.

[7] Tausanovitch and Warshaw, "Representation in Municipal Government"; Einstein and Kogan, "Pushing the City Limits." One very recent study suggests that there is a multidimensional structure to local political ideology – one that focuses on the traditional left–right conflict, and another distinctive dimension organized around the balance between community needs and individual freedoms with respect to land use. As we have noted, in this book we use a single-dimensional framework to study local political ideology. However, we acknowledge that the possible multidimensional structure of local ideology is a worthy subject of further research. See Damon M. Cann. "The Structure of Municipal Political Ideology." *State and Local Government Review* 50, no. 1 (2018): 37–45.

In this chapter, we reexamine the ideological tone of local politics, using the unique information we have gathered from Catalist to shed new light on the prospects for conflict and compromise in a representative sample of large cities, midsize communities, and small towns. In contrast to the conventional wisdom, we find strong evidence of ideological cleavages within many local communities, as well as indications that these differences are tied to race and, to a lesser degree, class. In this way, local politics does not seem to be very distinctive from national or state politics, even if the issues are not necessarily the same. In many municipalities, in fact, we find ideological differences that closely parallel those at other levels of government.[8]

As we show, local communities are characterized by a remarkable amount of ideological diversity. Indeed, a majority of the communities in our sample display a level of ideological diversity that is similar to that of the United States population as a whole! Equally striking, roughly one-quarter of municipalities have a level of ideological diversity *greater* than that of the US population. Far from being sites of ideological consensus, many local communities demonstrate substantial ideological differences, and quite a few exhibit what can only be described as ideological polarization.

Moreover, and very importantly, these ideological differences often map onto enduring social cleavages. Within local communities, African Americans, Latinos, and whites typically have distinctive ideologies, and in many communities, we find indications of significant racial ideological polarization (particularly between African Americans and whites). Class differences in ideology are less stark, but we do uncover ideological differences, especially between the least and most affluent. These cleavages generally mirror those found in national and state politics, with nonwhites and the less affluent typically adopting noticeably more liberal positions than whites and the well-to-do.

The portrait of municipal politics that emerges from our analysis departs from the conventional wisdom, but it should be familiar to followers of national and state politics in the United States. Local politics is not distinctive – and it certainly is not sleepy. To the contrary, many communities in our study exhibit as great a potential for racial and class tensions as their counterparts at higher levels of government.

---

[8] See also, e.g., Cheryl Boudreau, Christopher S. Elmendorf, and Scott A. MacKenzie. "Lost in Space? Information Shortcuts, Spatial Voting, and Local Government Representation." *Political Research Quarterly* 68, no. 4 (2015): 843–855.

The characteristics of local politics that we uncover in this chapter provide initial reasons for suspicion that local governments may demonstrate biases in their representation of different groups of residents. Existing research on representation at other levels of government suggests that less advantaged groups receive significantly less representation than do advantaged constituents. Moreover, this work indicates that one likely explanation for these findings is that disadvantaged groups have preferences that diverge noticeably from those of advantaged groups, at least on an important subset of political issues.[9] With these findings in mind, given that different racial and economic groups exhibit distinctive ideologies within communities, we think it quite plausible that local governments exhibit biases in representation toward advantaged groups as well. In the chapters that follow, we investigate whether this expectation is warranted.

IDEOLOGICAL DIVERSITY IN LOCAL COMMUNITIES

Just how much ideological diversity exists in American municipalities? Do the residents of a given community tend to have similar views – be they liberal or conservative – or do they often have divergent perspectives? To begin to answer this question, we examined variation in ideology within all of the communities in our sample. To justify our making an inference about all communities in the United States, we constructed sampling weights that account for the stratified nature of our sample. In Figure 3.1, we show the distribution of the standard deviation in ideology – a simple measure of the diversity in ideology within communities – for all of the communities in our sample, weighted to be representative of all American communities. The standard deviation helps to describe the degree to which residents in that community hold ideologies that differ from the ideology of the average resident in that community. A small standard deviation in ideology implies less ideological diversity, while a large standard deviation suggests more heterogeneity. We include a reference line for the standard deviation in ideology for the entire United States adult population as a point of comparison. We note that, in keeping with the notion that contemporary American politics is characterized by

---

[9] Gilens, "The Insufficiency of 'Democracy by Coincidence'"; Martin Gilens. "Preference Gaps and Inequality in Representation." *PS: Political Science and Politics* 42, no. 2 (2009): 335–341.

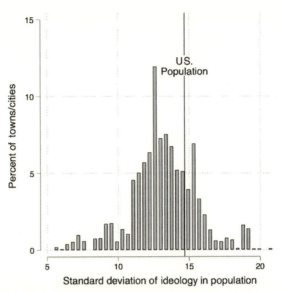

FIGURE 3.1 Variation in ideology in our sample of communities (with the United States as a reference)

Note: Sampling weights applied to make data representative of all American communities.

significant ideological polarization, this reference point indicates a fairly high level of ideological diversity.

If ideological diversity within most local communities is low, as the conventional wisdom suggests, we would expect the distribution of standard deviations in ideologies within our communities to be clustered around relatively small values. More pointedly, we would expect that most of this distribution would be distant from the standard deviation of ideology for the very ideologically diverse United States.

This is not what we find. The distribution of standard deviations in ideologies at the local community level is clustered around the median value of 13.1, which is quite close to the standard deviation in ideology for the entire US population (14.7). Even municipalities at the twenty-fifth percentile of the distribution have a standard deviation in ideology – 11.9 – that is not very distant from that of the United States population as a whole. And remarkably, roughly one-quarter of the communities have standard deviations in ideology that are larger than that of the United States adult population – meaning that 25 percent of communities have more ideological diversity than the US population as a whole! This is a far cry from the picture of ideological consensus presented in the

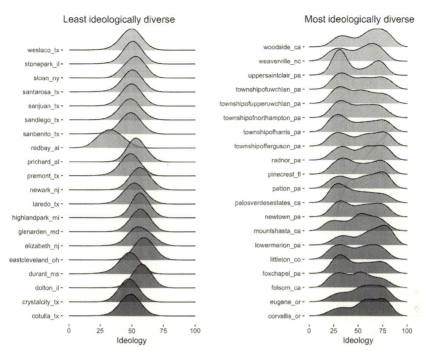

FIGURE 3.2 The least and most ideologically diverse communities

conventional wisdom about local politics. Indeed, the diversity of views within many communities provides ample reason to suspect that local politics may be more ideological than previously thought.

Just how much ideological disagreement is possible can be illustrated by comparing the least and most ideologically diverse communities. In Figure 3.2, we do just that, showing the distribution of ideology in the twenty least ideologically diverse communities (in the left-hand panel) and in the twenty most ideologically diverse communities (in the right-hand panel).

The communities in the left-hand panel closely resemble the consensus-oriented communities described by Oliver and others.[10] Interestingly, with the exception of Red Bay, Alabama, these communities also tend to have quite moderate residents (i.e. the distributions of ideology tend to be centered around fifty on the ideological scale). With relatively little ideological diversity among residents, these communities are unlikely to be characterized by ideology-based disagreement. Instead, disputes, when

---

[10] Oliver, Ha, and Callen, *Local Elections and the Politics of Small-Scale Democracy*.

they arise, are more likely to be related to personality clashes, unantici-
pated events, or reasoned differences over managerial decisions. Notably,
such consensus-oriented communities come in all types – from the
sprawling East Coast metropolis of Newark, New Jersey, to the largely
African American village of Dolton in Cook County, Illinois, to the
bustling border city of Laredo, Texas.

The communities in the right-hand panel are quite different, however.
These communities are characterized by substantial ideological diversity,
with residents occupying much of the ideological spectrum. Indeed, many
feature a bimodal distribution of ideology (that is, a distribution of
ideology with two distinctive and separate peaks) that is the hallmark of
ideological polarization. In such communities, it is hard to imagine that
politics will be confined to episodic disagreements over managerial
choices. Rather, it seems very likely that ideology-based disagreement will
play a prominent role in local politics. Importantly, too, these communities don't seem to represent a single "type," either: The most ideologically diverse communities range from Woodside, California, a San
Francisco–area small town that is among the wealthiest in the nation; to
Pinecrest, Florida, a prosperous suburban town in Miami-Dade County;
to Patton, Pennsylvania, a tiny, working-class community in rural Cam-
bria County. In other words, extreme ideological polarization doesn't
seem to be the exclusive province of any particular kind of community.

And remember: While the twenty communities presented in Figure 3.2
represent the most extreme examples of local ideological polarization, a
much larger share of communities exhibits a considerable degree of
ideological disagreement. As suggested by Figure 3.1, ideology-based
disagreement in local politics is likely to be the norm, rather than the
exception.

IDEOLOGICAL DIVERSITY AND RACIAL CLEAVAGES

Our analysis so far indicates that many American communities are quite
ideologically diverse, which could be expected to set the stage for
ideology-based disputes among residents. It remains an open question,
though, whether and to what extent ideological differences map onto
enduring social cleavages at the local level, such as those engendered by
racial or class differences. While ideology is fairly closely related to both
race and class in national and state politics – with people of color and the
less affluent tending to have more liberal ideologies than whites and the
well-to-do – it could be that this relationship doesn't hold within local

communities. Perhaps racial and class groups tend to agree *within* communities, but when it comes to state or national politics these commonalities within cities and towns are swamped by large differences in the views of racial or class groups *across* municipalities (or states or regions of the country). From the perspective of local politics, this would be the best-case scenario. While it is true that ideological differences can produce tensions in communities, such disagreements are more likely to be benign when they are weakly connected to other sources of difference. A less auspicious scenario is a close relationship between ideology and enduring markers of social difference, such as race or class. Such patterns tend to reinforce intergroup differences, paving the way to more intense and intractable political conflicts.[11]

With these considerations in mind we examine the relationship between ideology and identity in local communities, starting with race. As a first step in this analysis, we present in Figure 3.3 the distribution of ideology for whites, African Americans, and Latinos respectively, across all of the communities in our sample.

As the figure indicates, across all of our communities the distributions of ideology among whites, African Americans, and Latinos are quite distinctive. Among the three groups, whites have the greatest diversity in ideology. In the figure, the distribution of ideology among whites is relatively broadly dispersed across much of the range of possible ideological values, but the distributions of ideology among both African Americans and Latinos are much more tightly concentrated between the values of 25 and 75. A comparison of the standard deviations in ideology of these three groups tells the same story. Among whites, the standard deviation in ideology is 15.6; while among African Americans and Latinos, the standard deviations in ideology are noticeably smaller: 7.7 and 10.1, respectively. Of special note, the standard deviation in ideology among African Americans is less than half of that among whites.

More to the point, whites are the most conservative of the three racial groups overall. This can be observed in Figure 3.3, in which the distribution of ideology among whites has a relatively "fat" tail that corresponds with more conservative ideological leanings. The mean ideology among whites is 46.7 (St.Dev. = 15.6) – that is, on the more conservative side relative to the midpoint of 50 – and fully half of whites have ideologies below 50. African Americans are noticeably more liberal. The mean

[11] Liliana Mason, *Uncivil Agreement: How Politics Became Our Identity*. Chicago: University of Chicago Press, 2018.

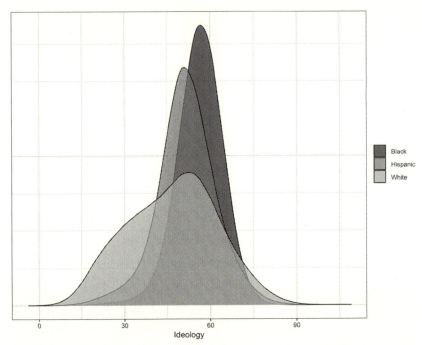

FIGURE 3.3 The distribution of ideology by race across communities in our sample

ideology among African Americans is 56.2 (St.Dev. = 7.7) – on the liberal side of the midpoint of 50 – and fewer than 25 percent of African Americans have ideologies below 50. It is important to underscore that African Americans and whites are, on average, quite ideologically distinct – a difference of nearly ten points (or 10 percent of the available scale) separates their respective means. But, of course, the fact that there is a great deal of ideological diversity among whites means that many whites overlap ideologically with blacks, even if on average whites are more conservative.

Relative to African Americans, Latinos have ideologies that are closer to those of whites, but they are still more liberal than whites overall. The mean ideology among Latinos is 51.6 (St.Dev. = 10.1), and about 50 percent of Latinos have ideologies below the midpoint of 50. Overall, the average Latino has an ideology that is almost exactly halfway between that of the average white (on the more conservative side) and the average African American (on the more liberal side).

Of course, while this analysis provides an initial look at ideological differences among racial groups in the communities in our sample, it does not grant insights into the magnitude of ideological differences between racial groups residing *within the same communities*. As noted, while the overall differences we observe could be reproduced within communities, it is also possible that the aggregate differences presented in Figure 3.3 reflect between-community variation more than within-community differences. The distinction matters, because only significant within-community racial differences in ideology would indicate the potential for race-based ideological conflict in *municipal* politics (as opposed to at the federal or state levels). Thus, to assess the scope of racial ideological difference within communities, we calculate differences between the mean ideologies of whites and the mean ideologies of African Americans/Latinos residing in the same community for all communities in our sample in which nonwhites constitute at least 10 percent of the population (we chose this cutoff to focus on communities in which nonwhites comprise nontrivial shares of the population). Keeping in mind that in any particular community either African Americans or whites could have more liberal/conservative ideologies, to ensure comparability across communities we calculate the *absolute value* of the difference in ideology between racial groups. A value of zero on this measure would mean that whites and blacks have the same average ideology, whereas a value of 10 would indicate that those groups are ten points apart on the ideological scale.

The distribution of absolute values in white–African American differences in ideology within these communities is presented in Figure 3.4. As a reference point, we plot the absolute difference in ideology between the adult population of the most conservative state (Alabama) and the adult population of the most liberal state (Massachusetts). That difference is seventeen points.

The figure suggests that, within communities with significant African American populations, there are large differences in ideology between African American and white residents. Within these communities, the mean absolute difference in ideology between African Americans and whites is 13.3 (St.Dev. = 6.4) – quite close to the seventeen-point absolute difference in ideology between the adult populations of the most conservative state and the most liberal state. Additionally, in more than one-quarter of these municipalities, the absolute difference in ideology between African Americans and whites is larger than the absolute difference in ideology between the adult residents of Alabama and those of Massachusetts. Simply put, in most communities with significant African American populations there are substantial ideological differences between African American and white adult residents. These patterns

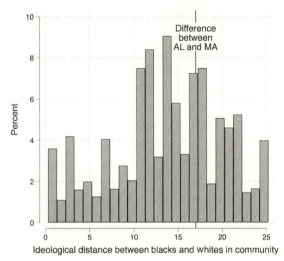

FIGURE 3.4 Distribution of communities based on ideological differences between black and white residents

Note: Plot includes only communities where African Americans comprise at least 10 percent of the population. Sampling weights applied.

suggest that, in municipalities with significant black populations, African American and white residents may frequently butt heads over important matters facing their communities.

We can zoom in on the prospects for ideology-based conflict between African Americans and whites within communities by comparing the twenty communities with the smallest differences and the twenty communities with the greatest differences in ideology between these two racial groups. This focused comparison is provided in Figure 3.5.

The communities in the left-hand panel of Figure 3.5 have the smallest African American–white differences in ideology among those in our sample with significant Black populations. As the information in the panel suggests, in these communities there is substantial overlap in ideology between African Americans and whites. Notably, though, in almost all of these communities the ideology of whites tends to be more broadly distributed, while that of African Americans is more concentrated. Contrast the image presented in the left-hand panel with that in the right-hand panel, however. In the communities in the right-hand panel, African Americans and whites are sharply polarized ideologically. Significantly, in every instance the distribution of ideology among whites is concentrated at the more conservative end of the ideological spectrum, while that of African Americans is either in the middle or toward the more liberal end.

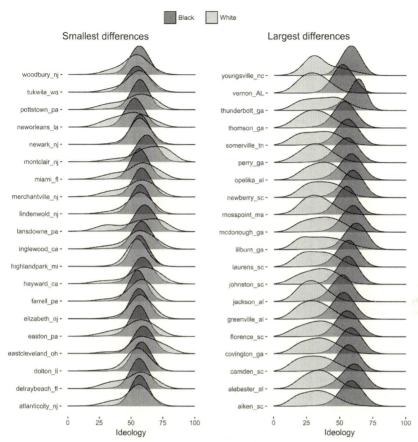

FIGURE 3.5 Communities with the smallest and greatest differences in ideology between African Americans and whites

Note: Analysis is limited to communities where African Americans are at least 10 percent of the adult population.

This is typical of the communities in our sample. When there are significant differences between the ideologies of African Americans and whites within communities, whites are almost always noticeably more conservative than African Americans. Notably, this pattern is virtually identical to that apparent in national politics, in which there are large ideological differences between African Americans and whites, with African Americans also tending to take more liberal positions on most issues than whites.

It is also important to note that the racially polarized communities presented in Figure 3.5 are *not* the large urban centers typically identified as seats of racial conflict in the prolific literature on urban politics. Rather,

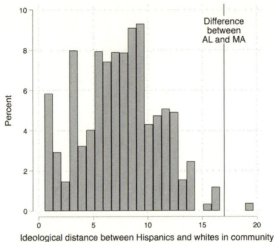

FIGURE 3.6 Distribution of communities based on ideological differences between Hispanic and white residents
Note: Plot includes only communities where Latinos comprise at least 10 percent of the population. Sampling weights applied.

the communities appearing in the right-hand panel of Figure 3.5 are largely small to medium-size towns, located in both rural and suburban areas, and scattered across the American South.[12] Consider, for example, the most racially polarized community in our sample, Youngsville, North Carolina. This semi-rural town, located in Franklin County (within the central region of the state) near Raleigh, had in 2010 a population of just 1,157 people, according to the US Census, and yet it exhibits here a stark ideological divide between African American and white residents. Notably, the town happens to be 28 percent African American, yet all five of the elected town officials are white. The example of Youngsville, along with the other patterns in Figure 3.5, reinforces our view that ideology-based conflict is not an exclusive characteristic of large metropolises, but is common to many communities throughout the United States.[13]

We see a somewhat more muted pattern when we examine ideological differences between Latinos and whites in communities with significant Latino populations, as in Figure 3.6.

---

[12] The pattern we find in southern communities is unsurprising given how the legacy of slavery still affects southern politics. See Acharya, Avidit, Matthew Blackwell, and Maya Sen. Deep roots: How Slavery Still Shapes Southern Politics. Princeton University Press, 2020.

[13] Hajnal and Trounstine, "Race and Class Inequality in Local Politics."

Within communities with significant Latino populations, the average absolute difference in ideology between Latinos and whites is 6.9 (St.Dev. = 3.8). This is not trivial, but it is only about half of the observed difference between African Americans and whites within all communities, on average, and less than half of the absolute distance in ideology between the adult residents of Alabama and those of Massachusetts. Even at the 75th percentile of the distribution, the absolute distance in ideology between Latinos and whites reaches only 9.6 – which, while significant (roughly 10 percent of the scale of ideology), is still less than the *average* distance between African Americans and whites. Thus, while Latinos tend to be more liberal than whites on average, the ideological differences between Latino and white groups within communities are less striking than the differences between African Americans and whites. And in the overwhelming majority of communities, the absolute difference in ideology between Latinos and whites is much smaller than the difference in ideology between adults in Alabama and adults in Massachusetts.

We can see this pattern again when we drill down into the data, contrasting the communities with the smallest and the largest absolute differences in ideology between Latinos and whites (shown in Figure 3.7).

As we can see in the left-hand panel (representing communities with the smallest Latino–white differences in ideology), such communities exhibit close ideological alignment between Latinos and whites. Strikingly, even in communities in which the distribution of ideology of either Latinos or whites is "lumpy" or irregular, the ideology of the other group is similar in shape.

In the right-hand panel, showing the communities with the largest Latino–white differences in ideology, we observe considerable ideological differences (though somewhat less polarization than is evident in Figure 3.5, which depicts communities with the largest racial divisions between African Americans and whites). Notably, communities with significant Latino–white differences in ideology include both relatively large urban areas such as Odessa, Texas (with a population of more than 116,000) and Oakland, California (with more than 425,000 residents) and small towns such as Robbins, North Carolina (population roughly 1,200) and Gering, Nebraska (population 8,500).[14] Again, we observe

---

[14] Oakland, CA may be an outlier in the sense that the differences in ideology between the Latino and white population are actually on a different side of the ideological spectrum than other localities. Oakland is a famously liberal city, which accounts for the observation that whites are actually further to the left – by a wide margin – than Latinos.

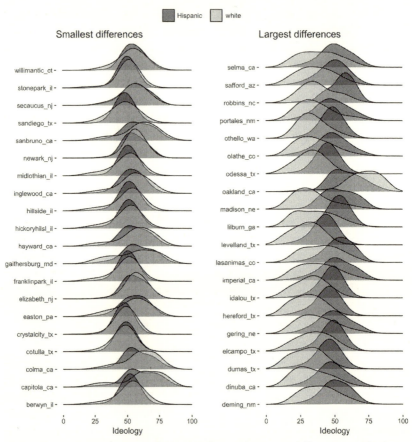

FIGURE 3.7 Communities with the smallest and greatest differences in ideology between Latinos and whites

Note: Analysis is limited to communities where Latinos are at least 10 percent of the adult population.

ideological polarization in communities of all sizes and across different areas of the country.

More generally, we note again the parallels between the racial ideological cleavages we observe and the ideological fissures between racial groups that are evident in today's state and national politics. Just as at the higher levels of government, there are within local communities significant racial differences in ideology between African Americans, Latinos, and whites, with residents of color (especially African Americans) tending to adopt more liberal positions. We also uncover more subtle differences in ideology between racial groups that parallel those found at the national level. Specifically, as is the case in national politics, we find that at the local level Latinos and whites tend to have more similar ideologies than do African Americans and whites.[15]

An important implication of our finding that, compared with those of African Americans, the ideologies of Latinos tend to be closer to those of whites, is that Latinos may be more likely than African Americans to benefit from coincidental representation in municipal politics. If we assume that local governments are most responsive to whites – a reasonable assumption given the nation's fraught racial history and continuing patterns of racial discrimination and unequal opportunity – the logic of coincidental representation favors groups that are ideologically more similar to whites, and disadvantages groups with ideologies that are more distant from those of whites. The closer ideological proximity of Latinos to whites points to the conclusion that Latinos may be favorably positioned, compared to African Americans, to become beneficiaries of coincidental representation in local politics.

IDEOLOGICAL DIVERSITY AND CLASS CLEAVAGES

The foregoing suggests significant prospects for ideology-based disagreements between racial groups (particularly between African Americans and whites) in many local communities. Do we see similar ideology-based cleavages among more and less affluent residents? Scholarly research on economic inequality in representation identifies important class differences in attitudes about taxation, redistribution, and poverty relief in national and state politics.[16] But it is unclear whether such ideological divisions also arise within local communities.

As in the previous section, we begin to assess ideology-based polarization among economic classes by examining the distributions of ideology for different wealth groups aggregated across all the communities in our sample. We examine the distributions of ideology for three wealth groups: a "low" wealth group composed of individuals in the bottom tercile (one-third) of the wealth distribution within their community; a "middle" wealth group including those in the middle tercile (one-third) of the wealth distribution within their community; and a "high" wealth group

---

[15] Rhodes, Schaffner, and McElwee, "Is America More Divided by Race or Class?"
[16] Gilens, *Affluence and Influence*; Gilens, "Inequality and Democratic Responsiveness"; Gilens, "Preference Gaps and Inequality in Representation."

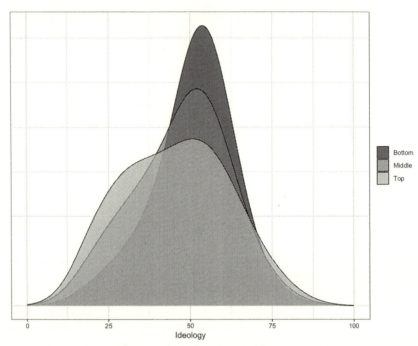

FIGURE 3.8 The distribution of ideology by wealth group across communities in our sample

comprising individuals in the top tercile (one-third) of the wealth distribution within their community. Keep in mind that these wealth groups are constructed to assign individuals to a tercile based on their place in the *local* wealth distribution rather than their position in the *national* distribution, so there is considerable diversity in the amount of wealth held by individuals within each tercile. However, we prefer this approach as it takes into account differences between communities in the local standard of living and thereby allocates individuals to terciles in ways that better represent their local class status, which is most relevant for assessment of representation of different class groups in municipal politics. These distributions are presented in Figure 3.8.

Figure 3.8 provides preliminary reasons for thinking that ideological differences among wealth groups are not as extreme as they are, say, between African Americans and whites. The respective distributions of ideology for the three groups overlap to a substantial degree, though the distribution for the top wealth group appears somewhat more diverse than does that of the other wealth groups. Consistent with existing research on the ideologies of different classes, we find that the top wealth tercile has the most conservative ideology – but the differences between the wealth groups are fairly small. The mean ideology of the top wealth group is 45.5 (St.Dev. = 16.4), compared with 47.5 (St.Dev. = 14.6) for the middle wealth group and 51.0 (St.Dev. = 12.1) for the bottom wealth tercile group. These differences are quite modest compared to the differences between African Americans and whites. However, the absolute difference in ideology between the low wealth group and the high wealth group (5.5 points) is similar in magnitude to the difference between Latinos and whites (6.9 points).

We can further assess the potential for ideology-based disagreements among class groups by examining the absolute value of the difference in ideology between class groups within communities. Within the communities in our sample, there is considerable ideological accord between the middle and high wealth groups. The average absolute difference in ideology between the middle and high wealth groups within the same community is only 3.0. Even at the 95th percentile of the distribution, the absolute difference in ideology between the middle and high wealth groups within the same community is only eight points. By comparison, recall that the absolute difference in ideology between Alabama adults and Massachusetts adults is seventeen points. Additionally, these figures indicate that the ideological differences between middle and high wealth groups are almost always much smaller than the *average* absolute difference in ideology between African Americans and whites, and they are typically smaller than the *average* absolute difference in ideology between Latinos and whites. In short, within the vast majority of communities the middle and high wealth groups tend to see eye to eye.

Ideological differences between low and high wealth groups within communities are a little larger – but are still relatively small compared to either the difference between the most conservative state and the most liberal state, or between African Americans and whites. The average absolute difference in ideology between the low and high wealth groups is a modest 5.8 points (St.Dev. = 3.0). Even at the 95th percentile of absolute differences in ideology between residents of low and high wealth, the difference between the low and high wealth groups is only 11.1 – less than the *average* difference between African Americans and whites! The absolute difference in ideology between the low and high wealth groups is most comparable to that between Latinos and whites (mean = 6.9, St. Dev. 3.8).

In short, class differences in ideology within local communities are not on average especially large. However, it is important to note that,

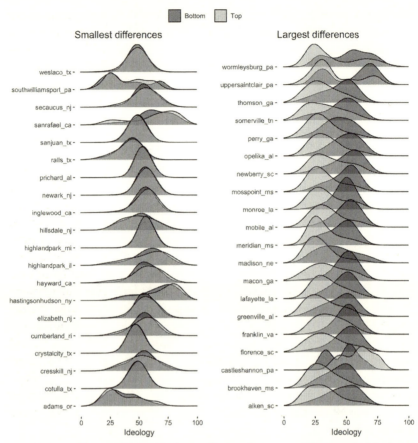

FIGURE 3.9 Communities with the smallest and greatest differences in ideology between low and high wealth groups

assuming that local elected officials are particularly responsive to high wealth residents (a not implausible assumption given the findings of most research on economic inequality in representation at other levels of government), the logic of coincidental representation appears to favor members of the middle wealth group. After all, as noted, on average middle and high wealth residents have very similar ideologies, while low wealth individuals have ideologies that are a bit more distinctive from those of the high wealth group. Under these circumstances, it may be that middle wealth individuals are more favorably positioned to benefit from coincidental representation.

A comparison of communities featuring the smallest and largest differences in ideology between low and high wealth groups, shown in

Figure 3.9, provides further insights into ideological disagreements on the basis of class. In the communities in the left-hand panel, we see striking accord between the low and high wealth groups. Suffice it to say, there is little indication of class-based ideological conflict in these municipalities. These communities conform to the conventional wisdom that ideological differences between economic groups are largely absent in most municipalities (especially outside of urban areas). The municipalities in the right-hand panel, in contrast, adhere to the stereotype of ideology-based tensions between the rich and the poor, with high wealth residents tending to adopt conservative positions and low wealth residents adopting noticeably more liberal views. For example, tiny Wormleysburg, Pennsylvania (population just over 3,000) – a community in Cumberland County, just across the Susquehanna River from the state capital of Harrisburg, exhibits a major ideological cleavage between conservative high wealth residents and much more liberal low wealth residents, many of whom are immigrants. The much larger Macon, Georgia – a city with more than 115,000 residents – is characterized by major differences in ideology between the wealthiest and poorest residents, though not quite on the scale of Wormleysburg. Many of the other communities with substantial class polarization are small to midsize towns scattered across rural and suburban America, giving lie to the notion that major class-based differences in ideology in municipal politics are confined to urban areas. Simply put, significant class differences in ideology within many communities create the potential for class-based political conflicts in those municipalities.

Even so, these communities – which are the most class-polarized in our sample – don't exhibit the same degree of ideological polarization as the most racially divided communities shown in Figure 3.5 (or even in Figure 3.7). Once again, it is hard to avoid the conclusion that, while present, ideology-based *class* conflict is less intense than is *racial* conflict in most municipalities. For the most part, the ideological differences between high, middle, and low wealth groups are smaller than the differences between racial groups or the differences between the most liberal and most conservative states.

A reasonable question is whether the class differences in ideology we observe in this chapter are to some degree attributable to racial differences (given that, in the racialized political economy of the United States, whites are on average more likely than nonwhites to have greater wealth holdings). In Chapter 6, we investigate this possibility in some detail. Although we save a detailed discussion for this later chapter, here we simply note that we find wealth-based differences in ideology of about the same size as reported here even in communities that are composed almost entirely of whites.

CONCLUSION

The perspective that local communities, especially outside large cities, are rarely sites of significant ideological disagreement has until recently been commonplace in both popular discourse and scholarly research.[17] While it is widely acknowledged that local politics can be conflictual, municipalities have typically been portrayed as insulated from the strong ideological cleavages that roil national and state politics.[18] Instead of exhibiting ideological conflicts, the conventional wisdom has suggested, local politics revolve around personality disputes and differences over managerial decisions. This perspective is consistent with a quip apocryphally attributed to former New York City Mayor Fiorello LaGuardia: "There is no Democratic or Republican way to fill a pothole."[19]

In this chapter we have used the unique data provided by Catalist to reexamine the ideological character of local politics in a stratified sample of large cities, midsize communities, and small towns from throughout the United States. Our findings provide a strong rejoinder to the conventional wisdom. As we show, residents of local communities have very diverse ideologies. Remarkably, the median standard deviation in ideology in the communities in our sample – a good measure of ideological diversity within communities - is very similar to that of the very ideologically diverse United States as a whole. This observation suggests that, contrary to popular belief, local politics are unlikely to be free from ideology-based differences. The patterns we reveal in this chapter point to the conclusion that there is substantial potential for ideology-based conflict in many US municipalities. Ideology, we suggest, plays a similarly central role in local politics and in national and state politics.[20]

Equally striking, we find that the ideological divisions we observe within communities map onto racial and class cleavages in predictable ways that likely reinforce the prospects for contention in local politics. Whites, African Americans, and Latinos within communities have

[17] Oliver, Ha, and Callen, *Local Elections and the Politics of Small-Scale Democracy*; Ferreira and Gyourko, "Do Political Parties Matter?"

[18] Warshaw, "Local Elections and Representation in the United States."

[19] Cann, "Structure of Municipal Political Ideology."

[20] Cann, "Structure of Municipal Political Ideology"; Tausanovitch and Warshaw, "Representation."

distinctive ideologies, with whites tending to hold more conservative positions and African Americans and Latinos tending to adopt more liberal views. The ideologies of whites and African Americans are particularly distant from each other. We also find important ideological differences between low wealth, middle wealth, and high wealth residents, though these are not quite as large as those between racial groups. Again, however, the pattern of class-based ideological differences within communities is familiar, with high wealth residents adopting more conservative positions than either middle wealth or low wealth residents.

The patterns of ideological cleavage within communities we explored in this chapter should raise concerns for those apprehensive about the prospects for effective local democracy in the United States. If national and state politics are characterized by substantial biases in representation against the interests of people of color and the less affluent, and local politics resemble national and state politics in their patterns of ideological disagreement, then it seems likely that local politics exhibit similar patterns of racial and economic biases in representation. Assessing whether this is in fact the case will be the task of the remainder of this book.

4

Local Political Participation, Municipal Elections, and the Prospects for Representation in Local Government

In 2017, researchers at Portland State University reached an eye-popping conclusion about the state of participation in local politics in the United States. Examining more than 23 million voting records, as well as information about community populations from the US Census, they estimated rates of voter turnout in the nation's fifty largest cities. Their findings were staggering – and depressing. Across the fifty communities, the median turnout rate in municipal elections was only 20 percent of the eligible electorate, and in Las Vegas, Ft. Worth, and Dallas, turnout was in the single digits. "low voter turnout is a problem in cities across the country," the study leaders concluded. "Too few people choose our local leaders."[1]

The findings from Portland State University are of a piece with those from other recent studies by academics and journalists that point to the sorry state of US participation in local politics. Contemporary headlines tell the tale: Some plaintively ask "Why Does No One Vote in Local Elections?" Others simply assert that "In the US, Almost No One Votes in Local Elections," while still others purport to explain "Why No One Votes in Local Elections."[2] In bemoaning the dismal patterns of participation in municipal politics, some commentators use language typically

---

[1] The quotes come from Portland State University's *Who Votes for Mayor?* project website, and can be found at www.whovotesformayor.org.
[2] Zoltan Hajnal, "Why Does No One Vote in Local Elections?," *The New York Times*, October 22, 2018, www.nytimes.com/2018/10/22/opinion/why-does-no-one-vote-in-local-elections.html; Jonathan Bernstein, "Why No One Votes in Local Elections," *Bloomberg Opinion*, April 29, 2019, www.bloomberg.com/opinion/articles/2019-04-29/why-no-one-votes-in-local-elections; Kriston Capps, "In the US, Almost No One Votes in Local

reserved for family interventions in cases of severe substance abuse. "Dallas is rock-bottom in voter turnout and we've got to pull together to change," an editor for the *Dallas News* exclaimed.[3]

This is also consistent with what we find in the communities from our own sample. We collected turnout data from the last general election held in ninety-nine towns and cities from our sample. In the average community, just 29 percent of registered voters participated in the last election. This means the rate would be much lower among *eligible* voters. In 15 percent of the communities, the turnout rate among registered voters did not even break 10 percent. Turnout is especially poor in communities that hold their elections separately from state or federal elections – just 20 percent of voters participated in local elections that were held off-cycle.

Given these facts, researchers and commentators have plausible reasons for concern. After all, a bedrock assumption among researchers, borne out by existing evidence, is that elected officials represent those who actively participate in politics much more than those who don't. As the Portland State University researchers warn, "When too few people elect local leaders, a small fraction of residents can have outsize influence in decisions about critical issues like schools, parks, housing, libraries, police, and transportation." And scholars of inequality in democracy at other levels of government have pointed to biases in turnout as an important contributor to inequities in representation.[4]

Ultimately, though, concerns about low turnout are warranted only if the small fraction of residents who participate in local politics are different in politically relevant ways from those who do not. The severity of the "problem" of low turnout in local elections hinges on the magnitude of the differences between participants and nonparticipants.

Are residents who participate in local politics different in important ways from those who abstain? And what are the likely consequences of low resident participation in local politics for racial and class inequality in representation? In this chapter, we address these questions by comparing the demographic and socioeconomic characteristics of regular participants

Elections," *CityLab*, November 1, 2016, www.citylab.com/equity/2016/11/in-the-us-almost-no-one-votes-in-local-elections/505766.

[3] Michael B. Lindenberg, "Dallas Is Rock-Bottom in Voter Turnout and We've Got to Pull Together to Change," *Dallas News*, September 27, 2018, www.dallasnews.com/opinion/commentary/2018/09/27/dallas-rock-bottom-voter-turnout-got-pull-together-change.

[4] See, e.g., William W. Franko, Nathan J. Kelly, and Christopher Witko. "Class Bias in Voter Turnout, Representation, and Income Inequality." *Perspectives on Politics* 14, no. 2 (2016): 351–368.

in local politics and of those who tend not to be engaged in municipal affairs. Our analyses justify the fear that the tendency toward limited overall participation in local politics does, in fact, increase the chances of racial and class biases in representation. Compared with residents overall, those who participate in local politics by voting or contacting local officials tend to be whiter and more affluent. Perhaps unsurprisingly, given these patterns and the trends we observed in Chapter 3, participants in local politics are also more conservative on average than are those who stay on the sidelines.

Notably, these biased patterns of participation appear to leave their mark on the composition of officials elected to municipal offices. As we show, local elected officials are, like the individuals who select them, unrepresentative of their communities. Local elected officials are more likely to be white, more likely to be wealthy, and more likely to be conservative than the communities they represent. Together – and especially in light of the findings from the previous chapter revealing that nonwhite and less affluent residents tend to have more liberal ideological leanings – the inequitable patterns in participation and the unrepresentative composition of local elected offices provide strong reasons to expect racial and class biases in representation at the municipal level.

BIASES IN VOTING IN LOCAL ELECTIONS AND THE
PROSPECTS FOR REPRESENTATION

Some seventy years ago, political scientist V. O. Key declared that "the blunt truth is that politicians and officials are under no compulsion to pay much heed to classes and groups of citizens that do not vote."[5] Social scientists generally agree. The consensus view is that those who vote in elections are much better represented by elected officials and in government policy than are those who do not.[6] There are three main reasons why this may be the case. First, voters' preferences may be especially influential because voters can select representatives who share their ideologies and policy preferences.[7] While elected officials presumably

---

[5] V. O. Key. *Southern Politics*. New York: Random House, 1949. 527.

[6] Arend Lijphart. "Unequal Participation: Democracy's Unresolved Dilemma: Presidential Address, American Political Science Association, 1996." *American Political Science Review* 91, no. 1 (1997): 1–14; Sidney Verba. "Would the Dream of Political Equality Turn Out to Be a Nightmare?" *Perspectives on Politics* 1, no. 4 (2003): 663–679.

[7] Warren E. Miller and Donald E. Stokes. "Constituency Influence in Congress." *American Political Science Review* 57, no. 1 (1963): 45–56.

have views that are relatively close to a majority of those who voted, this may or may not be so for nonvoters.[8] Second, voters may have more influence with elected officials than do nonvoters because voters are especially likely to communicate their preferences to elected officials.[9] Elected officials depend heavily on communications from constituents to ascertain the views of those they represent, and as voters are more likely than nonvoters to make their preferences known, their views likely carry more weight.

Finally, elected officials may be especially likely to cater to the preferences of voters because they believe that satisfying regular voters is the key to winning reelection.[10] If elected officials want to retain their offices – a foundational supposition in the social sciences – they must be closely attuned to what their constituents want. Indeed, research strongly suggests that elected officials who are out of step with their constituents quickly find themselves out of office.[11] Of course, in a perfect world elected officials would represent all their constituents. But when conflicts among constituents arise "vote-maximizing politicians must care more, other things being equal, about the views of regular voters than about the views of people who seldom or never get to the polls."[12] Thus, the incentives facing election-minded representatives favor the representation of voters.

Empirical research in American politics bears out the expectation that voters are generally better represented than nonvoters. For example, in their study of the US Senate, Griffin and Newman show that the preferences of voters predict the roll-call behavior of senators, while the preferences of nonvoters do not.[13] Martin and Claibourn compare the behavior of representatives across congressional districts to show that the preferences of constituents have a stronger influence on representatives' voting

---

[8] John D. Griffin and Brian Newman. "Are Voters Better Represented?" *The Journal of Politics* 67, no. 4 (2005): 1206–1227.

[9] Verba, "Would the Dream"; Verba, Brady, and Schlozman, *Voice and Equality*; Schlozman, Verba, and Brady, *The Unheavenly Chorus*.

[10] Morris P. Fiorina. *Representatives, Roll Calls, and Constituencies.* Lanham, MD: Lexington Books, 1974; Larry M. Bartels. "Where the Ducks Are: Voting Power in a Party System." In *Politicians and Party Politics*, ed. John Geer. Baltimore: Johns Hopkins University Press, 1998. 43–79.

[11] David Mayhew. *Congress: The Electoral Connection.* New Haven, CT: Yale University Press, 1974; Brandice Canes-Wrone, David W. Brady, and John F. Cogan. "Out of Step, Out of Office: Electoral Accountability and House Members' Voting." *American Political Science Review* 96, no. 1 (2002): 127–140.

[12] Bartels, "Where the Ducks Are," 45.

[13] John D. Griffin and Brian Newman. "Are Voters Better Represented?" *The Journal of Politics* 67, no. 4 (2005): 1206–1227.

behavior when district turnout is higher.[14] And looking at patterns of
state policymaking, Hill and Leighley demonstrate that states with higher
turnout among lower-income residents spend more on social welfare than
do those where turnout among the poor is lower.[15]

If, as these studies suggest, voters tend to enjoy better representation
than nonvoters, what are the implications for local government, the level at
which it is common for four-fifths of the eligible electorate to stay on the
sidelines? It would seem that the quality of local governance depends on
the extent to which the small set of people who are likely to vote in local
elections resemble the community's population as a whole. To examine
this issue, we need to look at the demographic characteristics and ideologies of those who are and are not likely to vote in local elections. Unfortunately, Catalist does not maintain turnout data for municipal elections for
most of the communities in our sample. It does, however, contain a
measure of how frequently each registered voter participated in elections
for which she was eligible. This variable is useful for our purposes because
it can help us identify our target population – people who are most likely to
vote in local elections – by accepting the reasonable assumption that people
who vote most of the time ("frequent voters") are likely to be, in large part,
the people who come to the polls in low-turnout municipal races.

Using a random sample of 3 percent of all registered voters across the
communities in our sample (a total of 511,964 individuals), Table 4.1
shows how frequent voters compare to those who participate infre-
quently. Importantly, this is a comparison of *registered voters*. People
who are registered to vote are already likely to be less racially diverse and
of higher socioeconomic status than unregistered individuals.[16] Nevertheless, we still see striking differences in the table when we compare
frequent voters to those who vote less often.

First, note that nearly three-fifths of all registered voters (59 percent)
participate in fewer than half of the elections for which they are eligible.
And only 17 percent of registered voters turn out in at least 75 percent of
elections. And it is this latter group that is likely to comprise the largest
share of voters in municipal elections. As we move from the lowest percent
of elections voted in (less than 25 percent) to the highest percent (75–100

---

[14] Paul S. Martin and Michele P. Claibourn. "Citizen Participation and Congressional
Responsiveness: New Evidence that Participation Matters." *Legislative Studies Quarterly* 38, no. 1 (2013): 59–81.
[15] Kim Quaile Hill and Jan E. Leighley. "The Policy Consequences of Class Bias in State
Electorates." *American Journal of Political Science* 36, no. 2 (1992): 351–365.
[16] Fraga, *The Turnout Gap*.

TABLE 4.1 *Racial composition and median wealth of frequent and infrequent voters*

Percent of elections voted in	Share of registered voters (%)	Median wealth	Percent of group that is ...		
			White (%)	Black (%)	Latino (%)
Less than 25	28	$80,000	67	16	11
25–50	31	$120,000	72	14	9
50–75	24	$160,000	79	11	7
75–100	17	$180,000	81	11	6

Note: Based on data from 511,964 registered voters from the Catalist voter file database.

percent), the white share of that group leaps by 14 percentage points, while the median wealth increases by $100,000. Put simply, individuals who are most likely to vote in municipal elections are much whiter and wealthier than are those who are least likely to vote in municipal elections. It is thus a virtual certainty that the electorate in municipal elections is a nonrepresentative – and quite privileged – sample of residents.

While Catalist does not keep turnout data for most municipal elections, it does keep this information for many of the largest cities. Notably, large cities like Chicago and New York provide a best-case scenario for turnout, since political campaigns in those cities attract widespread news coverage and are often the target of large amounts of spending. Nevertheless, even in municipal elections in those cities, we see clear disadvantages for racial minorities. For example, in the 2012 presidential election, Catalist estimated that whites and blacks made up an equal share of those voting in the city of Chicago (each group accounted for 41 percent of the electorate that November). Yet, in February 2015, when Mayor Rahm Emanuel ran for reelection against two minority candidates, less than half as many people came to the polls and whites enjoyed an eight-percentage-point advantage in their share of the electorate in that race (45–37 percent). Perhaps due to this edge, Emanuel won a plurality of the vote and eventually prevailed in the runoff election two months later. A similar pattern can be found in New York City. For the 2012 presidential election, well over 2 million people turned out to vote in New York City, with whites accounting for 42 percent of those who voted. However, when New York City held its mayoral election the following year, the number of people voting dropped by more than half, and whites accounted for 49 percent of those voting.

And, of course, large city mayoral elections featuring well-known politicians like Rahm Emanuel and Bill DeBlasio are the best-case scenarios for turnout in odd-year municipal elections. The situation is surely much worse in smaller cities and towns across America. Indeed, there is evidence that this is the case: in fact, the decline in nonwhite turnout is dramatically more pronounced in such communities than in the larger cities. For example, Schaffner, Van Erve, and La Raja compared turnout in Ferguson, Missouri, during the 2012 presidential election to turnout in the municipal election that was held in that town in April 2013.[17] While African Americans made up 71 percent of those who turned out in Ferguson in 2012, they accounted for just 47 percent of the electorate for the municipal elections of 2013.

So far, Table 4.1 has demonstrated that there are significant demographic differences between those who vote most frequently and the rest of the registered voters in our communities. But what about their underlying preferences? Using the same sample from Catalist, Figure 4.1 plots the distribution of ideology for four groups: all registered voters; those who voted in at least 25 percent of recent elections; those who voted in at least 50 percent of recent elections; and those who voted in at least 75 percent of recent elections. The patterns displayed in Figure 4.1 are striking. The distribution of ideology for all registered voters has the most liberal skew: It has the highest liberal peak (at around 60 on the Catalist ideology scale), and it lacks a significant conservative peak. However, as we move from the least frequent voters (those who vote at least 25 percent of the time) to the most frequent voters (those who vote at least 75 percent of the time), three things happen. First, the distribution of ideology becomes increasingly bimodal, with liberal and conservative peaks of more similar size. Second, the liberal peak at around 60 on the ideology scale progressively shrinks, indicating that, among more consistent voters, an ever-smaller share of individuals appears in this region of the distribution. Third, the conservative peak at around 20 on the ideology scale grows larger and larger, suggesting that, among more consistent voters, a growing proportion of individuals holds conservative views. Indeed, for the ideology distribution of those who vote at least 75 percent of the time, the conservative peak is nearly as large as the liberal peak. Putting all of these observations together, Figure 4.1 reveals that people who are most likely to vote in municipal elections are much more conservative than the population of registered voters.

In Figure 4.2, we provide insight into why this is the case. Figure 4.2 essentially replicates Figure 4.1, but breaks out the distribution for whites,

---

[17] Schaffner, Van Erve, and La Raja, "How Ferguson Exposes the Racial Bias in Local Elections."

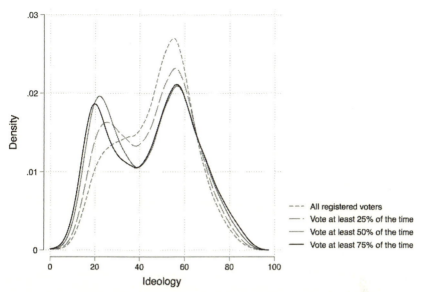

FIGURE 4.1 Distribution of ideology by frequency of voting
Note: Based on data from 511,964 registered voters from the Catalist voter file database.

African Americans, and Hispanics, respectively (note that this figure only compares all registered voters and the most frequent voters for each racial group). What we find is telling. Looking at the left-hand panel of Figure 4.2, we see that the ideological distribution of the most frequent white voters skews *much* more conservative than does the ideological distribution of all registered whites. In stark contrast, the ideological distribution of the most frequent African American voters is virtually identical to that of all registered black voters, as the center panel of Figure 4.2 shows. Finally, as suggested in the right-hand panel of Figure 4.2, the ideological distribution of the most frequent Hispanic voters is noticeably more conservative than is the distribution of all registered Hispanic voters, though this pattern is not nearly as extreme as it is for whites. These observations suggest that a major reason for the overall conservative skew of the most frequent voters is the very conservative orientation of the most frequent white voters.[18] As we noted in Chapter 3, white Americans are ideologically diverse, but *whites who*

---

[18] The somewhat more conservative orientation of frequent Hispanic voters may also play a role; however, because Hispanics represent a much smaller share of all frequent voters than do whites (6% vs. 81%, as shown in Table 4.1), their impact is much smaller.

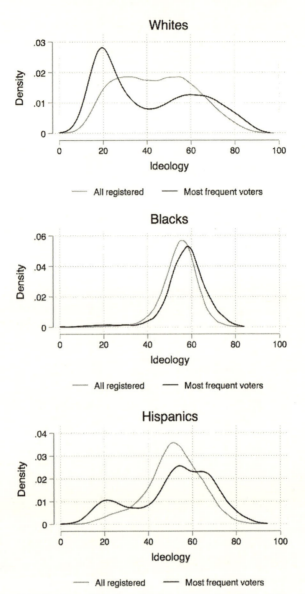

FIGURE 4.2 Distribution of ideology by frequency of voting, whites, African Americans, and Latinos

actually vote in local elections are less so. And when we compare the ideological distribution among whites who vote frequently to the plot of ideology among African Americans, we can quickly see that these groups hold distinctly different viewpoints.

The fact that the most frequent voters – i.e. those most likely to vote in municipal elections – are whiter, wealthier, and more conservative than all registered voters has major implications for our expectations about the functioning of local democracy. If elected officials are most responsive to voters, as existing theory and research suggest, and if the most likely voters in local elections are whiter, wealthier, and more conservative than residents in general, then it seems plausible that whiter, wealthier, and more conservative individuals receive outsized representation in local government.

BIASES IN PARTICIPATION IN LOCAL POLITICS AND THE PROSPECTS FOR REPRESENTATION

As noted, one likely reason for the superior representation enjoyed by voters is that voters (in addition to casting ballots) engage in other activities that inform the behaviors of elected officials. Perhaps most important, voters are particularly likely to contact elected officials about their concerns and demands, thus amplifying their influence.[19] Given that municipal elected officials view neighborhood meetings with constituents as one of the top two ways they learn about residents' views, we need to know more about the characteristics of the individuals who contact their local representatives.[20]

Existing research on contacts with elected officials gives us reason to suspect that individuals who contact their representatives are a nonrepresentative, and advantaged, sample of community residents.[21] Most notably, in a study of resident participation in local planning and zoning board meetings in Massachusetts – which matched speakers at local meetings to a voter file in order to identify their demographic and socioeconomic characteristics – researchers found that individuals who were

[19] Schlozman, Verba, and Brady, *The Unheavenly Chorus*; Hajnal and Trounstine, "Race and Inequality in Local Politics."

[20] Katherine Levine Einstein, David Glick, and Conor LeBlanc, "2016 Menino Survey of Mayors" (2017), www.bu.edu/ioc/files/2017/01/2016-Menino-Survey-of-Mayors-Final-Report.pdf.

[21] Naewon Kang and Nojin Kwak. "A Multilevel Approach to Civic Participation: Individual Length of Residence, Neighborhood Residential Stability, and Their Interactive Effects with Media Use." *Communication Research* 30, no. 1 (2003): 80–106; William A. Fischel. *The Homevoter Hypothesis: How Home Values Influence Local Government Taxation, School Finance, and Land-Use Policies.* Cambridge, MA: Harvard University Press, 2001.

older, male, longtime residents, and homeowners were more likely to make their views known to local elected officials at these events.[22]

Here, we took a different methodological approach, comparing the characteristics of those who reported attending a local political meeting on the 2016 CCES survey with the characteristics of other respondents to the survey who lived in the same community but did not report attending a local meeting. We did this through a process called matching. Since different communities may hold more or fewer public meetings, we wanted to be sure that we were making an apples-to-apples comparison. Therefore, our process was to first identify each respondent who said that they attended a local meeting and then compare that individual to all the other respondents who lived within the same municipal boundaries but did not report attending a local meeting. This allowed us to get a sense of how people who attend local meetings compare to those who don't, while controlling for the local context.

We also know that people tend to overreport the extent to which they engage in activities that might be viewed as socially desirable. For example, a large percentage of nonvoters in recent elections generally claimed on surveys that they did, in fact, vote.[23] Unfortunately, we cannot confirm whether CCES respondents actually attended local meetings. However, to attempt to mitigate some of the potential bias from people overreporting participation in local meetings, we used CCES vote validation information to identify individuals who, despite having no record of having voted, claimed to have done so. If a respondent who misrepresented their actual voting record also claimed to have attended a local meeting, we coded that individual as not having attended a meeting.[24] Once we made this adjustment, we found that about 8 percent of CCES respondents attended a local meeting during the previous year.

---

[22] Katherine Levine Einstein, Maxwell Palmer, and David M. Glick. "Who Participates in Local Government? Evidence from Meeting Minutes." *Perspectives on Politics* 17, no. 1 (2019): 28–46.

[23] Stephen Ansolabehere and Eitan Hersh. "Validation: What Big Data Reveal about Survey Misreporting and the Real Electorate." *Political Analysis* 20, no. 4 (2012): 437–459; Ted Enamorado and Kosuke Imai, "Validating Self-Reported Turnout by Linking Public Opinion Surveys with Administrative Records," *SSRN Working Paper* (2018), https://papers.ssrn.com/sol3/papers.cfm?abstract_id=3217884; Simon Jackman and Bradley Spahn. "Why Does the American National Election Study Overestimate Voter Turnout?" *Political Analysis* 27, no. 2 (2019): 193–207.

[24] The number of people who attend local political meetings but do not vote in a presidential election is likely to be very small.

TABLE 4.2 *Demographics of individuals who report having attended a local political meeting*

Trait	Did not attend a meeting	Attended a meeting
Black	9%	7%
White	74%	79%
Hispanic	10%	8%
Female	57%	46%
Median family income	$50,000–$60,000	$70,000–$80,000
Home owner	66%	75%
Invested in stock market	44%	61%
Average age	51	52

Note: Data from the 2016 CCES. $N = 31,249$ respondents in communities where at least one respondent attended a meeting and at least one respondent did not attend a meeting. Individuals who misreported having voted in 2016 are excluded from the second column. Sampling weights applied.

Our comparison of meeting attendees with people who did not attend meetings is presented in Table 4.2. Despite taking a different approach, our findings largely confirm those reported by Einstein, Palmer, and Glick (2019), and point to noticeable racial and class skews in local political participation. Just as our earlier examination of the characteristics of likely voters in municipal elections suggested the disproportionate influence of whites and the affluent, this analysis indicates that attendees at local meetings are whiter and wealthier than are survey respondents overall. While whites constitute 74 percent of CCES respondents who did not attend a meeting, they represent 79 percent of those who reported attending a local political meeting. In contrast, nonwhites are underrepresented among meeting participants. Blacks represent 9 percent of those not attending a meeting but 7 percent of meeting attendees, while Hispanics represent 10 percent of those not attending a meeting but only 8 percent of attendees at local meetings. In similar fashion, participants in local meetings are on average more affluent than other individuals. Those who report attending a local political meeting have a substantially higher median income than all respondents ($70,000–$80,000 vs. $50,000–$60,000). Additionally, in comparison with non-attendees, a larger share of local meeting participants own homes (75 percent vs. 66 percent) and invest in the stock market (61 percent vs. 44 percent).

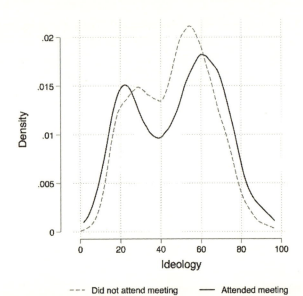

FIGURE 4.3 Distribution of ideology for meeting attendees and non-attendees
Note: Data from the 2016 CCES. N = 31,249 respondents in communities where at
least one respondent attended a meeting and at least one respondent did not attend
a meeting.

Equally important, local meeting attendees tend to have more extreme
ideological views than do those who did not attend meetings, as Figure 4.3
suggests. The ideological distribution of meeting attendees is more bimodal
than that for non-attendees. Additionally, compared to the distribution for
non-attendees, the two peaks of the distribution for attendees are further
apart, and both peaks are closer to the extremes of the ideological spectrum. Not surprisingly, people who attend local meetings tend to have
more extreme ideological views than their neighbors who stay home.

Thus, as was the case for individuals who vote, individuals who contact
local elected officials are unrepresentative of the broader population.
Importantly, these patterns are consistent with the hypothesis of racial
and/or class bias in representation in local politics. Those who contact
local elected officials are more likely to be white, more likely to be wealthy,
and more likely to hold extreme views than are those who do not.

WHO RUNS FOR OFFICE, AND WHO WINS MUNICIPAL COUNCIL SEATS

So far, we have provided evidence that participation in local politics is
dominated by an unrepresentative, and privileged, stratum of residents.

How, if at all, does this affect the composition of those elected to local office? One oft-stated reason for concern about the outsized influence of voters is that, compared with those with less opportunity, ability, or motivation to vote, they are able to exercise decisive influence over the selection of elected officials and thereby elect like-minded individuals to positions of power. But is this actually the case?

To answer this question, we first examine the composition of those who elect to *run* for local office. After all, those who win office must first run for office, so if the sample of individuals who run for office is biased toward advantaged community members, it is likely that the group of those who win office is unrepresentative also (unless disadvantaged community members tend to win the elections they contest at much higher rates). Notably, existing research on political ambition and the decision to run strongly suggests that those already enjoying advantages on the basis of race, affluence, and gender are more likely to run for elective office.[25] In addressing this question, the CCES is once again helpful in that it asks respondents whether they have ever run for elective office. Individuals who respond affirmatively can then indicate which office they have run for. Here, we examined respondents who reported that they had at some time run for mayor, city council, city or district attorney, school board, or some other local board or commission. After making our adjustment to account for people who were likely to have misrepresented their history of having run for office (because they were known to have misrepresented their voting history), we identified 943 respondents who had previously run for office (a little less than 2 percent of the CCES sample in 2016). In analyzing this group, we adopted the same approach as we did for people who said they attended local meetings – we matched them to other people in their community in order to make a comparison that would control for local context.

The patterns in Table 4.3 provide support for our expectation of demographic and socioeconomic biases favoring already privileged groups among those who report running for municipal offices. Whites

---

[25] Nicholas Carnes. *The Cash Ceiling: Why Only the Rich Run for Office-and What We Can Do about It*. Princeton, NJ: Princeton University Press, 2018; Jennifer L. Lawless and Richard L. Fox. *It Still Takes a Candidate: Why Women Don't Run for Office*. Cambridge: Cambridge University Press, 2010; Richard L. Fox and Jennifer L. Lawless. "To Run or Not to Run for Office: Explaining Nascent Political Ambition." *American Journal of Political Science* 49, no. 3 (2005): 642–659; Jennifer L. Lawless. *Becoming a Candidate: Political Ambition and the Decision to Run for Office*. Cambridge: Cambridge University Press, 2012.

TABLE 4.3 *Demographics of individuals who report having run*
for municipal office

Trait	Did not run for office	Ran for office
Black	7%	5%
White	76%	80%
Hispanic	10%	8%
Female	56%	29%
Median family income	$50,000 –$60,000	$70,000–$80,000
Home owner	67%	81%
Invested in stock market	45%	66%
Average age	51	57

Note: Data from the 2016 CCES. Individuals who misreported having voted in 2016 are excluded from the second column. Includes people who reported running for school board, local commissions or boards, city council, or mayor.

made up a larger share of those who ran for municipal office than of those who did not (80 percent vs. 76 percent), while African Americans and Latinos represented smaller shares of those who ran for local offices (5 percent vs. 7 percent, and 8 percent vs. 10 percent, respectively). Self-reported candidates for municipal offices were also significantly wealthier than non-candidates in general. Those who ran for office reported a median income of $70,000–$80,000, while the median family income for 2016 CCES respondents who did not run was only $50,000–$60,000. Self-reported candidates for municipal office were also much more likely to be homeowners and investors than noncandidates. Additionally, and in keeping with previous research, our analysis revealed an enormous gender bias in the decision to run for office, with women composing a much smaller share of those indicating a run for municipal office (29 percent). When it comes to the pool of municipal candidates, then, concerns about the overrepresentation of privilege seem to be warranted.

WHO ARE OUR LOCAL ELECTED OFFICIALS?

So far we have demonstrated the existence of substantial biases in the characteristics of individuals who are most likely to participate in local elections; most likely to show up and make their voices heard at local political meetings; and most likely to run for local office. But how is this finding reflected in the types of people who actually hold elected office in America's cities and towns? The characteristics of local officials – and in particular, their races and incomes – likely influence officials' patterns of representation, with officials of a particular race/income being especially likely to represent the interests of the members of their own group.[26]

To provide a picture of who represents us in local government, we return to our sample of communities and the 4,110 elected officials we matched with the Catalist database. Recall that the Catalist database provides us with information about the age, gender, race, income, and ideologies of these elected officials. Overall, local elected officials are much like politicians at higher levels of government – they are older, more male, more white, wealthier, and more ideologically polarized than the people they represent. The average age of the local elected officials in our sample is 58.2 years old. Notably, this is almost exactly the same as the average age of members of the 116th US Congress (elected in 2018). By comparison, the average age of American adults is 47.7. Fully 74 percent of the councilors in our sample are men, and only 26 percent are women. The fact that municipal councils are heavily dominated by men provides reason for concern that councils may not be equally responsive to all constituents; it also provides evidence that the substantial under-representation of women in politics extends even to local government.

The membership of municipal councils is also highly skewed toward whites. Indeed, 85 percent of all councilors in the communities in our sample are white. Of the nonwhite councilors, approximately two-thirds (or 10 percent of all councilors) are African American, one-quarter (or

---

[26] Robert R. Preuhs. "The Conditional Effects of Minority Descriptive Representation: Black Legislators and Policy Influence in the American States." *The Journal of Politics* 68, no. 3 (2006): 585–599; Robert R. Preuhs. "Descriptive Representation as a Mechanism to Mitigate Policy Backlash: Latino Incorporation and Welfare Policy in the American States." *Political Research Quarterly* 60, no. 2 (2007): 277–292; Robert R. Preuhs and Rodney E. Hero. "A Different Kind of Representation: Black and Latino Descriptive Representation and the Role of Ideological Cuing." *Political Research Quarterly* 64, no. 1 (2011): 157–171; John D. Griffin and Claudia Anewalt-Remsburg. "Legislator Wealth and the Effort to Repeal the Estate Tax." *American Politics Research* 41, no. 4 (2013): 599–622; Michael W. Kraus and Bennett Callaghan. "Noblesse Oblige? Social Status and Economic Inequality Maintenance among Politicians." *PloS One* 9, no. 1 (2014); Nicholas Carnes. "Does the Numerical Underrepresentation of the Working Class in Congress Matter?" *Legislative Studies Quarterly* 37, no. 1 (2012): 5–34; Nicholas Carnes. *White-Collar Government: The Hidden Role of Class in Economic Policy Making.* Chicago: University of Chicago Press, 2013.

4 percent of all councilors) are Hispanic/Latino, and the remainder are of other races. As we demonstrate empirically in the next chapter, the racial membership of municipal councils does not resemble that of their respective communities, showing a substantial overrepresentation of whites (and underrepresentation of African Americans and Latinos).

Interestingly, the wealth differences between local elected officials and the overall US population are less dramatic. To be sure, the poorest Americans are less likely to hold local office – while 32 percent of American adults have wealth of less than $30,000, just 22 percent of local elected officials are in that same low-wealth grouping. By contrast, 40 percent of local elected officials have estimated wealth between $100,000 and $300,000, which is a bit higher than the share of American adults in that same wealth group (33 percent). But local office is not especially dominated by millionaires – 4.5 percent of local elected officials have an estimated wealth of greater than $1 million (compared to 2.7 percent of Americans in that wealth group). While the US Congress is often said to be run by millionaires, the same is not quite true of municipal politics.

But one dimension where local elected officials do seem to resemble members of Congress is on ideological polarization. Figure 4.4 shows the ideological distribution of local elected officials in our sample. Note that this distribution is clearly bimodal. One large block consists of liberal-leaning municipal officials while another, even larger, block consists of conservative officials. The conservative block of elected officials is particularly noteworthy, as it peaks around an ideological score of 20. Overall, the average ideology of municipal councilors is 37.9, a score that is substantially more conservative than either the average for white adults (47.6) or the average for the most affluent residents (45.5). In short, many local elected officials are quite conservative, a fact that may not be surprising when we remember that most municipalities are small rural towns.

Additionally, it may be worth returning to Figure 4.1 as a point of comparison with Figure 4.4. In particular, the solid line in Figure 4.1 – which shows the ideological distribution of the voters who are most likely to turn out in municipal elections – is remarkably similar to the distribution for local elected officials. If local elected officials are ideologically polarized and conservative-leaning, this may be because they are a fairly good reflection of the voters who elect them. Unfortunately, they look much less like the vast majority of citizens who do not make it to the polls during municipal elections.

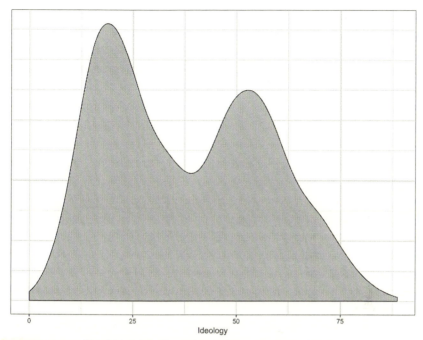

0   25   50   75

Ideology

FIGURE 4.4 The ideological distribution of local elected officials

Together, the patterns described in this section point to the conclusion that municipal councils represent a relatively privileged stratum of society. Councils disproportionately comprise older white men – in short, those who enjoy disproportionate power and influence in American political life. They are also quite conservative. The extremely strong representation of the privileged in the halls of power of local government raises concerns about the capacity of municipalities to represent all their constituents fairly and equitably.

CONCLUSION

Participation in municipal politics is typically quite low. In most communities, less (often much less) than a majority turns out to vote in local elections, and even fewer engage in other forms of participation such as contacting local elected officials and running for municipal office. Ironically, the very governments that are "closest to the people" inspire the lowest levels of political engagement among citizens.

However, as we show in this chapter, the deeper issue is that dismal overall rates of participation in local political affairs greatly increase the chances of racial and class biases in representation in municipal government. The crux of the problem is that residents who are active in local politics are different in systematic ways from those who abstain. Voters in local elections are more likely to be white, more likely to be affluent, and more likely to be conservative than are residents overall. Additionally, the sample of residents who contact municipal officials are whiter, wealthier, and more ideologically extreme than their communities. Since elected officials tend to be more responsive to those who engage actively in politics than to those who stay on the sidelines, the racial and class biases in local political participation we observe in this chapter set the stage for similar biases in representation.

Indeed, the patterns we describe point to the conclusion that already advantaged residents are disproportionately able to elect like-minded individuals to office. The pool of candidates for municipal offices is heavily skewed toward whites, more affluent residents, and men. Perhaps unsurprisingly, then, whites, wealthy people, and men also predominate among those elected to local offices. Strikingly, we also find among these individuals ideologies that are far more conservative than those of the communities they represent.

The substantial overrepresentation of the already advantaged among both politically active residents and municipal elected officials provides strong justification for suspecting considerable bias in representation in local government in favor of privileged racial and economic groups. Starting in Chapter 5, we begin to assess whether and how much the advantages in participation enjoyed by privileged groups in fact translate into superior representation in municipal politics.

5

Racial Inequality in Representation on Municipal Councils and in Policy

A rural, working-class community of about 12,000 residents (38 percent of whom are African American), Brookhaven, Mississippi, is located in Lincoln County, approximately 60 miles south of Jackson, the state's capital. Traditionally, Brookhaven has been dominated by timber and cotton concerns, and these industries still play a major role in the community, along with light industry and warehousing and distribution services. In tacit acknowledgment of the economic and social challenges the town has faced in an era of globalization and rising economic inequality, a local history describes the town as "a charismatic survivor" that persisted in the face of "vicissitudes similar to those which resulted in the diminishment or disappearance of [other] formerly flourishing Lincoln County villages and towns."[1]

Despite its resilience, however, all is not well politically in Brookhaven. The town was recently roiled by allegations that municipal councilors used a variety of strategies to shield their deliberations from public scrutiny. According to the local paper, the *Daily Leader*, town aldermen routinely violated the state's Open Meeting Act by retiring without adequate justification to "executive sessions" closed to the public.[2] It was especially troubling that such violations occurred during consideration of not only mundane issues, but also major issues with profound implications for the community's future. For example, the Board of

---

[1] Brookhaven Chamber of Commerce, "How We Got Where We Are Today," http://brookhavenchamber.org/wp/work-here/about-brookhaven.

[2] Adam Northam, "Complaint Filed over City Alderman Meeting – Closed Door Meeting Prompts Request for Ethics Opinion," *Daily Leader*, May 9, 2018.

Aldermen repeatedly met in closed session with representatives from the local Chamber of Commerce to discuss proposals for economic development – even though, as the *Daily Leader* pointed out, "there is no Open Meetings Act exemption for 'economic development.'"[3]

Aldermen have also exploited quorum rules in an apparent attempt to avoid public oversight of councilors' discussions of planning and economic development strategies. As the *Daily Leader* reported, "When discussing the city's comprehensive plan project recently … aldermen have been meeting two at a time with consultants about the project. Doing so allows aldermen to keep the public out of the meetings, since a quorum is not present."[4] City councilors apparently used the same ploy when discussing a feasibility study for a controversial proposal to build a new community center and swimming pool.[5] Notably, the Mississippi Supreme Court has ruled that efforts to skirt the requirements of the Open Meeting Act by intentionally holding sub-quorum meetings violate the Act.

Such chicanery by municipal officials would be unacceptable in any community. But it is especially problematic in a community like Brookhaven, which is characterized by racial divisions and a large racial gap in ideological representation on the municipal council. According to our calculations, Brookhaven has one of the largest racial gaps in ideological congruence representation among communities that are composed of at least 30 percent African American residents. While whites on average are only 3.4 points away from the ideological mean of the city council, African Americans are on average 20.8 points away. Under such racially inequitable circumstances, attempts by municipal councilors to avoid public oversight threaten both the overall quality of local democracy

[3] Adam Northam, "Closed Meetings Keep Public in the Dark – Attorney: Local Boards Not Following Letter of the Law," *Daily Leader*, March 23, 2018.

[4] Our viewpoint, "Openness Not Always Easy, but It's Right," *Daily Leader*, May 4, 2018.

[5] Adam Northam, "Are Brookhaven City Officials Meeting in Secret? Aldermen Deny Access to Committee Meeting; also Skirting Law by Meeting in Pairs to Avoid Quorum," *Daily Leader*, May 4, 2018.

The community center and swimming pool were advocated by Alderman Shannon Moore, who represents the poorest ward in Brookhaven, which is comprised of predominantly black residents. In a controversial vote the council voted against these projects, with the majority claiming they were too expensive for the town and would not get sufficient use. Information based on Donna Campbell, news editor, *The Daily Leader*, interview by coauthor, June 28, 2019. See also Donna Campbell, "Mayor: Pool 'Not Be in the Best Interests of Our City.'" *The Daily Leader*, May 16, 2018, https://m.dailyleader.com/2018/05/16/mayor-pool-not-in-the-best-interest-of-our-city.

and the civil rights of the community's black residents. As local attorney and first amendment expert Leonard Van Slyke emphasized in criticizing the council's actions, "An informed voting public is essential to maintaining a free society."[6]

Of course, Brookhaven may represent an extreme case of government malfeasance and lack of responsiveness to the ideologies of residents of color. But this tale raises broader questions about the quality of representation at the local level in the United States. To what extent do the racial demographics of municipal councils resemble those of the communities they represent? How well do municipal councils represent the ideologies of their residents of color? And to what extent are the demands of African American and Latino residents reflected in the policies formulated by local governments?

In this chapter we tackle these questions, using our data to yield unprecedented insights into the quality of representation that municipal governments provide to African American and Latino residents in communities around the United States. Our findings should shock and disturb everyone concerned about the quality of local democracy in this country. Across a range of measures of representation in municipal government, African Americans and Latinos enjoy far less representation than do whites. Racial inequality in representation is, disturbingly, the norm rather than the exception.

Residents of color do not enjoy descriptive representation on municipal councils on par with their shares of the population. While African Americans and Latinos compose 13.6 and 10.1 percent of all persons in the communities in our sample, they represent respectively only 8.1 and 3.9 percent of municipal councilors. Moreover, relative to whites, the ideologies of African American and Latino residents are poorly reflected on municipal councils. Only when they constitute a large majority of the community population do African American and Latino residents receive ideological congruence representation on municipal councils at a level similar to that routinely enjoyed by whites. For example, it is only when blacks make up 80–100 percent of the community population that they receive the same amount of ideological congruence representation that whites receive when they represent 20–40 percent of the population. Although it is difficult to make direct comparisons between our findings and estimates of racial inequalities in representation at other levels of

---

[6] Northam, "Are Brookhaven City Officials Meeting in Secret?"

government, we believe the inequities we uncover are substantively quite significant.[7]

Finally, while the overall ideology of local government policy is closely related to the ideology of white constituents, this is not the case for African Americans and Latinos. Shockingly, our statistical models suggest that after controlling for the preferences of white residents, the ideology of local government policy is completely unrelated to the ideology of Latinos, and it is actually the opposite of that preferred by African Americans.

We conclude that while the details of the case of Brookhaven may be unusual, the broader problems that it symbolizes are much more common than we would like to admit. Contrary to oft-repeated claims that democracy works best when it is closest to the people, we find profound and systematic biases in local government against people of color. Indeed, the chronic racial inequality in representation we find at the local level is quite similar to that identified by other scholars in federal and state politics.

Our results suggest that a fundamental reappraisal of the quality of our democratic politics is in order. If local governments do not do a good job representing constituents of color, even when these constituents compose a sizeable proportion of the population, are they truly democratic? Our findings also raise pressing questions for concerned citizens. Why have so many local governments failed to meet basic standards of democracy? What differentiates the worst-performing local governments from those that do better in providing representation to residents of color? And what can be done to bring more local governments into alignment with democratic ideals?

DESCRIPTIVE REPRESENTATION ON MUNICIPAL COUNCILS

Theorists of democracy have made a compelling case that *descriptive representation*, especially of historically marginalized groups, is a crucial indicator of the health of democracy.[8] Descriptive representation refers to representation on a governing body of a particular group within a

---

[7] See, e.g., Griffin and Newman, "The Unequal Representation of Latinos and Whites"; Griffin and Newman, *Minority Report*; Griffin and Flavin, "Racial Differences in Information, Expectations, and Accountability."

[8] Lani Guinier. "The Supreme Court, 1993 Term: [E]Racing Democracy: The Voting Rights Cases." *Harvard Law Review* no 1. (1994): 109–137; Jane Mansbridge. "Should Blacks Represent Blacks and Women Represent Women? A Contingent 'Yes.'" *The Journal of Politics* 61, no. 3 (1999): 628–657; Phillip Paolino. "Group-Salient Issues and Group Representation: Support for Women Candidates in the 1992 Senate Elections." *American Journal of Political Science* no. 2 (1995): 294–313.

community by a representative who shares one or more identities (race, gender, class, sexual orientation, etc.) with the members of that group.[9] Thus, for example, if Latinos in a congressional district succeeded in electing a Latino to the House of Representatives, we would say that they were receiving from their congressperson descriptive representation on the basis of shared race/ethnicity.[10]

Descriptive representation is important for several reasons. The repeated betrayals of historically disadvantaged groups by relatively privileged community members strongly suggest that advantaged groups cannot be trusted to represent the interests of marginalized members of society.[11] With this historical context in mind, increased descriptive representation at the local level may provide a partial compensation for groups victimized by past and present betrayals by privileged groups.[12] At the same time, descriptive representation of disadvantaged groups may provide a number of positive benefits for democracy. First, descriptive representativeness may send an inspiring signal that can positively affect the self-esteem and political efficacy of group members.[13] Second, group representation may enable historically marginalized groups to introduce onto the political agenda distinctive viewpoints, issues, and policy proposals that might otherwise be ignored.[14] And third, the presence of descriptive representation may send a signal to all community members of the local community's commitment to democratic renewal through broad inclusion in the political process.[15] A substantial body of empirical research suggests that descriptive representation of marginalized groups

---

[9] Hanna F. Pitkin. *The Concept of Representation.* Berkeley: University of California Press, 1967.

[10] Mansbridge, "Should Blacks Represent Blacks."

[11] Virginia Sapiro. "Research Frontier Essay: When Are Interests Interesting? The Problem of Political Representation of Women." *American Political Science Review* 75, no. 3 (1981): 701–716.

[12] Anne Phillips. "Democracy and Representation: Or, Why Should It Matter Who Our Representatives Are?" In *Feminism and Politics*, ed. Anne Phillips. Oxford: Oxford University Press, 1998: 224–241.

[13] Lawrence Bobo and Franklin D. Gilliam. "Race, Sociopolitical Participation, and Black Empowerment." *American Political Science Review* 84, no. 2 (1990): 377–393; David E. Campbell and Christina Wolbrecht. "See Jane Run: Women Politicians as Role Models for Adolescents." *The Journal of Politics* 68, no. 2 (2006): 233–247; Suzanne Dovi. "Preferable Descriptive Representatives: Will Just Any Woman, Black, or Latino Do?" *American Political Science Review* 96, no. 4 (2002): 729–743.

[14] Anne Phillips. *The Politics of Presence.* Oxford: Clarendon Press, 1995.

[15] Suzanne Dovi. "In Praise of Exclusion." *The Journal of Politics* 71, no. 3 (2009): 1172–1186.

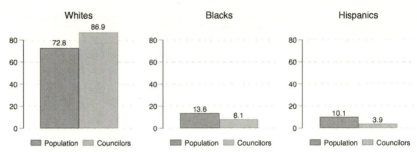

FIGURE 5.1   Share of community population and municipal council seats held by whites, blacks, and Latinos in communities in sample
Note: Sampling weights applied to calculations.

can strengthen representational links, foster more positive attitudes toward government, and encourage political participation.[16]

For these reasons, we have assessed how well officials elected to municipal councils descriptively represent their constituents. Using the data we acquired from Catalist, we have been able to estimate the racial demographics both of communities and of municipal councils for every community in our sample. We began by simply comparing the racial demographics of constituents and councilors across all of the communities in our sample. Figure 5.1 charts the proportion of constituents and councilors in each of three racial categories: whites, African Americans, and Latinos.[17] We weighted these figures to ensure that the results would be representative of the situation in American communities as a whole.

---

[16] Susan A. Banducci, Todd Donovan, and Jeffrey A. Karp. "Minority Representation, Empowerment, and Participation." *The Journal of Politics* 66, no. 2 (2004): 534–556; David E. Broockman. "Distorted Communication, Unequal Representation: Constituents Communicate Less to Representatives Not of Their Race." *American Journal of Political Science* 58, no. 2 (2014): 307–321; Jeffrey A. Karp and Susan A. Banducci. "When Politics Is Not Just a Man's Game: Women's Representation and Political Engagement." *Electoral Studies* 27, no. 1 (2008): 105–115; Adrian D. Pantoja and Gary M. Segura. "Does Ethnicity Matter? Descriptive Representation in Legislatures and Political Alienation among Latinos." *Social Science Quarterly* 84, no. 2 (2003): 441–460; Rene R. Rocha, Caroline J. Tolbert, Daniel C. Bowen, and Christopher J. Clark. "Race and Turnout: Does Descriptive Representation in State Legislatures Increase Minority Voting?" *Political Research Quarterly* 63, no. 4 (2010): 890–907; Kenny J. Whitby. "The Effect of Black Descriptive Representation on Black Electoral Turnout in the 2004 Elections." *Social Science Quarterly* 88, no. 4 (2007): 1010–1023.

[17] Catalist includes an "Other" racial category, which comprises individuals who do not fit into any of the other racial groups. However, individuals in the Other category represent only about 4 percent of observations in our sample, so we focus on representation among whites, African Americans, and Latinos in our analyses.

As the figure suggests, whites are overrepresented on councils relative to their share of the total population across all of the communities in our sample, while African Americans and Latinos are underrepresented. Whites constitute 72.8 percent of the population of all of the communities in our sample, but 86.9 percent of all councilors. Put another way, the additional 14.1 percent of their representation, compared to their 72.8 percent share of the population in the communities in our sample, means that whites are overrepresented on municipal councils by 19 percent. This represents a substantial degree of overrepresentation, which may reinforce the political power of whites in local government (especially given, as we showed previously, that whites tend to have ideologies that are quite distinctive from those of African Americans or Latinos).

In contrast to whites, residents of color are underrepresented on municipal councils relative to their shares of community populations. African Americans represent 13.6 percent of the population of all the communities in our sample but only 8.1 percent of councilors. This means that blacks' share of municipal councils is only about 60 percent of their share of the population of the communities in our sample. The situation facing Latinos is even worse. While Latinos constitute 10.1 percent of the population in the communities in our sample, they represent only 3.9 percent of municipal councilors. Thus, Latinos' share of municipal councils is only about 40 percent of their share of the population of the communities in our sample.

These figures provide preliminary indications that residents of color are substantially underrepresented on municipal councils compared to their shares of community populations, and they suggest that these groups may suffer from diminished influence in local politics. However, this bird's-eye view provides only partial insight into the actual degree of descriptive representation (or lack thereof) of nonwhites in each of the communities in our sample. If we simply combine observations from across all our communities, we may be obscuring the presence or absence of descriptive representation within particular communities. What we would really like to know is how much, on average, the proportion of municipal councilors in a given community comprising whites, African Americans, and Latinos deviates from the proportion held by each of these racial groups in the same community. Figure 5.2 plots the share of seats held by members of each racial group against the proportion of the community that each group composes within each of the communities in our sample. The first panel of Figure 5.2 illustrates the situation for whites, the second panel for African Americans, and the third panel for Latinos. Each panel also includes a solid

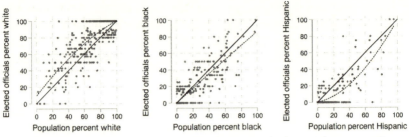

FIGURE 5.2 Scatterplot of share of council composed of a racial group against population share of the group in the community

45-degree line, which presents the hypothetical scenario in which a perfect one-to-one correspondence between population share and share of council seats is present, as well as a dashed line fitted to the data, which describes the actual empirical relationship between population share and council seat share across communities for each racial group in our sample. A fitted line closely following the 45-degree line would suggest that, on average, the racial group was descriptively represented on councils almost exactly in proportion to its share of the local population. A fitted line appearing above the 45-degree line would suggest that a racial group tended to be descriptively overrepresented on municipal councils relative to its share of the community population, and a fitted line falling below the 45-degree line would indicate that a racial group tended to be descriptively under-represented on municipal councils relative to its share of the population.

On the whole, Figure 5.2 mirrors the patterns presented in Figure 5.1, providing confirmation of racial biases in descriptive representation on municipal councils in the communities in our sample. As panel 1 of Figure 5.2 indicates, whites are descriptively overrepresented on municipal councils regardless of community population share. The degree of overrepresentation is quite substantial. When whites make up less than 70 percent of the population, they are generally overrepresented on municipal councils by more than 10 percentage points. This considerable degree of overrepresenta-tion on councils declines as the proportion of whites in a community rises above 70 percent, but this is only because it becomes increasingly difficult mathematically to maintain overrepresentation of this magnitude as the share of whites in a community approaches 100 percent. When it comes to descriptive representation in local government, whites enjoy a highly envi-able situation in communities throughout the United States.

As might be expected given the overrepresentation of whites, African Americans and Latinos are consistently underrepresented on municipal councils relative to their shares of the community population. For example, when blacks make up 40 percent or more of the population, they tend to be consistently underrepresented on councils by at least 5 percentage points. Similarly, Latinos are underrepresented on councils by a magnitude of at least 10 percentage points when they make up 20 percent or more of the population.

Relative to whites, then, residents of color tend to be significantly disadvantaged when it comes to descriptive representation on municipal councils. In some communities in our sample, the descriptive underrepresentation of nonwhite residents is particularly extreme. Consider the example of Smyrna, Georgia, a community of about 55,000 residents in the northwestern suburbs of Atlanta. Smyrna is probably most famous for being the hometown of actress Julia Roberts, but it hardly resembles the sleepy community that she grew up in during the 1960s and 1970s. Like many Atlanta suburban communities, Smyrna has seen tremendous population growth in the past few decades, nearly doubling in size since 1990. With this growth has also come increasing diversity; in 1990, Smyrna's population was only about 15 percent black and 4 percent Hispanic. By 2017, however, Smyrna has become a majority-minority city, with non-Hispanic whites constituting just 45 percent of the population.

African Americans are now one-third of Smyrna's population. Yet, when we collected our data on city councils in 2016, all of Smyrna's elected officials were white. In fact, Smyrna had never elected a black city councilor until December, 2017, when Maryline Blackburn won a special election runoff by a margin of seventy-two votes (511 to 439). Blackburn is the embodiment of what is changing in Smyrna. She moved to the city about two decades ago, relocating from her home state of Alaska, where she once defeated Sarah Palin to win the Miss Alaska pageant. Her opponent in Smyrna, Travis Lindley (a white man), emphasized his long-standing roots in the community, noting, "The main difference between my four opponents and myself is I'm a native. I came home from the hospital nearly 43 years ago, and Smyrna has been part of my life ever since." While Blackburn also emphasized her ties to the community, she focused on a platform of ensuring inclusivity for all residents of Smyrna and helping to bring more mass transit options to the city.[18]

---

[18] Ross Williams, "5 Candidates Battle It Out for Smyrna Ward 3 Council Seat," *Marietta Daily Journal*, October 24, 2017, www.mdjonline.com/news/candidates-battle-it-out-for-smyrna-ward-council-seat/article_5edb3978-b921-11e7-b45d-5f76e002cf17.html.

Blackburn's victory was historic, but it is just a first step toward equal representation for African Americans in the city. After all, the fact that Blackburn is the sole African American member of the city council means that African Americans now compose just 14 percent of the council, still lagging far behind their share of the population. And we see gaps such as these across all the communities we focus on. Such patterns provide preliminary indications that local democracy is not serving residents of color as it should. Indeed, if the quality of democracy is to be judged at least in part by the extent to which it provides inspiration and compensation to marginalized communities, enables representation of diverse viewpoints, and signals the importance of inclusion, many communities in our sample are performing poorly.

IDEOLOGICAL CONGRUENCE REPRESENTATION ON MUNICIPAL COUNCILS

While we have demonstrated that residents of color are descriptively underrepresented on municipal councils, it is still premature to conclude that the actual ideologies of African Americans and Latinos are poorly represented on councils. Although descriptive representation is undoubtedly related to the substantive representation of nonwhite interests at the local level,[19] the strength of this relationship is uncertain.[20] Because, as we showed in Chapter 3, the ideologies of racial groups are not uniform, the relationship between the ideologies of racial groups and those of descriptively representative elected officials is necessarily imperfect. Furthermore, while descriptively representative elected officials are generally more motivated to represent their constituents than are officials who are not descriptively representative, some descriptively representative elected officials may be more motivated or skillful than others in representing the ideologies of their constituents, thus weakening the link between

---

[19] David L. Leal, Valerie Martinez-Ebers, and Kenneth J. Meier. "The Politics of Latino Education: The Biases of At-Large Elections." *The Journal of Politics* 66, no. 4 (2004): 1224–1244.

[20] Peter K. Eisinger. *The Politics of Displacement: Racial and Ethnic Transition in Three American Cities.* New York: Academic Press, 1980; Zoltan Hajnal. *America's Uneven Democracy: Turnout, Race, and Representation in City Politics.* Cambridge: Cambridge University Press, 2010; Albert K. Karnig and Susan Welch. *Black Representation and Urban Policy.* Chicago: University of Chicago Press, 1980; John A. Straayer, Robert D. Wrinkle, and Jerry L. Polinard. *State and Local Politics.* New York: St. Martin's Press, 1994.

descriptive representation and ideological representation on the council.[21] And, of course, elected officials who do not share the race or ethnicity of a given group of constituents may nonetheless represent the group's ideological positions well. In short, for various reasons we should expect some slippage between descriptive representation and ideological representation of racial groups on municipal councils, making a direct examination of ideological representation essential if we are to fully assess racial bias in representation in local government.

In order to do this, however, we must first define more precisely what we mean by *ideological representation*. An important normative expectation of democracy is that, at least to some degree, the preferences of elected officials are "close to" those of the constituents they represent. Noted political scientist Christopher Achen suggests that

When a very conservative Congressman serves a moderate constituency, one may occasionally hear it said that the man is "not very representative of his district." The implicit definition of representativeness draws on notions of ideological distance. The good representative resembles his constituents; by some measure, he is "close" to them.[22]

Achen's comments suggest that a crucial consideration in evaluating ideological representation is the "closeness" or similarity between the ideologies of constituents and those of their elected representatives. An equally important expectation is that, especially once relative group sizes are taken into account, the preferences of distinctive groups within a constituency should be represented by an elected representative to a similar degree. As Larry Bartels (2010), a preeminent scholar of American politics, argues, "one of the most basic principles of democracy is the notion that every citizen's preferences should count equally in the realm of politics and government." In the social sciences, a very large literature has investigated the "closeness" between constituents and their elected officials.[23]

[21] David E. Broockman. "Black Politicians Are More Intrinsically Motivated to Advance Blacks' Interests: A Field Experiment Manipulating Political Incentives." *American Journal of Political Science* 57, no. 3 (2013): 521–536.

[22] Christopher H. Achen. "Measuring Representation." *American Journal of Political Science* 22, no. 3 (1978): 475–510.

[23] Matt Golder and Gabriella Lloyd. "Re-evaluating the Relationship between Electoral Rules and Ideological Congruence." *European Journal of Political Research* 53, no. 1 (2014): 200–212; Matt Golder and Jacek Stramski. "Ideological Congruence and Electoral Institutions." *American Journal of Political Science* 54, no. 1 (2010): 90–106; G. Bingham Powell Jr. "The Ideological Congruence Controversy: The Impact of Alternative Measures, Data, and Time Periods on the Effects of Election Rules." *Comparative Political Studies* 42, no. 12 (2009): 1475–1497; G. Bingham Powell Jr. "Representation

Following this work, we dub this form of representation *ideological congruence representation* because it is focused on the correspondence or "congruence" between constituent ideologies and the ideologies of elected officials.

In this section we take up the task of evaluating the ideological congruence representation received by African Americans and Latinos on municipal councils in the communities in our sample. The data that we have gathered for this project are ideally suited for this objective. The measures of ideology of racial groups and councilors provided by Catalist are calculated on the same scale. Thus, these measures allow us to estimate directly ideological congruence representation – the distance between the ideology of the mean group member and the mean ideology of the municipal council – for each racial group in each community in our sample. This measure provides an intuitive sense of "how far away" municipal councils are from each of the different racial groups in their respective communities. Using this approach, smaller distances between racial groups and their councils indicate better ideological congruence representation, while larger distances point to worse ideological congruence representation.

Before turning to this more detailed analysis, however, we will assess how well municipal councils provide ideological congruence representation to the mean resident of the community as a whole, irrespective of race. This exercise allows us to determine whether municipal councils meet a basic expectation of democracy – that they are on average relatively close ideologically to the residents they represent – and provides a baseline for our subsequent group-based analysis. Figure 5.3 presents a scatterplot of the mean ideology of elected officials on the council against the mean ideology of the population in the same community, along with a linear regression line summarizing this relationship.

As Figure 5.3 suggests, there is a relatively strong association between the mean ideology of the municipal council and the mean ideology of the population in the same community. Indeed, for all communities in our sample, the correlation between these two variables is .69. This indicates that – at least when it comes to the average resident – municipal councils are meeting a basic test of democracy.

in Context: Election Laws and Ideological Congruence between Citizens and Governments." *Perspectives on Politics* 11, no. 1 (2013): 9–21; Jesse H. Rhodes and Brian F. Schaffner. "Testing Models of Unequal Representation: Democratic Populists and Republican Oligarchs?" *Quarterly Journal of Political Science* 12, no. 2 (2017): 185–204.

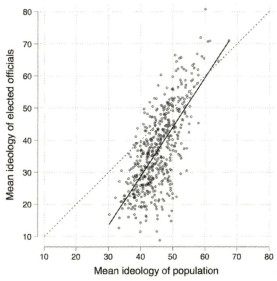

FIGURE 5.3 Scatterplot of the mean ideology of the municipal council against the mean ideology of the population in the same community

Note, however, that a broken diagonal line appears in the graphic. This line is drawn as a reference – communities that fall along this line have elected officials whose average ideologies are equal to those of members of the community. Thus, if a community falls close to this line, the ideological congruence representation enjoyed by that community's residents is very good. Once we consider representation with regard to this reference line, we must reconsider our conclusions to some extent. After all, on average, elected officials have lower values on the ideology scale than do their constituents, meaning that in most communities, they are more conservative than the people they represent. Thus, while municipal councilors are fairly close to their constituents on average, there is also a definite conservative bias to ideological congruence representation in American communities.

Additionally, the closeness of municipal councils to constituents from different racial groups remains to be examined. The reasonably close correspondence between the ideology of the average resident and the ideology of municipal councils could mask significant inequities in ideological congruence representation of different racial groups. In other words, if some groups within communities are generally very well represented, while others within the same communities are very poorly represented, it could nonetheless appear at the aggregate level that the *average* resident was reasonably well represented.

We return, therefore, to our primary question: To what extent are whites, African Americans, and Latinos represented ideologically by municipal councils in their towns and cities? Figure 5.4, which plots the mean ideological distance between the municipal council and each racial group at different levels of community population share, provides an answer to this question. We report ideological congruence representation at various levels of population share for each group because we expect that "closeness" should be positively related to population share. After all, a reasonable expectation is that as a group makes up a larger share of a community, their views will be better reflected among elected officials in that community, simply because larger groups should (all things being equal) be better situated to elect similarly minded representatives to municipal councils. This view is broadly consistent with "political power" models of representation in local government that highlight the importance of group size in determining representation.[24]

Strikingly, however, the plot for whites shows no such relationship, while the plots for blacks and Latinos are more nuanced. The top plot in Figure 5.4 indicates that the mean ideological distance between whites and their councils is less than 10 (mean = 9.83, St.Dev. = 7.09), and that the distance between whites and councils changes only slightly depending on how much or how little of a community's population is made up of whites. Indeed, and counterintuitively, as whites compose a larger share of the community population, the distance between them and the council actually increases very slightly (i.e. the line tends upward, possibly due to increased diversity of views among whites in communities in which whites

[24] Of course, the traditional "political power" school emphasized the importance of group size in determining descriptive representation on municipal councils. We adapt this insight to the question of ideological congruence representation; see Charles S. Bullock III and Bruce A. Campbell. "Racist or Racial Voting in the 1981 Atlanta Municipal Elections." *Urban Affairs Quarterly* 20, no. 2 (1984): 149–164; Charles S. Bullock III and Susan A. MacManus. "Staggered Terms and Black Representation." *The Journal of Politics* 49, no. 2 (1987): 543–552; Richard L. Engstrom and Michael D. McDonald. "The Election of Blacks to City Councils: Clarifying the Impact of Electoral Arrangements on the Seats/Population Relationship." *American Political Science Review* 75, no. 2 (1981): 344–354; Tim R. Sass and Stephen L. Mehay. "Minority Representation, Election Method, and Policy Influence." *Economics & Politics* 15, no. 3 (2003): 323–339; Delbert Taebel. "Minority Representation on City Councils: The Impact of Structure on Blacks and Hispanics." *Social Science Quarterly* 59, no. 1 (1978): 142–152; Susan Welch. "The Impact of At-Large Elections on the Representation of Blacks and Hispanics." *The Journal of Politics* 52, no. 4 (1990): 1050–1076.

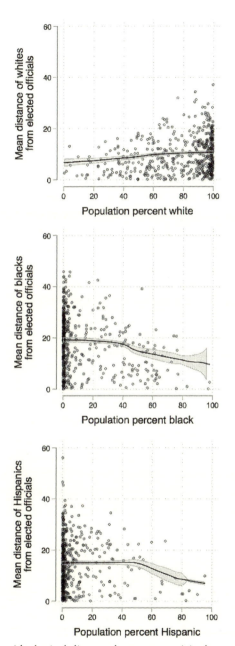

FIGURE 5.4 Mean ideological distance between municipal councils and racial groups, by group population share

Note: Sampling weights applied. Shaded areas are 95 percent confidence intervals.

constitute a supermajority). It is quite remarkable – and very advantageous to whites – that the ideological congruence representation that members of this group enjoy is not very sensitive to whites' share of the community population. Also of note is the fact that the ideological distance between whites and elected officials (mean = 9.83, St.Dev. = 7.09) is much smaller on average than is the distance between African Americans and elected officials (mean = 17.60, St.Dev. = 10.68) or between Latinos and elected officials (mean = 13.96, St.Dev. = 9.44). Thus, the ideologies of whites are typically much more congruent with those of municipal councils than are those of blacks or Latinos, *even in communities in which whites are a distinct minority.*

The relationship between population share and elected official representation is more conditional and nuanced for blacks and Latinos. The center plot shows this relationship for African Americans. When blacks make up a small to medium share of the community (between 0 and 40 percent), their ideological distance from their local elected officials remains well above 10 – noticeably further than the distance between whites and councils at similar community population levels. It is only when blacks make up a supermajority of the community population (between 80 and 100 percent of the population) that the ideological distance between them and their councils approaches a similar level of closeness to that attained by whites when they represent a much smaller share of the community population. The bottom plot shows a similar pattern for Latinos, with increasing representation only kicking in once members of this group compose more than 40 percent of the population. Like African Americans, Latinos have to constitute a supermajority of the community population before they attain a level of ideological congruence representation similar to that achieved by whites at a much smaller population proportion. In other words, whites typically enjoy a level of ideological congruence representation on municipal councils that African Americans and Latinos obtain only in special, and relatively rare, circumstances. More generally, while whites enjoy a substantial amount of ideological congruence representation independent of their share of the local population, the amount of ideological congruence representation enjoyed by African Americans and Latinos is very sensitive to their respective shares of the community population.

A closer look at the towns in our sample reveals that there are numerous instances in which the council is ideologically distant from African Americans and/or Latinos even though these groups represent a substantial share of the community population. For example, Opelika, Alabama, a city of more than 33,000 residents, is nearly one-third African American, but there is a twenty-seven-point gap between the ideology of African American residents and the ideology of the council (the mean gap for all communities with at least 30 percent black residents is 12). Newberry, South Carolina's population of more than 14,000 residents is nearly 42 percent African American, but the ideology of the council is 24 units away from the ideology of its African American residents (twice the average distance for communities that are at least 30 percent black). Evans, Colorado, is a community of nearly 11,000 residents, one-third of whom are Latino. But the ideology of the Evans municipal council is an enormous 35 units away from that of the average Latino resident – three times the average distance for communities that are at least 30 percent Hispanic.

Our findings that African Americans and Latinos receive less ideological congruence representation from local elected officials resonate with recent research revealing similar inequities at other levels of American government. In the next chapter, we build on these descriptive results, estimating models to reveal which factors are most predictive of ideological congruence representation. The results of these models reinforce our descriptive findings, providing further quantitative evidence of the much stronger ideological congruence representation enjoyed by whites relative to African Americans and Latinos.

HOW DESCRIPTIVE AND IDEOLOGICAL CONGRUENCE REPRESENTATION ARE RELATED

So far, we have demonstrated the existence of racial inequalities when it comes to both descriptive representation and ideological congruence representation. But to what extent are these two types of representation related? For example, do racial minorities achieve more ideological congruence representation when they increase their descriptive representation by electing more members of their racial group into office?

The left-hand panel of Figure 5.5 shows the relationship between the percentage of councilors who are black (on the x-axis) and the ideological distance between blacks and their local elected officials (on the y-axis). The right-hand panel of the figure shows the same relationship for Hispanics. As one might expect, minorities receive better ideological congruence representation when members of their group make up a larger share of the council; however, this relationship is not linear. Blacks experience only a modest improvement in ideological congruence representation as

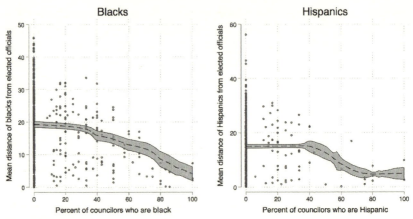

FIGURE 5.5 The relationship between descriptive and ideological congruence representation for blacks and Hispanics
Note: Sampling weights applied. Shaded areas are 95 percent confidence intervals.

the share of the council that is African American increases from 0 to 40 percent. Beyond the 40 percent mark, representational gains for blacks are much more pronounced. We see something very similar in the plot for Hispanics, but this is not as observable because there are many fewer communities where Hispanics make up more than half of the council.

One plausible reason for a lack of immediate gains in descriptive representation among these minority groups is that minority elected officials may often be ideological outliers on councils that are majority white. (Recall that, on average, African Americans and Latinos have distinctly more liberal ideologies than do whites, so it is plausible that members of these groups tend to elect descriptive representatives who are also more liberal than white representatives.) If this is the case, then nonwhite elected officials may find it more challenging to influence policy by creating coalitions with a majority of the council. Indeed, this is the situation in many communities. Of the 124 communities with at least one African American councilor working among a majority of white councilors, the most conservative black member of the council is on average 7.8 points more liberal than the mean councilor. In fact, in about 40 percent of these communities, the most conservative black councilor is more liberal than the *most liberal* white councilor. Hispanic councilors, by contrast, are less likely to be ideological outliers when they are elected to office, even in communities where whites constitute a majority of elected officials.

Another way to understand the relationship between descriptive representation and ideological congruence representation is to examine how well councilors from a particular racial group represent their co-racial citizens from the community. To explore this question, Figure 5.6 plots the mean ideology for whites, blacks, and Hispanics against the median ideology of white, black, and Hispanic elected officials in each community. Each plot also includes a diagonal (45-degree) line; in a community that falls on this line, the racial group's ideology is perfectly represented by councilors from that racial group. In communities above the line, the councilors from the racial group are more liberal than their co-racial constituents; and in communities below the line, the councilors are more conservative than their co-racial constituents.

Overall, Figure 5.6 reveals significant variance in the match between descriptive representation and ideological congruence representation. In some cases, for example, African American councilors are very close to the ideologies of the African American constituents in their community, but in many cases there is a substantial departure. Perhaps more notably, for each racial group, elected officials tend to be more conservative than their constituents from the same racial group. For example, in nearly two-thirds of the communities in our sample, African American elected officials are more conservative than the black populations in their communities. A similar share of Hispanic elected officials are more conservative than the Hispanics in their communities. For whites, the pattern is even stronger – in nearly three-fourths of the communities, white elected officials are more conservative than their white constituents.

Thus, we can draw the preliminary conclusion that descriptive representation does indeed help to facilitate ideological congruence representation, but that this effect is not quite linear. Part of the reason that this relationship is less than perfect may be that elected officials are often more conservative than the communities they represent. However, in the following chapter we will return to this discussion to show that in some types of communities, descriptive representation is more influential than it is in other types.

POLICY RESPONSIVENESS

Analyzing racial inequality in descriptive representation and in ideological congruence representation are important objectives. But they are only interim steps in evaluating inequality in municipal politics. Ultimately, we want to know whether there is racial inequality in the relationship between constituent ideology and the overall ideological orientation

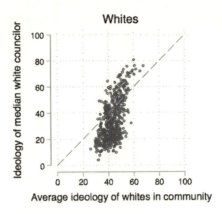

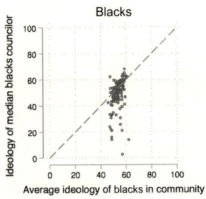

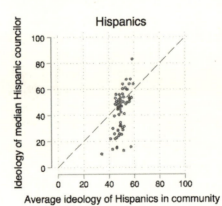

FIGURE 5.6 The relationship between elected officials and citizens among each racial group

of local government policy.[25] Thus, in this section, we seek to determine whether and to what extent there are racial inequalities in overall policy representation in local government.

Scholars have long been interested in understanding racial differences in policy representation in municipal government. Typically, research has conceptualized "policy representation" in terms of representation of particular minority interests – for example, access to public jobs and contracts, redistribution of certain government expenditures, and implementation of police reforms.[26] Following Tausanovitch and Warshaw (2014), we take a broader view of policy responsiveness, conceptualizing it as the relationship between the overall ideology of a constituent group and the overall "ideology" of policy.[27] Although policies do not have "ideologies" in the same way individuals do, it is possible to extract meaningful information about the overall ideological orientation of government outputs from information about municipal policy choices across a wide array of issue domains. To this end, we developed a scaled measure of "policy liberalism" using data from the International City/County Management Association (we call our measure "policy liberalism" because larger values represent a more liberal overall policy orientation). Using information about community adoption of policies focused on supporting disadvantaged groups and reducing inequalities in society, this scaled measure provides a simple, one-dimensional summary of each community's policy ideology.

Because this measure of policy liberalism is scaled differently than the constituent ideology measure we extracted from Catalist, we cannot simply measure ideological "closeness," as we did with our measure of ideological congruence representation. Instead, we must rely on a measure of what social scientists sometimes call "responsiveness."[28] That is,

[25] Zoltan Hajnal and Jessica Trounstine. "Identifying and Understanding Perceived Inequities in Local Politics." *Political Research Quarterly* 67, no. 1 (2014): 56–70.

[26] Rufus P. Browning, Dale Rogers Marshall, and David H. Tabb. *Protest Is Not Enough: The Struggle of Blacks and Hispanics for Equality in Urban Politics.* Berkeley: University of California Press, 1984; Karnig and Welch, *Black Representation and Urban Policy*; Kenneth J. Meier, Eric Gonzalez Juenke, Robert D. Wrinkle, and Jerry L. Polinard. "Structural Choices and Representational Biases: The Post-Election Color of Representation." *American Journal of Political Science* 49, no. 4 (2005): 758–768; Kenneth R. Mladenka. "Blacks and Hispanics in Urban Politics." *American Political Science Review* 83, no. 1 (1989): 165–191; Sass and Mehay, "Minority Representation"; Susan Welch. "The Impact of At-Large Elections on the Representation of Blacks and Hispanics." *The Journal of Politics* 52, no. 4 (1990): 1050–1076.

[27] Chris Tausanovitch and Christopher Warshaw. "Representation in Municipal Government." *American Political Science Review* 108, no. 3 (2014): 605–641.

[28] Achen, "Measuring Representation."

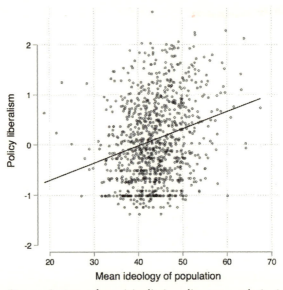

FIGURE 5.7 Responsiveness of municipality's policy to population's ideology

our measure of ideological representation in policy outputs is the extent to which the mean ideology of a particular group of citizens is associated statistically with the policy liberalism of the government. This responsiveness measure is derived from a simple regression model, where the policy liberalism for a particular local government is regressed on the mean ideology of the group of constituents in that community. In this framework, larger coefficients indicate greater policy responsiveness.

As with our analysis of ideological congruence representation on municipal councils, we start by simply evaluating municipal policy responsiveness to the average community resident, regardless of racial group. Figure 5.7 plots each community on our measure of policy liberalism against the mean ideology for the population of all adult citizens in that community.

Consistent with the findings of Tausanovitch and Warshaw (2014), we observe an overall trend of policy responsiveness to the average resident.[29] For example, the figure shows that more conservative communities (i.e. those with a mean ideology around 30 on the 100-point Catalist scale) enact policies that are, on average, more conservative (about one-half of a standard deviation below the mean policy liberalism).

[29] Tausanovitch and Warshaw, "Representation in Municipal Government."

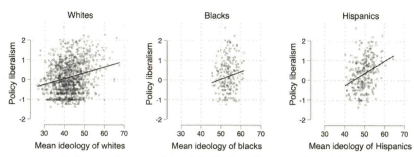

FIGURE 5.8 Responsiveness of municipality's policy to each racial group's ideology

Note: Each plot includes only communities where the racial/ethnic group constitutes at least 10 percent of the population.

By comparison, towns and cities whose populations have a more liberal mean ideology (around 60 on the Catalist scale) tend to enact more liberal policies (about one-half standard deviation above the mean). The correlation between the population's ideology and policy liberalism is 0.32.[30] Local governments therefore appear to be at least somewhat responsive to the average ideologies of their populations, providing more conservative or more liberal policies in line with the ideological preferences of community residents.

So far, so good. But is local government policy liberalism differentially responsive to distinctive racial groups within communities? We begin to answer this question by constructing bivariate plots of the relationship between the mean ideology of each racial group and policy liberalism in each community, along with a linear regression line (Figure 5.8). For each plot, we limit the communities to those where the racial group makes up at least 10 percent of the population. These plots are conceptually identical to the plot in Figure 5.7, except that the relationship between resident ideology and policy liberalism is plotted separately for whites, African Americans, and Latinos, respectively.

The bivariate plots seem to tell a mixed story about the relationship between racial group ideology and the ideological orientation of local government policy. The left-hand panel suggests a fairly robust positive

---

[30] This compares well with the data from Tausanovitch and Warshaw's study of policy responsiveness in municipalities. Their data indicates a 0.34 correlation between the ideology of a community's population and the liberalism of the policies produced by the local government. If we limit our sample to communities with populations greater than 25,000, the correlation is 0.39.

relationship between the mean ideology of whites and the ideological direction of local government policy. However, the center panel, which shows the bivariate relationship between the mean ideology of African Americans and policy liberalism, suggests a quite different pattern. Here, the slope of the line is flatter, suggesting that there is a weaker relationship between the ideology of blacks and the ideology of local policy. Finally, the right-hand panel appears to indicate that there is a reasonably strong positive relationship between the mean ideology of Hispanics and policy liberalism.

While informative in some ways, however, such bivariate plots may be misleading. First, each plot fails to account for the potential effect of the ideology of the other racial groups, and thus may over- or underestimate the true effect of the ideology of each racial group on policy liberalism. To be consistent with previous research on inequality in representation, what we really want to know is whether government is responsive to the ideology of a given group *after accounting for the influence of the ideology of other groups*. Only if the ideology of a group is associated with policy liberalism after the ideologies of the other groups are taken into account can we say with confidence that the ideology of the group has an independent effect on local government outputs. Second, each bivariate plot ignores factors in addition to racial group ideology that also likely contribute to policy liberalism. In order to accurately assess how a group's ideology influences municipal policy liberalism we need to take these contextual factors into account. Otherwise, we might attribute influence on policy liberalism to a group's ideology, when the influence is actually due to another factor that is correlated with the group's ideology (a phenomenon known as a "spurious relationship").

Thus, to provide a clearer answer to the question of differential responsiveness, we estimate a multivariate regression model that includes a separate term for the mean ideology of each racial group. In this way, we can estimate the unique effect of each racial group's ideology on municipal policy liberalism, while controlling for the effects of the ideologies of other racial groups. We also control for other factors that likely to influence municipal policy liberalism, including the community's population size, its median income, and the proportion of its population that is white.[31] This analysis includes only communities where blacks and Hispanics make up at least 10 percent of the community's citizens, since it is

---

[31] Tausanovitch and Warshaw, "Representation in Municipal Government."

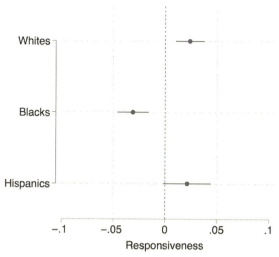

FIGURE 5.9 Responsiveness of municipality's policy to ideologies of racial groups
Note: Analysis includes only communities where blacks and Hispanics make up at least 10 percent of the population.

unrealistic to expect robust responsiveness to their views in places where those groups constitute only a small share of the population. Rather than presenting the results of the full model here, we plot in Figure 5.9 the coefficient estimate of the effect of each racial group's ideology on municipal policy liberalism, along with a confidence interval (note that each estimate takes into account the effects of the control variables).

In Figure 5.9, for each racial group, a positive coefficient with a confidence interval that does not overlap with 0 indicates that municipal policy ideology is responsive to the ideology of that group. The model shows that local policy is on average responsive to the views of white constituents. The coefficient of 0.03 for ideology among whites, combined with a confidence interval that does not overlap with zero, suggests that for every ten points more liberal the white population of a community is, government tends to produce policies that are three-tenths of a standard deviation more liberal. This finding is broadly consistent with the results of the bivariate analysis in Figure 5.8 and reinforces the view that the ideological direction of local government policy is indeed responsive to the ideology of whites.

However, Figure 5.9 also underscores how bivariate results of the type presented in Figure 5.8 can be misleading when considering the effect of racial group ideology on municipal policy liberalism. Once we account for the effect of white ideology and other factors associated with municipal policy liberalism, neither the ideology of African Americans nor the ideology of Latinos has a positive, statistically significant effect on the ideology of municipal policy. The coefficient for African American ideology is actually *negatively* signed and statistically distinguishable from o. That is to say, the coefficient of −0.04 among blacks suggests that for every ten points more liberal the black population of a community is, government tends to produce policies that are four-tenths of a standard deviation *in the more conservative direction*. This is a truly disturbing finding that implies that municipal policy liberalism typically moves in the direction opposite to that preferred by African American residents. Not only are African American preferences ignored on average, African American residents actually tend to get the opposite of what they want, after we account for the ideologies of whites and Hispanics.

The story for Latinos is more encouraging. The estimated effect of Latino ideology on municipal policy liberalism is positive, though the confidence interval for the estimate overlaps with o. This result indicates that we cannot say with confidence that Latino ideology has any effect on municipal policy liberalism. However, the effect is almost surely not negative, as it is for African Americans.

It is important to note here that in Figure 5.9, our estimates of responsiveness are not based on a model that accounts for the size of each group within a community. Even though we limit our focus in this model to communities where minorities make up at least 10 percent of the population, it is still important to consider whether policy is more responsive to minority groups in communities where they make up a larger share of the population. Unfortunately, however, we find that this is not the case. When we estimate a model that accounts for the size of each group in our communities, the results do not change.[32] That is, controlling for the ideologies of whites and Latinos, local government policy is not responsive to African American opinion even in places where African Americans make up a large share of the population.

It is worth pausing to further underscore the implications of these results. In the final analysis, the responsiveness of local government must

---

[32] This version of our model includes interaction terms for the percent of the community comprised by each racial group. None of these interaction terms is statistically significant and the size of the coefficients for the interaction terms is quite small, indicating that responsiveness to each group's ideology does not increase (or decrease) based on the group's share of the population.

be judged on how well it meets the policy demands of its constituents.[33] With this in mind, our results paint a dire portrait of the unresponsiveness of municipal government policy to the ideologies of residents of color. Our findings suggest a profound and systematic bias of local government policy liberalism in favor of the ideologies of whites and against those of African Americans and Latinos. Only whites enjoy ideological responsiveness from local government policy outputs; on average, residents of color experience indifference or, even worse, policy that moves in the opposite direction from what is preferred. With respect to policy responsiveness, local governments seem to be utterly failing residents of color.

CONCLUSION

At the beginning of this chapter we introduced readers to Brookhaven, Mississippi, a community marked by stark racial inequities in ideological congruence representation and apparent efforts by municipal councilors to evade public oversight in important matters affecting the common good. Although the lengths to which municipal councilors in Brookhaven went to avoid transparency may be extreme, our research suggests that – at least with respect to the representation of citizens of color – Brookhaven is not an exception. As we showed in this chapter, local governments are, across several dimensions, typically much less representative of African American and Latino constituents than they are of white constituents. Municipal councils descriptively underrepresent black and Latino residents; municipal councils are, on average, much more ideologically distant from African American and Latino constituents than they are from white constituents; and the ideological orientation of local policy outputs is, on average, unresponsive to the ideologies of members of these groups.

In sum, as our results suggest, local governments are systematically biased against residents of color. In a nation ostensibly dedicated to a government "of the people, by the people, and for the people," the patterns described in this chapter raise fundamental questions about the legitimacy of municipal government in the United States. While many Americans cherish bright dreams of "local democracy," the reality of local government is far bleaker. Many municipal governments around the nation, it seems, fail basic tests of representation of, and responsiveness

---

[33] Hajnal and Trounstine, "Identifying and Understanding Perceived Inequities in Local Politics."

to, many of their residents, and thus are not truly democratic governments at all.

However, while our research shows that local governments fail on average to serve African American and Latino residents, not all local governments do an equally bad job in representing residents of color. In fact, some actually serve African Americans and Latinos very well. Thus, as grim as they are, the results of this chapter also raise important questions about factors that may either remediate or exacerbate the inequities we described here. How do institutional and social characteristics of communities affect the representation received by African American and Latino residents? Why is it that residents of color in some communities are well represented, even though on average members of these groups receive little or no representation from local governments? In the next chapter we take up these questions, investigating whether and how electoral institutions, the dynamics of coincidental representation, and patterns of racial inequality within communities affect the prospects for more or less equitable representation in local politics.

6

Predictors of Racial Inequality in Representation

For many Americans of color, the promise of local democracy seems unfulfilled. On average, African Americans and Latinos are underrepresented descriptively on municipal councils, ideologically distant from local elected officials, and poorly represented in the overall ideological orientation of local government policy. At the same time, however, the picture is not uniformly bleak: There are perceptible differences in how well or how poorly different local governments perform in substantively representing the preferences of African American and Latino constituents.

Indeed, we have found numerous examples of communities in which minorities are represented fairly well, even though structural circumstances limit the capacity of governments to maintain robust services. In small towns in the rural South, such as Ashburn, Georgia, or Baldwin, Louisiana, blacks make up as much as 65 percent of the population and hold most or all of the seats on the city council. Like many rural communities, these two towns struggle with severe financial problems due to globalization, out-migration, and rising economic inequality. Ashburn is in Turner County, which is among the poorest counties in the state of Georgia. It ranks 148 out of 159 on a recent statewide benchmark of social and economic factors, which assesses important indicators, such as child poverty, educational attainment, and crime.[1] And yet, the community has not surrendered to despair: The town of Ashburn tries to support

---

[1] University of Wisconsin Population Health Institute, School of Medicine and Public Health, "County Health Rankings and Roadmaps" from the 2018 County Health Rankings, www.countyhealthrankings.org/app/georgia/2018/rankings/turner/county/outcomes/overall/snapshot.

a local recreation center for its children, and it helped to attract a chicken processing plant to replace local jobs lost when an air conditioning parts factory closed years ago. Moreover, members of the Ashburn City Council are not reluctant to intervene with the police department when African American members of the community complain about being harassed.[2] Similarly, Baldwin, Louisiana, struggles with maintaining its water and sewer infrastructure in the face of falling tax revenues due to the decline in oil industry jobs and retail shopping. The town is on the brink of bankruptcy as it gamely attempts to arrest the downward spiral in jobs and tax revenues. Despite the town's daunting financial situation, Baldwin's leadership has tried to keep taxes and fees low as a way to support poor and elderly residents.[3] It has even tried saving money by having police officers patrol on foot rather than in cars.[4]

Notably, we also find that African American residents in these communities receive considerable ideological congruence representation. In Ashburn, the mean ideology among black citizens is 50.5 while among whites it is 32.8. The town's elected officials have a mean ideology of 49.1, meaning that they closely represent the town's black population (at the expense of representing whites less closely). In Baldwin, both blacks and whites find themselves ideologically about six to seven points distant from the mean elected official. In both instances, then, the ideological congruence representation enjoyed by African Americans is much better than the level that this group enjoys on average.

Nor is local government responsiveness to residents of color limited to Ashburn or Baldwin. Substantial variation in the degree of representation is evident when considering all of the communities in our sample – a fact that points to numerous instances of excellent (as well as poor) representation of African Americans and Latinos. To illustrate the range of ideological congruence representation on municipal councils, Figure 6.1 plots the distribution of distances between the mean ideologies of African Americans and Latinos, respectively, and the mean ideologies of the municipal councils that represent them, across all communities in our sample. Essentially, the figure shows a wide range of ideological congruence representation experienced by residents of color in those

---

[2] Ben Baker, Editor, *The Wiregrass Farmer*, interview by coauthor, March 26, 2018.

[3] Roger Emile Stouff, managing editor, *Banner Tribune*, interview by coauthor, May 9, 2018.

[4] Billy Gunn, "Little Town, Big Problems: Budget Crunch Forces Baldwin Police to Patrol on Foot," *The Advocate*, August 4, 2016, www.theadvocate.com/acadiana/news/crime_police/article_e3e25756-5a76-11e6-9a4a-cbf9c8a4fd52.html.

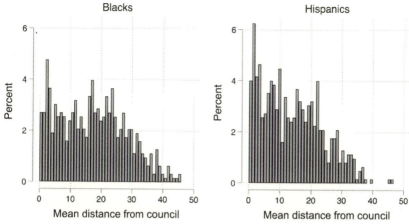

FIGURE 6.1 Distribution of mean ideological distance from municipal council

communities. Recall that larger distances between the mean ideology of a group and the mean ideology of the council signify a lower level of ideological congruence representation.

As the figure suggests, there is great cross-community variation in the amount of ideological congruence we find between African Americans/ Latinos, on the one hand, and municipal councils, on the other. In some communities, the distances between African Americans/Latinos and councils are very large, suggesting relatively little ideological congruence between these groups and their councils. Indeed, in half of the communities in our sample, African American citizens are seventeen points or farther from the mean elected official and in 10 percent of the communities the African American population is more than thirty points away from the council average. Likewise, in half of the communities in our sample, Hispanics are more than twelve points away from the average elected official. On the other hand, in some communities the distances are much smaller, indicating that constituents of color in those communities receive considerable ideological congruence representation on municipal councils. For example, in one quarter of our communities African Americans are less than nine points from the council mean and the Latino community is less than six points away. In such communities, residents of color enjoy a degree of ideological congruence representation from their councils that is similar to what whites enjoy on average.

When it comes to policy representation, we find much the same story. Although on average the preferences of African Americans and Latinos have little influence on municipal policy, as we showed in the previous chapter, in some communities the preferences of these groups seem to be very well represented. After all, as Figure 5.7 in the previous chapter revealed, in some communities there appears to be considerable policy responsiveness to the ideologies of residents of color.

These observations point toward a single vital question: What distinguishes communities that do a good job representing African Americans and/or Latinos from those that do not? Unfortunately, although scholars of inequalities in American politics have provided compelling evidence that communities of color generally receive worse representation than do whites, they have provided somewhat less guidance on the contextual factors that either reduce or exacerbate these biases.[5] Uncertainty about the factors that moderate racial inequalities in representation both limits our understanding of the political world and stands in the way of practical efforts to make democracy work more effectively for residents of color.

Fortunately, the great variation in institutional and social contexts across American communities provides an ideal opportunity for understanding how such factors affect the representation received by communities of color. Thus, in this chapter we use the unique information we have gathered about resident preferences, council ideologies, municipal policy outputs, local institutions, and patterns of economic and racial inequality within communities to investigate why residents of color receive better representation in some communities than in others. These data allow us to train our three theoretical lenses on the problem of variation in racial inequality in representation across municipalities.

Recall that we are evaluating the prospects for achieving equality by looking at the interplay of institutions (the institutional lens), the degree to which racial groups share similar preferences (the coincidental representation lens), and the interplay of racial and economic inequality (the racial and economic inequality lens). This chapter focuses on the extent to which any of these factors moderate biases in representation. Our initial hope and expectation is that local institutions, which are the most amenable to transformation, would have a powerful effect on improving equality of representation. Our framework contrasts the Political and Professional models of elections and governance, with the proposition that the Political model – with its emphasis on maximizing voter interest

---

[5] Griffin, Hajnal, Newman, and Searle, "Political Inequality in America."

and mobilization – will engage, and therefore better represent, the preferences of marginalized communities. At the same time, and building on previous research, we are also attuned to the possibility that factors that are less amenable to political control – specifically, the degree of overlap between the preferences of advantaged and disadvantaged groups, and the level of local racial inequality – may also influence how well disadvantaged groups are represented.

Our findings suggest hard truths about the prospects for reform of local institutions to better reflect the ideologies of African American and Latino residents. It turns out that the ideological congruence representation received by residents of color is strongly influenced by two factors – population share and ideological similarity to whites in the same community – that are not readily amenable to political influence or reform. Our analyses indicate that municipalities do a good job representing African Americans and Latinos when these groups make up a large share of the community population and/or have ideologies that are similar to those of whites in the same community. Returning to the examples that framed this chapter, we observe that black ideological congruence representation in Ashburn and Baldwin appears to be very good, owing largely to the fact that these two towns have large shares of black residents.

On the other hand, municipalities do a relatively poor job when non-whites represent a smaller share of the population and/or have ideologies that are very distinctive from those of whites. We observe the latter phenomenon in a town like Opelika, Alabama, not far from Auburn and Tuskegee universities, where blacks are as much as one-third of the population of 33,310. However, black Opelika residents have very different political views than do the community's white residents: According to our estimate, the difference between the mean ideology of African Americans and the mean ideology of whites in the community is 21.41. Perhaps unsurprisingly, therefore, the distance between the mean ideology of African American residents and that of the city council is twenty-six points.[6] This is not to say that Opelika's leadership fails to advance the community with policies that promote jobs, education, and public works.

---

[6] Perhaps significantly, there had not been a contested mayoral race since 2008 until an African American county commissioner challenged the incumbent in 2016. Jim Little, "Harris Challenges Fuller for Opelika Mayors Seat," *Opelika-Auburn News*, July 20, 2016, www.oanow.com/news/harris-challenges-fuller-for-opelika-mayor-s-seat/article_62453b86-4efb-11e6-a7bd-87f11beeec32.html.

We see plenty of evidence that they do.[7] However, we note that the ideological preferences of African Americans are not robustly reflected in the preferences of town leadership, which (as the analysis in this chapter suggests) has potential downstream consequences for policy decisions affecting the lives of African Americans in this community.

Furthermore, at least for African Americans, the prospects for coincidental representation in local government are closely related to the structure of local racial inequality. When there is less racial inequality on socioeconomic indicators like income, education, and the employment rate, African Americans and whites have more similar ideologies, creating better conditions for coincidental representation of African Americans on municipal councils. However, under conditions of greater racial inequality, African Americans and whites tend to have more distinctive ideologies, which in turn sharply limits the prospects for coincidental representation of African Americans. This disturbing pattern points to the conclusion that African Americans will likely have the least ideological representation on municipal councils in precisely the communities in which they need it most.

Because factors like ideological similarity and population share are not readily influenced by ordinary political activities such as voting, political advocacy, or litigation, our findings suggest that the substantial biases of municipal governments against the ideologies of residents of color are endemically resistant to change. Similarly, although racial inequality is amenable to political resolution, the politics of doing so are extraordinarily difficult, again pointing to the obstacles to remediating racial biases in representation.

To be sure, our analysis provides modest support for the notion that political institutions can play a role in reducing biases in municipal politics against African American and Latino residents. Consistent with our Political Model of Representation, we find indications that communities with significant nonwhite populations that hold local elections concurrent with federal and state elections (or off-cycle, but still in November) provide better representation of the ideologies of African

---

[7] See, e.g., Keith Hoffman, "Local Nonprofits Grateful for Approved Funds from Opelika City Council," *Opelika-Auburn News*, April 9, 2018; Keith Hoffman, "Aerocosta Global Systems Holds Ribbon-Cutting for New Distribution Center," *Opelika-Auburn News*, April 10, 2018; Keith Hoffman, "Workforce Development Initiative Underway in Opelika," *Opelika-Auburn News*, May 9, 2018; Keith Hoffman, "Opelika Fire, Police Departments, Looking Forward to New Headquarters Facilities," *Opelika-Auburn News*, April 29, 2018.

American and Latino residents on municipal councils than do communities that hold local elections at other times.[8] On the whole, however, the characteristics of local institutions play a very modest role in determining the amount of representation received by nonwhite residents and fall far short of producing equal representation.

WHAT PREDICTS IDEOLOGICAL CONGRUENCE REPRESENTATION ON MUNICIPAL COUNCILS?

As we have shown, municipal councils on average exhibit considerable ideological biases against both African Americans and Latinos; yet a notable fraction of councils appear to provide considerable ideological representation of residents of color. With these considerations in mind, we begin our analysis by investigating which institutional and/or contextual factors are the strongest predictors of how much ideological congruence representation African Americans, Latinos, and whites receive from municipal councils. To do this, we use an approach called a *random forest regression model*. This is an algorithmic method that tests the predictive power of a set of variables on some particular outcome. A random forest model is preferable to a typical regression analysis in this case for a number of reasons. First, by design, random forest models account for interactions and nonlinearities in the variables of interest, thereby freeing the researcher from having to specify these relationships in advance. Second, random forest models produce a useful summary measure of which variables are most predictive of the outcome of interest (in this case, representation of racial groups). And third, random forest models can easily handle a large number of predictors, even when those predictors might be highly correlated (which is often the case with some of our key contextual and institutional variables). However, we emphasize that this modeling approach is not geared toward causal inference, but rather toward identifying the variables that are the best predictors of the representation accorded to each racial or ethnic group.

To examine how different institutional and contextual factors influence the amount of ideological congruence representation received by African Americans, Latinos, and whites, we estimate random forest models of this relationship – one for each racial group. The dependent variable in each model is our measure of ideological congruence

---

[8] See also, Zoltan L. Hajnal and Paul G. Lewis. "Municipal Institutions and Voter Turnout in Local Elections." *Urban Affairs Review* 38, no. 5 (2003): 645–668.

representation – the distance between the mean ideology of each racial group and the mean ideology of the council in the same community. We include several contextual variables in each model – the proportion of the community composed of each racial group; the distance between the mean ideology of each nonwhite racial group and the mean ideology of whites; and the variance in the ideology of the group. We include each group's share of the total community population because it is likely that groups receive more representation from municipal elected officials as they constitute a larger proportion of the community simply because larger groups are better positioned to elect similarly minded representatives to the municipal council.[9]

We include measures of the distance between the ideology of each racial group and the other racial groups in the community to test for the extent to which minority groups benefit from "coincidental representation."[10] As we have argued, since the advantaged group typically receives considerable representation, disadvantaged groups that happen to share the ideological predilections of the advantaged group will likewise enjoy representation. Importantly, a review of our sample indicates that coincidental representation of the ideologies of residents of color in some communities is likely. Although on average whites and nonwhites have distinctive preferences, there is considerable cross-community variation in the degree of these differences, with some communities exhibiting great distance between the preferences of whites and nonwhites and others showing considerable similarity in preferences. Figure 6.2 shows how communities are distributed when it comes to this metric. When comparing the two plots, it is clear that Hispanic residents generally have ideologies that are closer to those of whites than do

---

[9] Charles S. Bullock III and Bruce A. Campbell. "Racist or Racial Voting in the 1981 Atlanta Municipal Elections." *Urban Affairs Quarterly* 20, no. 2 (1984): 149–164; Charles S. Bullock III and Susan A. MacManus. "Staggered Terms and Black Representation." *The Journal of Politics* 49, no. 2 (1987): 543–552; Richard L. Engstrom and Michael D. McDonald. "The Election of Blacks to City Councils: Clarifying the Impact of Electoral Arrangements on the Seats/Population Relationship." *American Political Science Review* 75, no. 2 (1981): 344–354; Tim R. Sass and Stephen L. Mehay. "Minority Representation, Election Method, and Policy Influence." *Economics & Politics* 15, no. 3 (2003): 323–339; Delbert Taebel. "Minority Representation on City Councils: The Impact of Structure on Blacks and Hispanics." *Social Science Quarterly* 59, no. 1 (1978): 142–152; Susan Welch. "The Impact of At-Large Elections on the Representation of Blacks and Hispanics." *The Journal of Politics* 52, no. 4 (1990): 1050–1076.
[10] Peter K. Enns. "Relative Policy Support and Coincidental Representation (Reflections Symposium)." *Perspectives on Politics* 13, no. 4 (2015): 1053–1064.

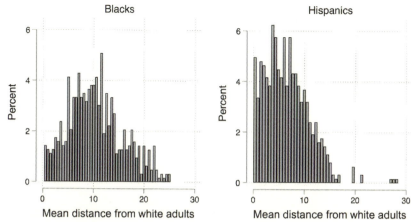

FIGURE 6.2 Distribution of ideological overlap between whites, African Americans, and Latinos

African Americans. In three-quarters of the communities we examine, the mean Latino resident is less than ten points from the mean white resident. Blacks, by contrast, generally hold opinions that coincide somewhat less closely with the views of their white neighbors. In over half of these communities, the average African American citizen's ideology is more than ten points away from the average white citizen's ideology.

If, as our analysis in the previous chapter suggests, whites typically receive high levels of ideological congruence representation from municipal councils, nonwhites residing in communities where their ideologies are fairly close to those of whites are also likely to enjoy high levels of representation. However, when the respective ideologies of nonwhites and whites are more distant, then nonwhites might receive much less representation on municipal councils than do whites.

Finally, we include a measure of the variance in the ideology of each racial group. We include this measure on the basis that, all things being equal, groups with more homogeneous ideologies are easier to represent, from the perspective of elected officials, while those with more diverse ideologies are more difficult to represent.[11] After all, when members of a group have similar ideologies, their elected official will usually not have to choose among opposing positions in order to represent the group; but

---

[11] Yosef Bhatti and Robert S. Erikson. "How Poorly Are the Poor Represented in the US Senate?" In *Who Gets Represented?*, eds. Peter K. Enns and Christopher Wlezien. New York: Russell Sage Foundation, 2011. 223–246.

when members of a group have diverse ideologies, their elected official may be forced to take sides on issues that split the group. Thus, we expect that groups that have more homogeneous ideologies will receive on average more ideological congruence representation, while those with less homogeneous ideologies will receive less ideological congruence representation.

Alongside these contextual variables, the models we estimate include a series of variables to test whether, as posited by our institutional lens on representation, the presence of various electoral institutions affects minority representation. We include indicators for whether a municipality uses partisan (versus nonpartisan) elections; whether council members are elected at-large (the baseline), by districts, or in a mixed system; and whether local elections are held on-cycle, off-cycle in November, or off-cycle at another time of year (typically the spring). As we suggested in Chapter 1, we anticipate that institutions associated with the Political model (partisan elections, districted representation, and on-cycle elections/off-cycle in November elections) will tend to be associated with greater ideological congruence representation of disadvantaged groups.

THE MOST IMPORTANT PREDICTORS
OF IDEOLOGICAL CONGRUENCE

What factors are powerful predictors of ideological congruence representation, and which have little predictive power? Figure 6.3 is a plot showing the importance of each variable in predicting how much ideological congruence representation each racial group receives. The random forest model measures the importance of a variable by replacing the actual values of each variable (one at a time) with random values and then calculating the change in the mean squared error between the amount of ideological congruence representation that the model predicts from that local government and what we actually observe in our data. When the mean squared error increases by a greater extent when a particular variable has been randomly perturbed, that indicates that the variable is more important for predicting values of the dependent variable (because effectively removing that variable has made the predictions much less accurate).

The top plot in Figure 6.3 shows the importance of the variables for predicting how much ideological congruence representation whites receive. The two most important variables for white representation are the percent of the community's population made up of whites and African

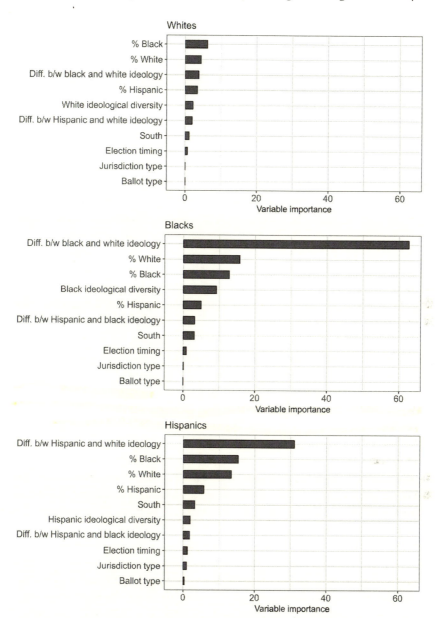

FIGURE 6.3 Importance of factors in predicting ideological congruence representation for whites, blacks, and Hispanics

Note: Variable importance is measured as the change in the mean squared error when values of each variable are replaced with randomly assigned values.

Americans, respectively. However, as we will soon show, even these variables are not particularly strong predictors of the ideological congruence representation of whites. After those first two factors, the difference between the views of whites and African Americans and the distance between the views of whites and Latinos are the next most important predictors. Finally, note that the least predictive variables are the electoral institutions variables – they are all close to zero, though election timing does show some modest predictive value.[12]

The second plot in Figure 6.3 shows the predictive importance of these variables for African American representation. Here, the most important factor by a wide margin is the distance between the mean ideology of blacks and whites in the community. What this tells us is that coincidental representation is very important in accounting for the amount of ideological congruence representation received by African American residents. After that, the racial composition of the community is also important, followed by the diversity of ideology within the black community and the difference between the views of blacks and Hispanics. Once again, electoral institutions are of modest, if any, predictive value. As we show shortly, election timing and ballot type provide some modest benefits to black communities with respect to ideological congruence representation; but on the whole, the institutional lens provides limited insight into the representation received by African Americans. It is clear from this plot that coincidental representation is by far the most important predictor of how much ideological congruence representation blacks receive.

The third plot in Figure 6.3 tells a similar story for Hispanics, highlighting the importance of coincidental representation and the insignificance of institutions in accounting for the representation received by members of this group. The bar for the variable measuring the average difference between whites and Hispanics in a community is the largest by far and is followed by variables capturing the racial composition of the community. Once again, the impact of electoral laws appears to be minimal.

A final important note about Figure 6.3 is the difference between the plot for whites and those for blacks and Hispanics. All three plots are on the same scale, and yet the bars for the random forests predicting black and Latino representation are much larger than those for whites. What

---

[12] Random forest models tend to privilege continuous variables (like our contextual measures) over categorical ones (like our variables for institutional rules). However, even when we replicate this analysis with a more traditional regression model, we still find a very limited role for electoral institutions.

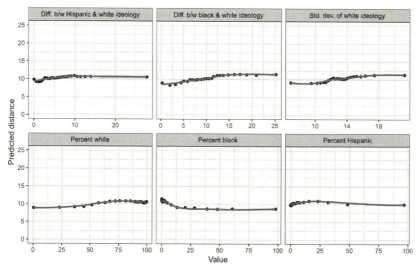

FIGURE 6.4 Contextual factors and ideological congruence representation of whites

Note: Figure presents partial dependence plots, which account for the role of other variables in our random forest model.

this means is that contextual factors are far more predictive of how much ideological congruence representation racial minorities receive compared to how much representation whites receive. To illustrate the extent to which ideological representation is sensitive (or insensitive) to context, depending on residents' race, we show in Figure 6.4 the relationship between each of the contextual variables and the distance of the average white citizen from the average elected official in the community. The panels in Figure 6.4 are partial dependence plots, which show the relationship between each factor and the dependent variable, while adjusting for the other variables in the model. What is striking from this figure is *just how little context matters* for the amount of ideological congruence representation that whites receive. The most important predictors are the percent white and percent black in the community, and yet changing values of these variables are associated with only a small change in the distance between whites and local elected officials. The fitted line is virtually flat, suggesting that the relationship hardly varies. The overall story from Figure 6.4 is that whites find themselves, on average, about ten points away from their local elected officials, regardless of contextual factors in the community.

For whites, this is very good news. On average, whites can count on a comparatively good amount of ideological congruence representation without regard to their share of the community population, the diversity of views among whites, or the degree to which their preferences overlap with those of African Americans or Latinos. And, at least for whites, the institutional context has virtually no impact on the amount of representation they receive. *Whites receive good representation from local governments – full stop.*

However, as we describe in detail shortly, the situation is quite different for residents of color: Local contexts are strongly associated with the amount of ideological congruence representation these groups receive from municipal councils. These findings are important for our understanding of inequality in American democracy in general, because they move beyond the mere identification and measurement of racial biases and toward a more comprehensive understanding of *where* and *how* these biases occur.[13]

For African Americans, local context matters a great deal for predicting how much ideological congruence representation they will receive. For example, the top left-hand plot in Figure 6.5 shows the enormous importance of coincidental representation for blacks. When blacks and whites in a community have similar ideologies, blacks find themselves quite close ideologically to the local elected officials. But as the distance between black and white ideologies increases, blacks find themselves increasingly unrepresented. The change in representation is dramatic, as demonstrated in the top left panel of the figure. For example, when blacks and whites in a community have views that are just five points apart on the ideological scale, the predicted distance of African Americans from the municipal council is just 12.5 points. However, when blacks and whites have views that are ten points away from those of whites, their distance from local elected officials increases by about five points. Indeed, there is roughly a one-to-one translation for much of the scale – for each point further away blacks in the community find themselves from whites, they find themselves about one point further from the government's elected officials as well. This suggests that the amount of representation that African Americans receive from local government is both highly uncertain

---

[13] Griffin, Hajnal, Newman, and Searle, "Political Inequality in America"; Flavin, "Campaign Finance Laws, Policy Outcomes, and Political Inequality"; Flavin, "Lobbying Regulations and Political Equality"; Patrick Flavin. "Labor Union Strength and the Equality of Political Representation." *British Journal of Political Science* 48, no. 4 (2018): 1075–1091.

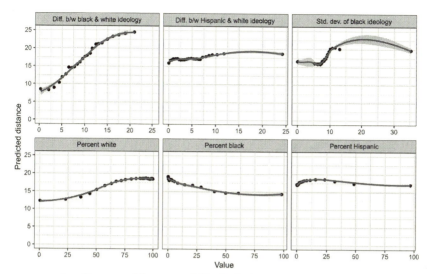

FIGURE 6.5 Contextual factors and ideological congruence representation of blacks

Note: Figure presents partial dependence plots, which account for the role of other variables in our random forest model.

and ultimately contingent on a relationship (ideological congruence with whites) that is very resistant to change.

African American representation is also related to how diverse the opinions of blacks are. When African Americans have relatively homogeneous ideologies, the ideological distance between African Americans and the municipal council is smaller. However, as the top right panel of Figure 6.5 suggests, as the ideologies of African Americans become more diverse, the distance between African Americans and municipal councils increases appreciably. This pattern is consistent with the view that groups with more diverse ideologies are more difficult for elected officials to represent, leading to diminished ideological congruence representation.

Finally, the ideological congruence representation enjoyed by African Americans is predicted by their share of the community population – but not nearly as much as might be expected. To be sure, blacks see some modest improvement in representation when they make up a higher share of the population. For example, moving from approximately o to 50 percent of a community's population reduces the distance between blacks and elected officials by a predicted five points. But this is a very small improvement in representation in relation to the change in community population share. Perhaps because African Americans have ideologies that

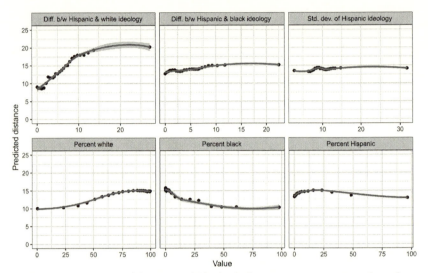

FIGURE 6.6 Contextual factors and ideological congruence representation of Hispanics

Note: Figure presents partial dependence plots, which account for the role of other variables in our random forest model.

are, on average, quite distinctive from those of whites, they do not benefit in terms of ideological congruence representation from an increased share of the community population as much as we might expect.

For Latinos, we observe a very similar pattern in terms of the relationship between ideological similarity with whites in the community and distance from those who are elected to office. This is shown in Figure 6.6. When Latinos are ideologically similar to whites, they are ideologically close to their municipal councils; but when they are ideologically distant from whites, they are also ideologically quite distant from their councils. Thus, like African Americans, Latinos depend to a significant degree on the dynamic of coincidental representation for ideological congruence representation on municipal councils. Meanwhile, the ideological distance between whites and their councils is almost completely unaffected by the ideological distance between whites and Latinos. There is a (small) silver lining for Latinos, however. Recall from Figure 6.2 that Latinos are on average much closer ideologically to whites in their communities than are African Americans. For this reason, Latinos are likely to be much more frequent beneficiaries of coincidental ideological congruence representation than are African Americans.

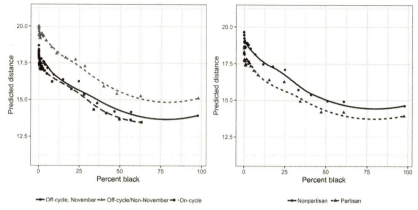

FIGURE 6.7 Role of institutions on ideological congruence representation of blacks
Note: Figure presents partial dependence plots, which account for the role of other variables in our random forest model.

These findings indicate that both population composition and coincidental representation – two factors that are not readily amenable to political influence – play important roles in predicting the degree of ideological congruence representation enjoyed by African Americans and Latinos. We now turn to a consideration of how more obviously political factors – namely, the characteristics of local electoral institutions – are associated with ideological congruence representation. Figure 6.7 plots the relationship between the percent of a community that is African American and the expected distance between African Americans and the average elected official in that community. The left-hand plot in the figure shows this relationship based on when the community schedules its elections, while the right-hand plot shows this relationship based on whether the local government holds partisan versus nonpartisan elections. Note that these institutions do have some modest associations with the amount of ideological congruence representation received by African Americans. Specifically, when communities hold their elections in November of either an odd year (black dashed line) or even year (black solid line), African Americans tend to be about one point closer to elected officials ideologically than when the community holds off-cycle non-November elections (grey dashed line). The adjacent figure on the right shows that partisan elections (dashed line) also help bring elected officials a bit closer to blacks in the community, but again the effects are modest, usually amounting to improving ideological congruence representation by less than one point on the 100-point ideological scale.

Notably, the type of jurisdictions (districted or at-large) that a community uses for its elections appears to have no real relationship with ideological congruence representation. In fact, it may be surprising to discover the limited role that jurisdictional type plays in producing ideological congruence representation for minority populations, since the presence of districted elections was often a key focus of "preclearance" scrutiny when the Department of Justice (DOJ) considered local government submissions for changes in voting procedures under the Voting Rights Act of 1965. In fact, before the 2013 US Supreme Court decision in *Shelby County* v. *Holder* effectively eliminated the preclearance process for such changes, voting rights attorneys within the DOJ often expressed a preference for district-based representation in communities with racially polarized voting on the expectation that such arrangements would promote greater *descriptive* representation for residents of color.[14] Our unexpected "non-findings" with respect to the effects of jurisdictional type on *ideological congruence* representation deserve further exploration, and we will provide additional analysis in the next section.

Our findings suggest complex conclusions about the factors associated with the ideological congruence representation received by African Americans and Latinos on municipal councils. Troublingly, we find that some factors that are not readily amenable to political influence – population share and ideological similarity between whites and residents of color – play very important roles in predicting the amount of ideological congruence representation enjoyed by nonwhite racial groups.

---

[14] Chandler Davidson and George Korbel. "At-Large Elections and Minority-Group Representation: A Re-examination of Historical and Contemporary Evidence." *Journal of Politics* 43, no. 4 (1981): 982–1005; Bernard Grofman and Chandler Davidson. "The Effect of Municipal Election Structure on Black Representation in Eight Southern States." In *Quiet Revolution in the South*, eds. Chandler Davidson and Bernard Grofman. Princeton, NJ: Princeton University Press, 1994. 301–334; Robert J. Mundt and Peggy Heilig. "District Representation: Demands and Effects in the Urban South." *Journal of Politics* 44, no. 4 (1982): 1035–1048; Tim R. Sass and Stephen L. Mehay. "The Voting Rights Act, District Elections, and the Success of Black Candidates in Municipal Elections." *The Journal of Law & Economics* 38, no. 2 (1995): 367–392; Tim R. Sass and Bobby J. Pittman. "The Changing Impact of Electoral Structure on Black Representation in the South, 1970–1996." *Public Choice* 104, no. 3–4 (2000): 369–388; Paru R. Shah, Melissa J. Marschall, and Anirudh V. S. Ruhil. "Are We There Yet? The Voting Rights Act and Black Representation on City Councils, 1981–2006." *The Journal of Politics* 75, no. 4 (2013): 993–1008.

The news is not all bad, however. Our findings provide some evidence for the efficacy of the Political model, and thereby suggest that political institutions can provide some help for ensuring that minority groups receive better representation on municipal councils. Specifically, we show that communities that hold local elections in November provide marginally better ideological representation on municipal councils of African Americans and Latinos than do communities that hold their local elections during other parts of the year (typically in the spring).

What accounts for the relationship between the timing of elections and ideological congruence representation of African Americans and Latinos? As we have suggested, the timing of elections may help make participation easier and more attractive to citizens, and may thus increase the likelihood that citizens, particularly those from more disadvantaged circumstances, will vote and elect councilors with whom they share ideological leanings. Notably, our finding – and the underlying logic of our argument – is consistent with research that shows that moving local contests to coincide with national elections substantially increases representation of disadvantaged groups in local government.[15]

However, our results suggest that other municipal institutions have little effect on the amount of ideological representation received by African Americans and Latinos on municipal councils. Since some of our findings – particularly the finding that the organization of districts has little effect on ideological representation – are unexpected, we explore them in greater detail.

DISTRICTS VERSUS AT-LARGE ELECTIONS

Some research suggests that districted council seats may yield gains in descriptive representation for nonwhite residents,[16] implying that such

[15] Sarah F. Anzia. "Election Timing and the Electoral Influence of Interest Groups." *The Journal of Politics* 73, no. 2 (2011): 412–427; Hajnal and Lewis, "Municipal Institutions and Voter Turnout"; Zoltan L. Hajnal, *America's Uneven Democracy: Turnout, Race, and Representation in City Politics*. New York: Cambridge University Press, 2010.

[16] Albert K. Karnig. "Black Representation on City Councils: The Impact of District Elections and Socioeconomic Factors." *Urban Affairs Quarterly* 12, no. 2 (1976): 223–242; Albert K. Karnig. "Black Resources and City Council Representation." *Journal of Politics* 41 (1979): 134–149; Melissa J. Marschall, Anirudh V. S. Ruhil, and Paru R. Shah. "The New Racial Calculus: Electoral Institutions and Black Representation in Local Legislatures." *American Journal of Political Science* 54, no. 1 (2010): 107–124; Susan A. MacManus. "City Council Election Procedures and Minority Representation: Are They Related?" *Social Science Quarterly* 59 (1978): 153–161; Jerry Polinard, Robert

arrangements should also yield increases in ideological congruence representation for these groups. However, recent research suggests a more nuanced view, in which districted systems increase descriptive representation only when underrepresented groups are highly concentrated and compose a substantial proportion of the population.[17] Moreover, as political scientist Paru Shah notes, scholars are divided on whether districted systems increase descriptive representation of Latinos.[18] Nevertheless, our findings depart from an important implication – though not the explicit empirical findings – of some existing research: that the use of districts should improve representation for racial and ethnic minorities.

What explains the apparent lack of a relationship between district-based representation and ideological congruence representation on municipal councils? Scholarship on race and districting has shown that an overriding focus on ensuring descriptive representation for African Americans may limit the extent to which blacks are able to achieve substantive representation of their ideologies in public policy.[19] This occurs because redistricting often packs African Americans into a small number of districts, allowing other districts to be dominated by more conservative constituencies. In a similar fashion, there may be a trade-off between maximizing descriptive representation and maximizing ideological congruence representation on municipal councils. In fact, Trebbi, Aghion, and Alesina go so far as to suggest that, especially in communities with relatively large nonwhite populations, whites may actively seek to pack nonwhite residents into a relatively small number of districts within a jurisdiction in order to maintain their own preponderant political influence.[20] Here we use our data to provide a preliminary assessment

Wrinkle, and Tomas Longoria. "The Impact of District Elections on the Mexican American Community: The Electoral Perspective." *Social Science Quarterly* 72, no. 3 (1991): 608–614; Shah, Marschall, and Ruhil, "Are We There Yet?"; Engstrom and McDonald, "The Election of Blacks to City Councils"; Welch, "The Impact of At-Large Elections."

[17] Jessica Trounstine and Melody E. Valdini. "The Context Matters: The Effects of Single-Member versus At-Large Districts on City Council Diversity." *American Journal of Political Science* 52, no. 3 (2008): 554–569.

[18] Paru Shah. "Racing toward Representation: A Hurdle Model of Latino Incorporation." *American Politics Research* 38, no. 1 (2010): 84–109.

[19] David Lublin. "Racial Redistricting and African-American Representation: A Critique of 'Do Majority-Minority Districts Maximize Substantive Black Representation in Congress?'" *The American Political Science Review* 93, no. 1 (1999): 183–186.

[20] Francesco Trebbi, Philippe Aghion, and Alberto Alesina. "Electoral Rules and Minority Representation in US Cities." *The Quarterly Journal of Economics* 123, no. 1 (2008): 325–357.

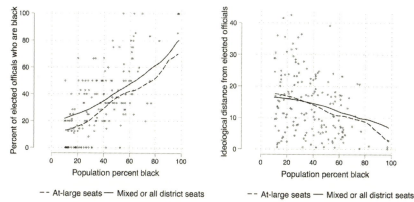

FIGURE 6.8 Descriptive and ideological congruence representation of African Americans on municipal councils

Note: Plots include only communities where African Americans are 10 percent or more of the adult population.

of the possibility that there is a trade-off between descriptive representation and ideological congruence representation.

Figure 6.8 shows the relationship between the percent of a community that is black and the amount of descriptive representation and ideological congruence representation African Americans receive on the council. In each plot, the solid line represents the amount of representation for blacks in towns and cities that elect councilors in districts or in a mix of districts and at-large seats. The dashed line shows representation in municipalities that elect all seats at-large. The plots include only communities where at least 10 percent of the population is African American.

We start with the pattern in the left-hand plot, which shows descriptive representation in terms of the percentage of elected officials who are black. This plot shows that using districts or a mix of districts and at-large seats does, as previous work would suggest, produce higher levels of descriptive representation. For example, our data show that when a community is 30 percent black, about 23 percent of that community's elected officials will be black under an at-large arrangement, while 29 percent will be black if the community uses districts to elect at least some of its council members. The increase in descriptive representation associated with the use of districts is significant and actually brings representation on the council close to parity with the percentage of African Americans in the community.

By contrast, the right-hand plot shows how the type of jurisdiction affects the amount of ideological representation blacks receive on the council. Here, we see little difference between municipalities that use at-large seats versus those that use districts or a mixed system. To the extent that there are differences, the patterns depend on whether or not African Americans make up a sizable share of the population. In communities that are less than 30 percent black, blacks are marginally (about two points) closer to elected officials when those officials are elected in districts. However, when blacks make up more than 40 percent of the population, the outcome for them is marginally better (about 2.7 points) when all officials are elected at large. Thus, while electing councilors in districts does appear to help African Americans achieve significantly greater descriptive representation on municipal councils, there appears to be no consistent effect of jurisdiction type on ideological congruence representation for African Americans.

We conducted a parallel analysis for Latinos (results not shown), with similar results. Again, the most important finding was that the amount of ideological representation received by Latinos on the council was not noticeably affected by the type of election used to select councilors. The amount of ideological congruence representation enjoyed by Latinos was virtually identical in districted and at-large systems.

WHEN DOES DESCRIPTIVE REPRESENTATION PRODUCE BETTER IDEOLOGICAL REPRESENTATION?

In the previous chapter, we showed that increasing descriptive representation does not uniformly improve ideological congruence representation. The findings presented so far in this chapter provide one clue as to why that might be the case – minority groups receive better representation from local elected officials when they agree more with their white neighbors. An important implication of this finding is that, in communities where the ideologies of whites and blacks overlap a great deal, it may not matter as much *for the purposes of ideological congruence representation* whether African Americans enjoy descriptive representation on the council. To be clear, though, descriptive representation matters greatly for other purposes, such as compensating for past injustices, providing a clear signal of inclusion, or encouraging broader citizen participation. But when larger differences exist between whites and blacks in the community, electing more African Americans to office may help to bring the city or town council closer to the views of blacks.

To assess this possibility, Figure 6.9 plots the relationship between descriptive representation (on the x-axis) and ideological congruence

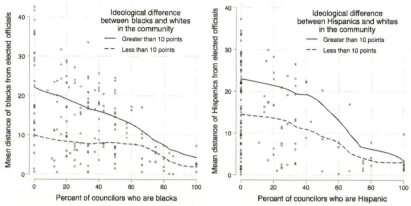

FIGURE 6.9 The relationship between descriptive and ideological congruence representation for blacks and Hispanics, by ideological context
Note: Plots include only communities where the minority group comprises at least 10 percent of the population. Lines represent local means based on local polynomial smoothing.

representation (on the y-axis) for communities with differential levels of overlap between the ideologies of blacks and Hispanics and those of whites. In each case, we include only communities where the minority group makes up at least 10 percent of the population. The left-hand plot in the figure displays this relationship for African Americans. As we have already documented at length, blacks find themselves much closer to local elected officials in communities where their views overlap more with those of whites (the broken line in the plot). But the fact that the broken line is also relatively flat in this plot is evidence of the expectation outlined previously: For blacks to achieve ideological congruence representation, it is less crucial to have descriptive representation when their views largely overlap with those of whites in the community. After all, in these communities, blacks will be the beneficiaries of coincidental representation.

By contrast, the solid line plots the relationship between descriptive and ideological congruence representation where blacks in the communities have more distinct views from their white counterparts. It is in these communities where increasing descriptive representation appears to produce clear and immediate payoffs, as shown by the downward sloping line. In one of these more racially divided communities, increasing the percentage of elected officials who are black from 0 to 33 percent produces about a five-point improvement in the distance between black citizens and their elected officials.

The right-hand plot in Figure 6.9 shows a similar – though less dramatic – pattern for the representation of Latinos. Overall, then, these plots help us to understand more profoundly the circumstances in which increased descriptive representation is associated with improved ideological congruence representation. Increasing descriptive representation will help bring elected officials ideologically closer to minority communities in places where the views of minorities are more disparate from the views of their white counterparts. While there are many other reasons to endorse descriptive representation across the board, our results suggest that descriptive representation is most important *for the purposes of increasing ideological representation of African Americans and Latinos* in those communities in which the views of these groups are most distant from those of whites.

SOCIOECONOMIC DISPARITIES AND IDEOLOGICAL OVERLAP

So far, we have shown that the most consistent and powerful predictor of whether African Americans receive better ideological congruence representation from their local governments is when their ideologies overlap more with the ideologies of whites in those communities. In other words, blacks appear to get better representation outcomes only when whites share their views. Notably, the same is not true for whites, who receive good representation regardless of their ideological overlap with other racial groups. But this raises a vitally important question – in which communities are the ideologies of whites and blacks most, and least, likely to overlap?

In this section, we use the racial and economic inequality lens we have developed in this book to shed new theoretical and empirical light on this question. Important research on racial inequality and the provision of public goods points in the direction of the hypothesis that racial differences in socioeconomic circumstances within communities may have important implications for ideological overlap between whites and nonwhites (and thus for the ideological congruence representation enjoyed by nonwhites).[21] This work indicates that greater racial economic inequality

[21] Alberto Alesina, Reza Baqir, and William Easterly. "Public Goods and Ethnic Divisions." *Quarterly Journal of Economics* 114, no. 4, (1999): 1243–1284; Brian An, Morris Levy, and Rodney Hero. "It's Not Just Welfare: Racial Inequality and the Local Provision of Public Goods in the United States." *Urban Affairs Review* 54, no. 5 (2018): 833–865; Rodney E. Hero and Morris E. Levy. "The Racial Structure of Inequality: Consequences for Welfare Policy in the US." *Social Science Quarterly* 99 (2018): 459–472; Erzo F. P.

(that is, greater inequality attributable to inequitable allocation of socio-economic resources between racial groups within a community) is associated with reduced provision of public goods such as welfare, education, hospitals, police, and parks.[22] The theoretical mechanism underlying this relationship – backed by research demonstrating that privileged racial groups typically oppose policies they perceive as transferring resources to less privileged racial groups[23] – is that increasing between-race inequality also increases the between-race gap in preferences for public goods. That is, as between-race inequality increases, the privileged racial group (typically whites) tends to become even less supportive of the provision of public goods due to the even greater perception that these goods will primarily benefit the disadvantaged racial group. Meanwhile, the less privileged racial group (typically nonwhites) will tend to become even more supportive of public goods.[24]

These findings strongly suggest that greater inequalities in socioeconomic outcomes between racial groups may also be associated with greater ideological differences between whites and nonwhites. Put simply, if increased racial inequality leads to a larger gap in *preferences for public goods* between whites and nonwhites, this dynamic should also be reflected in a larger overall *ideological gap* between members of these two races. This conclusion follows from the general observation that preferences for public goods are theoretically and empirically closely related to more general left–right ideology.

To understand the role that racial socioeconomic disparities might play in determining the degree of ideological overlap between racial groups within communities, we create a scale capturing the extent to which each community experiences racial disparities on four important indicators: (1) the poverty rate; (2) the unemployment rate; (3) the attainment of college degrees; and (4) family income. We take these indicators from the US

Luttmer. "Group Loyalty and the Taste for Redistribution." *Journal of Political Economy* 109, no. 3 (2001): 500–528; Tetsuya Matsubayashi and Rene R. Rocha. "Racial Diversity and Public Policy in the States." *Political Research Quarterly* 65, no. 3 (2012): 600–614; Lyle Scrugg and Thomas J. Hayes. "The Influence of Inequality on Welfare Generosity: Evidence from the US States." *Politics & Society* 45, no. 1 (2017): 35–66.

[22] Hero and Levi, "Racial Structure of Inequality"; An, Levi, and Hero, "It's Not Just Welfare."

[23] Alberto Alesina and Edward Glaeser. *Fighting Poverty in the US and Europe: A World of Difference.* New York: Oxford University Press, 2004; Martin Gilens. *Why Americans Hate Welfare: Race, Media, and the Politics of Antipoverty Policy.* Chicago: University of Chicago Press, 1999; Luttmer, "Group Loyalty."

[24] An, Levi, and Hero, "It's Not Just Welfare."

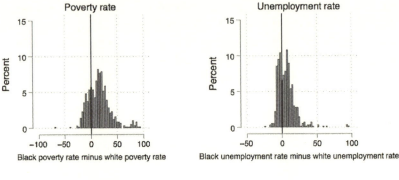

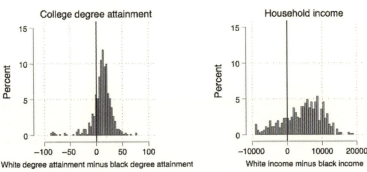

FIGURE 6.10 The distribution of communities along measures of black–white socioeconomic inequality

Census and map them to each of our communities, highlighting first the differences between whites and blacks. Figure 6.10 shows the distribution of communities based on values for whites and blacks along each of these indicators. For example, the top left plot in Figure 6.10 shows the distribution of communities based on the numerical difference between the black poverty rate and the white poverty rate. Communities to the right of the zero-line in the plot are those where blacks are more impoverished than whites. Note that while there are some communities where African Americans fare better than whites, it is much more common for the reverse to be true. Looking at the average community across all four indicators in our sample, the poverty rate is 15.3 percentage points higher for blacks than for whites; the unemployment rate is 6.1 percentage points higher for blacks; the percentage of whites with a college degree is 10.6 percentage points higher than it is for blacks; and the household income is $4,550 higher for whites than for blacks.

In each community, we calculated the difference between the value for whites on each of these variables and the value for each of our nonwhite

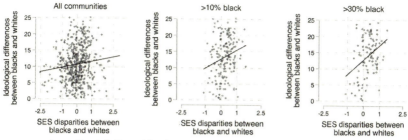

FIGURE 6.11 Racial disparities in socioeconomic indicators and ideological divergence among whites and blacks

Note: Plots show our scale of racial disparities in socioeconomic status on the x-axis. This scale is standardized with a mean of 0 and standard deviation of 1. The y-axis shows the difference between the average ideology of whites and blacks in the community.

groups (blacks first and then Latinos). We then used factor analysis to combine these metrics into a single scale that captures overall socioeconomic disparities. Lower values of the scale indicate that outcomes on these measures are relatively similar for white and nonwhite residents, respectively, whereas larger values suggest larger racial differences in outcomes favoring whites compared to nonwhites.

Figure 6.11 shows the relationship between the black–white disparities in socioeconomic indicators and our measure of the ideological distance between blacks and whites in our communities. The left-hand panel plots the relationship for all communities, and the second and third panels limit the analysis to communities with increasingly larger populations of African Americans. The line in each plot shows the linear relationship between these two measures. While there is a great deal of variance across the communities, the general trend is clear – communities that have larger racial disparities on socioeconomic indicators are also more likely to have larger differences in ideology between whites and African Americans. Even more notably, this pattern is stronger in communities where African Americans constitute a larger share of the population. For example, in communities that are more than 30 percent black, a one standard deviation increase in socioeconomic racial disparities is associated with blacks and whites being 4.5 points further apart ideologically.

These findings indicate that, consistent with our expectations, racial inequality plays a powerful moderating role in determining the ideological congruence representation enjoyed by African Americans. More pointedly, the patterns in Figure 6.11 raise serious concerns about the prospects for representation of African Americans by their local governments. Not only do we find that whether African Americans do or do not receive representation is heavily influenced by whether they agree with whites ideologically; we also demonstrate that such agreement is significantly less likely to occur in precisely the circumstances in which African Americans would benefit the most from it. It is in local communities where blacks are worst off relative to whites that they are also least likely to be ideologically similar to whites – and where they are therefore least likely to benefit from coincidental representation on municipal councils.

It is notable that, when we analyzed the data pertaining to socioeconomic disparities between Hispanics and whites, no such pattern emerged. However, this is an understandable finding when we recall that the views of Hispanics tend to overlap more with those of whites than do those of blacks, and that Hispanics generally receive more ideological congruence representation from their elected officials as a result. As we feared – and as the results presented throughout this book have implied – in many communities African Americans face particularly severe obstacles to obtaining equitable representation in local government.

DOES THIS MATTER FOR POLICY REPRESENTATION?

Nonwhite residents, and particularly African Americans, receive less ideological congruence representation from their local elected officials than do whites. Furthermore, this gap in representation is largely a function of contextual factors, with electoral institutions playing only a minor role in helping to bridge these differences. But how important is this for the type of policies that communities consider and enact? That is, how much does it matter if particular racial and ethnic groups are not well represented by their local city or town councils?

To answer this question, we turn to the information on policy enactments that we have for a subset of our communities. We estimate a simple regression model where our policy liberalism scale is the dependent variable and our two key independent variables are the mean ideology of the community's adult population and the mean ideology of the community's elected officials. The coefficients on each of these items will provide us with an estimate of how much each matters while controlling for the other. The crux of our analytic strategy is this: *If the ideology of councilors is more important in explaining policy liberalism than is the mean ideology of the population, then the representational biases that we uncovered in this and the previous chapter are likely to have real policy consequences. But if the ideology of the community's population is a*

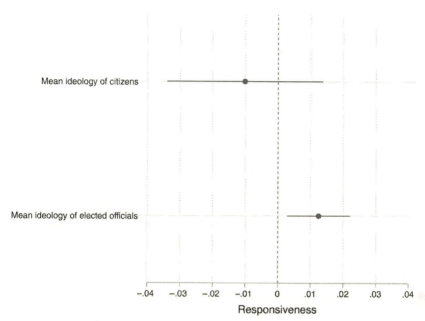

FIGURE 6.12 Policy responsiveness to citizens and elected officials in local communities
Note: Plots show coefficients and 95 percent confidence intervals from a regression model with the policy scale as the dependent variable and controlling for population size and the community's median income. Weights are applied to make results representative.

stronger predictor of policy, then some of the biases we documented may be less consequential, because policy is still more responsive to the views of the people than to the wishes or tastes of elected officials.

Figure 6.12 shows the responsiveness of policy to the ideologies of a community's population and to the ideology of its elected officials. In this analysis, we implement the weights that enable our sample to be representative of all American communities. We also implement additional weights that adjust for the fact that we do not have policy information available in all of our communities. Further, our model controls for other factors that have been shown to be related to policy liberalism, such as the size of the community's population and its median income.

The top coefficient in the plot, which measures the effect of the public's mean ideology, is actually negative, though with a wide confidence interval. A negative coefficient would mean that policy becomes more conservative even as the public's ideology becomes more liberal. However, the wide confidence interval means that we cannot be certain whether this relationship is positive, negative, or nonexistent. By contrast, the bottom coefficient in the plot is positive with a smaller confidence interval, indicating that when a local government's elected officials are more liberal, that local government is more likely to adopt policies that address inequality. The coefficient here means that for every ten points more liberal a community's elected officials are on average, policy will become about one-eighth of a standard deviation more liberal. To give a sense of what an increase in one-eighth of a standard deviation might mean, we can consider how that translates to the probability of adopting each item that went into our policy liberalism scale in the first place. For instance, a one-eighth of a standard deviation increase in policy liberalism for an average community would translate to a more than five-percentage-point greater chance that the local government would provide financial support or incentives for affordable housing.

Of course, it is important to remember two things about this analysis. First, this model merely shows the extent to which policy is correlated with the ideology of office holders and the public, we cannot claim here that policy liberalism is necessarily caused by the views of these two groups. Second, the ideology of office holders is, of course, related to the ideology of the population. That is, more liberal communities tend to elect more liberal municipal officials. Thus, what this model suggests is that most of the relationship between the ideology of a community and the types of policies its local government produces is a function of who that community elects to office.

In this way, these results provide further evidence of the potential consequences of the inequality in ideological congruence representation that we described. If, as we have shown, municipal councilors provide significantly more ideological congruence representation to whites than they do to African Americans or Latinos, and if, as we show in Figure 6.12, policy liberalism is largely responsive to the mean ideology of elected officials, then the ideology of whites must be better represented in the ideological orientation of municipal policy than is the ideology of either African Americans or Latinos.

CONCLUSION

In Chapter 5, we illustrated the troubling fact that, on average, nonwhites tend to have limited descriptive representation, ideological congruence representation, and policy responsiveness compared to what whites enjoy. In this chapter, we sought to understand the factors that influence the degree of municipal government bias against nonwhite residents, and to assess whether and to what extent institutions, contextual factors, and coincidental representation play a role in remediating inequalities in representation.

We observe that African Americans and Latinos receive much better representation of their ideologies when they make up a very significant share of the electorate. Generally speaking, this finding is consistent with a long line of research in municipal politics suggesting that the political power of nonwhite racial groups hinges to a significant degree on their share of the community population. However, our research also points to limitations in this perspective. For example, even where nonwhites make up a large fraction of the community population, in places like Ferguson, Missouri (66 percent), Louisville, Georgia (61 percent), or Bolivar, Tennessee (51 percent), we still find very large gaps between the average preferences of African American voters and those elected to the city council.

We found that the coincidental representation lens provides very important insights on variation in the ideological congruence representation received by African Americans and Latinos. Nonwhites get better representation when their ideologies happen to overlap considerably with those of white residents. In other words, they benefit from the happy coincidence of having similar ideologies as whites. However, when the ideologies of nonwhites *diverge* from those of whites, nonwhites receive relatively little representation. This problem is especially acute for African Americans, because the ideologies of African Americans and those of whites are, on average, quite distinctive, with African Americans expressing substantially more liberal preferences than whites. Because Latinos, compared with blacks, tend to have ideologies that overlap to a much greater degree with those of whites, they may be more likely to benefit from coincidental representation.

Additionally, this finding suggests the types of communities where we might see the largest racial disparities in representation. For the most part, African Americans' ideologies overlap with those of whites to a much greater degree in places where whites have a liberal bent. A consistent finding in contemporary American politics is that white liberals tend to live in large cities whereas smaller towns have become a haven for conservative whites. For example, the 2018 Cooperative Congressional Election Study shows that whites living in big cities are twice as likely to identify as liberal compared to whites living in rural areas and small towns. The fact that small town whites are generally much more conservative than those in larger cities suggests that racial inequalities in representation will be especially pronounced in America's smaller towns, a pattern we confirm in Chapter 9.

We also found that the racial and economic inequality lens shed important light on why African Americans are represented much more in some communities than in others. As we show, patterns of racial inequality within communities have major implications for the representation received by African Americans. The ideologies of African Americans and whites are most different in communities with the greatest racial inequality in socioeconomic outcomes, meaning that African Americans are least likely to receive representation (in the form of coincidental representation) in the communities *in which they need it most*. This is a profoundly disturbing finding about political representation in local communities. In sharp contrast, Latinos are not penalized in terms of ideological congruence representation in communities in which there is more inequality in socioeconomic outcomes between Latinos and whites.

An important focus of this chapter has been to understand if observed gaps in representation might be mitigated by the design of political institutions. In particular, we expected that a Political model of institutions, with its emphasis on political engagement rather than government effectiveness, might mitigate the underrepresentation of the interests of residents of color. We found only limited grounds for optimism. Most local institutions are unrelated to the ideological congruence representation of African Americans and Latinos. However, having local elections in November, at the same time as state or federal elections, tends to improve the ideological congruence representation of nonwhites. This makes sense because turnout tends to be considerably higher among nonwhite populations during these salient elections.[25] Yet although scheduling local elections in November tends to increase ideological congruence representation, the results of our study of policy representation suggests that this institutional reform has little if any effect on how much policy representation African Americans or Latinos receive. Put differently, increased ideological congruence representation as a result of institutional reform does not seem to translate directly into greater policy responsiveness.[26]

[25] Hajnal and Lewis, "Municipal Institutions and Voter Turnout"; Zoltan Hajnal and Jessica Trounstine. "Where Turnout Matters: The Consequences of Uneven Turnout in City Politics." *Journal of Politics* 67, no. 2 (2005): 515–535.
[26] Chris Tausanovitch and Christopher Warshaw. "Representation in Municipal Government." *American Political Science Review* 108, no. 3 (2014): 605–641.

Our findings in this chapter rely on the assumption that municipal politics is intrinsically linked to ideological viewpoints and that governments can produce policy outputs that are more or less representative of those ideological viewpoints.[27] The ideological mappings of different racial groups do not always overlap at all points, and when they do not, we observe significant disparities in representation, even when non-white groups make up a significant share of the local population. On the positive side, we observe that some changes in elections and governing institutions can ameliorate, but not resolve, the situation. In the next two chapters we see if the same dynamics apply to economic class structure.

[27] Tausanovitch and Warshaw, "Representation in Municipal Government."

7

Economic Inequality in Representation
on Municipal Councils and in Policy

Mount Pleasant, Wisconsin, is a village of 26,000 residents in Racine County, Wisconsin, a suburban area approximately 30 miles south of Milwaukee. Although historically devoted to agriculture, the village economy is now dominated by the retail, industrial, and health care sectors. Mount Pleasant boasts numerous local, national, and international companies, "including Putzmeister, Case New Holland, SC Johnson, Diversey, Horizon Retail Construction, Racine Federated, and many others."[1] The village is fairly prosperous: The median family income ($59,584) is slightly above the state median of $59,305, and more than 40 percent of residents possess at least an associate's degree. Nearly 72 percent of residents own homes, with a median home value of $172,292.[2]

All things considered, the residents of Mount Pleasant – as the name of their town suggests – find themselves in a fairly enviable position, with a solid economy, close proximity to a major city, and a good standard of living. Yet in recent years the town has been engulfed in class-tinged economic conflict. The controversy is rooted in an agreement by local elected officials with Taiwan-based Foxconn Technology Group, an enormous technology and communications manufacturing firm, to build a $10 billion dollar manufacturing plant in Mount Pleasant. Some community members allege that this agreement was reached in secret, failed to

---

[1] Village of Mount Pleasant and Racine County Economic Development Corp. "Village Economic Snapshot," www.mtpleasantwi.gov/DocumentCenter/View/1286/2018-Mount-Pleasant-at-a-Glance?bidId.

[2] Village of Mount Pleasant, "Village Economic Snapshot."

provide residents with adequate opportunities for discussion or consultation, and imposed huge costs on residents.[3]

The Foxconn project in Mount Pleasant resulted from a more than $3 billion dollar deal engineered by then-governor Scott Walker to lure the electronics giant to Wisconsin.[4] In exchange for this record-setting package of subsidies and tax gifts, which was announced in June 2018, Foxconn agreed to build a large factory – initially touted as employing up to 13,000 blue-collar workers – somewhere in the state.[5]

While the state was negotiating terms with Foxconn, Mount Pleasant officials were simultaneously engaged in secret discussions with the corporation to site the factory in the community. In the end, Mount Pleasant's elected officials struck a deal with the electronics behemoth – including the donation by the town of a six square mile parcel of land and a huge incentives package (which it would have to borrow heavily to finance) – without public notice or any opportunity for community deliberation.[6] Indeed, according to a group of local residents, "The public was not allowed to read the development agreement between Mount Pleasant and Foxconn until it was approved by the Village Board in late November 2017, and Trustees who met in closed session negotiation meetings were prohibited from discussing the details with residents."[7] Adding to the controversy is the fact that the Village Board engaged in some hard-hitting tactics to advance the agreement, including designating a huge swath of community land as "blighted" as a way both to lower the cost of borrowing to finance its incentives package to

[3] Dan Kaufman, "Did Scott Walker and Donald Trump Deal Away the Wisconsin Governor's Race to Foxconn?," *The New Yorker*, November 3, 2018, www.newyorker.com/news/dispatch/did-scott-walker-and-donald-trump-deal-away-the-governors-race-to-foxconn.
[4] Bruce Murphy, "Wisconsin's $4.1 Billion Foxconn Boondoggle," *The Verge*, October 29, 2018.
[5] Danielle Paquette, "Wisconsin Offered Foxconn More than Virginia and New York Did for Amazon," *The Washington Post*, November 15, 2018, www.washingtonpost.com/business/2018/11/15/wisconsin-offered-foxconn-more-than-virginia-new-york-did-amazon/?fbclid=IwAR3Ebhztg1mBqgIuWNgNLh8zGDmuo9XEKj8duMRYMnqBh81s5xlhbdtUP6U&noredirect=on&utm_term=.6185ce1983a1.
[6] Sruthi Pinnamaneni, "Foxconn and the Village: The $10B Factory Deal That Turned One Small Wisconsin Town Upside Down," interview by Josh Dzieza, *The Verge*, December 6, 2018, www.theverge.com/2019/4/10/18296793/foxconn-wisconsin-location-factory-innovation-centers-technology-hub-no-news.
[7] A Better Mount Pleasant, "Mount Pleasant Village Officials Threaten and Censor Foxconn Area Residents," Urban Milwaukee, May 14, 2018, https://urbanmilwaukee.com/pressrelease/mount-pleasant-village-officials-threaten-and-censor-foxconn-area-residents.

Foxconn and to facilitate the use of eminent domain to seize property for development.[8]

Even as local conflict over the development intensified, Foxconn backtracked from its initial promises to Mount Pleasant. The company originally pitched its development as a huge manufacturing site that would produce large LCD screens and employ thousands of blue-collar workers (a major reason for initial enthusiasm for the project among less affluent Wisconsinites). But it subsequently scaled back these plans, suggesting that the site would be a more modest "technology hub" that might engage the services of a smaller number of well-educated, high-skilled research- and science-oriented employees.[9] As this book went to press, state officials led by new Democratic governor Tony Evers and Foxconn leaders were still negotiating the scope of the development.[10] Meanwhile, the state's Legislative Fiscal Bureau estimates that, given the huge scope of the subsidies, Wisconsin's investment in Foxconn will not break even until 2050 or later.[11] For the time being, the state and community both appear to be saddled with an enormously expensive commitment that does not seem poised to deliver benefits for Wisconsin's less affluent residents.

The Foxconn episode in Mount Pleasant, Wisconsin, is a cautionary tale of how the pursuit of economic development can come at the expense of local democracy and, quite possibly, the interests of less affluent residents. It is fair to say that the decision-making process surrounding the village's agreement with Foxconn did not conform to democratic norms. In particular, residents were never permitted the opportunity to directly evaluate a deal with huge consequences for town finances and the character of the community.[12] Meanwhile, the combination of lavish costs associated with the economic incentives package (which led Moody's to downgrade the town's credit rating) and the apparent disappearance of high-paying jobs for blue-collar workers suggests that the deal

---

[8] Dan Kaufman, "Did Scott Walker and Donald Trump Deal Away the Wisconsin Governor's Race to Foxconn?"; Joy Powers, "Mount Pleasant Declares Homes in Footprint of Foxconn 'Blighted,'" WUWM 89.7 *NPR*, June 8, 2018.

[9] Jake Swearingen, "Foxconn Is Good at Grifting Governments, and the US Is an Easy Mark," *New York Magazine*, January, 31, 2019, http://nymag.com/intelligencer/2019/01/foxconn-consistently-lies-about-jobs-and-were-an-easy-mark.html.

[10] Jay Sorgi, "Foxconn Disputes Report That Investment in Wisconsin Is 'Suspended and Scaled Back,'" WTMJ Radio, January 31, 2019, www.wtmj.com/news/report-foxconn-10b-investment-in-wisconsin-suspended-and-scaled-back-due-to-evers-negotiations/9966 37002.

[11] Murphy, "Wisconsin's $4.1 Billion Foxconn Boondoggle."

[12] Pinnamaneni, "Foxconn and the Village."

may hit less affluent residents the hardest. After all, resources committed to the project are unavailable for spending on public goods that Wisconsinites depend on, such as schools, hospitals, parks, and roads – especially when the town, because of its lowered credit rating, cannot borrow at reasonable cost. Finally, the good blue-collar jobs that arguably provided the best rationale for the enormous expense – at least for less affluent residents – have not materialized (yet). In January 2019, Foxconn announced that it had 178 full-time employees on the payroll in the *entire state of Wisconsin* – falling short of its hiring target by 82 percent.[13]

The story raises important questions about the functioning of local democracy. Is the Foxconn episode an extreme outlier? Or does it illustrate broader patterns of dysfunction in local politics? More pointedly, does this affair illustrate a more general trend in which the interests of the less affluent are inadequately represented?

In this chapter we investigate economic inequality in representation at the local level, through the lens of several distinctive forms of representation – descriptive representation, ideological congruence representation, and policy responsiveness. Although our analysis in this chapter closely parallels that of our earlier chapter on racial inequality in representation, our findings are different in important ways. In a departure from research on economic inequality in representation at other levels of government, we find that residents in the middle of the wealth distribution are relatively well served by local democracy.[14] Yes, elected officials tend to be more affluent than residents on average, and they provide more ideological congruence representation to wealthy residents than to other wealth groups. But residents in the middle wealth tercile do quite well in terms of descriptive representation on municipal councils. And policy appears to be more responsive to residents in the middle of the wealth distribution than to either the poorer or wealthier groups in a community. With the important caveat that the close proximity between the ideologies of middle wealth residents and the ideologies of their wealthier neighbors complicates efforts to distinguish between the amount of representation received by each of these two groups, we conclude that local government seems to be working fairly well for middle-class Americans.

[13] Austin Carr, "Inside Wisconsin's Disastrous $4.5 Billion Deal with Foxconn," *Bloomberg Businessweek*, February 6, 2019, www.bloomberg.com/news/features/2019-02-06/inside-wisconsin-s-disastrous-4-5-billion-deal-with-foxconn.

[14] See, most prominently, Gilens, "Inequality and Democratic Responsiveness"; Gilens and Page, "Testing Theories of American Politics"; Bartels, *Unequal Democracy*.

Unfortunately, however, not all of our news about economic representation in local government is good. Quite the contrary, in fact. As we show, poorer residents do not share in the advantages in representation enjoyed by those in the middle wealth group. The least affluent are woefully underrepresented on municipal councils. Perhaps unsurprisingly, then, local elected officials are on average relatively distant ideologically from residents in the bottom wealth tercile, and local policy is *almost completely unresponsive* to the preferences of members of the least affluent group. If democracy is judged in significant part on the extent to which it represents the interests of its most vulnerable residents, our analysis suggests that democracy at the local level is falling far short of expectations. This finding resonates with research on representation at other levels of American government, which also concludes that the least affluent are largely unrepresented by elected officials and in policy.

The limited representation of poorer residents by local governments is similar to the unhappy experience of Latinos and, especially, African Americans that we charted in previous chapters. Because African Americans and Latinos tend to have accumulated less wealth than whites due to past and present patterns of discrimination and unequal opportunity, our findings raise the question whether the economic inequities in representation that we observe are actually attributable, at least to some degree, to the racial inequalities in representation that we have already documented. However, even when we look only at municipalities with very small nonwhite populations, biases in representation against the least affluent residents remain. It seems clear, then, that class differences in representation – and, in particular, biases in representation against poorer residents – are a distinctive, and important, dimension of local politics in many municipalities in the United States.

While the image of economic inequality in representation at the local level presented in this chapter is not as stark as in our portrait of racial inequality, our findings nonetheless reinforce the view that local democracy is in a serious state of disrepair. It might be comforting, at least to some, to imagine that this conclusion applies to huge cities only; unfortunately, this is not the case. Because our sample draws from large cities, midsize communities, and small towns, our findings apply to smaller communities such as Mount Pleasant as well as urban centers like San Diego. In fact, as we show in this chapter, some of the grossest inequities appear in relatively small communities. More generally, our results bolster the growing consensus among social scientists that the interests of the least affluent are substantially underrepresented in the halls of government. There is mounting evidence that Congress, state legislatures, and (as revealed in our work) municipal councils largely discount the concerns of their least affluent constituents; this finding challenges time-worn assumptions about the adequacy of representative democracy as it is currently practiced in the United States.[15] At a minimum, our analysis suggests that – at least when it comes to representation – Americans may be mistaken to express greater faith in their local governments than in the federal government or their state governments.[16]

DESCRIPTIVE ECONOMIC REPRESENTATION ON MUNICIPAL COUNCILS

As we suggested in Chapter 5, descriptive representation of racial groups on municipal councils is an important indicator of the well-being of local democracy, serving as it does to increase the political confidence of group members, provide partial compensation for past and present injustices, empower group members to set the political agenda, and increase the likelihood of ideological and policy representation of group members. For similar reasons, examining descriptive economic representation in local government is an important starting point for assessing how well – or poorly – local governments represent less affluent residents. Nicholas Carnes, a prominent scholar of class and representation in American politics, has made a strong argument that the election to office of representatives from middle- and especially working-class backgrounds plays a large role in determining the quality of representation received by less affluent constituents. Along with coauthor Noam Lupu, Carnes has shown that ordinary citizens view candidates from less affluent backgrounds as equally qualified as those from the upper class, and rate them as more relatable than affluent candidates.[17] This work suggests that the

---

[15] Gilens, "Inequality and Democratic Responsiveness"; Gilens and Page, "Testing Theories of American Politics"; Bartels, *Unequal Democracy*; Gilens, *Affluence and Influence*; Benjamin Page and Martin Gilens. *Democracy in America? What Has Gone Wrong and What We Can Do about It.* Chicago: University of Chicago Press, 2017; Flavin, "Income Inequality and Policy Representation in the American States"; Christopher Ellis. "Understanding Economic Biases in Representation: Income, Resources, and Policy Representation in the 110th House." *Political Research Quarterly* 64, no. 4 (2012): 938–951; Christopher Ellis. *Putting Inequality in Context: Class, Public Opinion, and Representation in the United States.* Ann Arbor: University of Michigan Press, 2017.

[16] McCarthy, "Americans Still More Trusting of Local than State Government."

[17] Nicholas Carnes and Noam Lupu. "What Good Is a College Degree? Education and Leader Quality Reconsidered." *Journal of Politics* 78, no. 1 (2016): 35–49.

presence of less affluent representatives likely contributes to greater feelings of efficacy and more positive attitudes about government among less well-to-do constituents.

More pointedly, Carnes suggests that the election of nonaffluent representatives to decision-making bodies may be a precondition for the representation of the actual interests of less advantaged constituents. As he notes, "politicians from different lines of work tend to bring different economic perspectives with them to public office." "[T]hese differences in how politicians think and behave," Carnes suggests, "can ultimately have enormous consequences for economic policy."[18] The systematic underrepresentation of less affluent individuals (particularly those from the working class, who tend to be more liberal on economic issues) in Congress and state legislatures "appears to bias policy on issues like the minimum wage, taxes, and welfare spending towards the more conservative positions typically favored by affluent Americans."[19] To the degree that elected officials from different economic classes approach political issues in fundamentally different ways, equitable representation of the interests of lower-class residents in local government may depend, at least in part, on economic descriptive representation on municipal councils.

With these considerations in mind, we investigate how well or poorly officials elected to the municipal councils in our sample of communities descriptively represent groups with differing amounts of wealth. In Figure 7.1, we compare the shares of residents and elected officials in a variety of wealth groups, across all the communities in our sample. Note that, in Figure 7.1, we present information about the amount of wealth held by residents and councilors, rather than about the position of residents and councilors in the overall distribution of wealth across communities or the particular distributions of wealth within communities. This facilitates direct comparisons of population shares and council shares

---

[18] Nicholas Carnes. "Adam Smith Would Be Spinning in His Grave." *The Forum* 15, no.1 (2017): 156.

[19] Nicholas Carnes. "Why Are There So Few Working-Class People in Political Office? Evidence from State Legislatures." *Politics, Groups, and Identities* 4, no. 1 (2016): 85; see also Nicholas Carnes and Noam Lupu. "Rethinking the Comparative Perspective on Class and Representation: Evidence from Latin America." *American Journal of Political Science* 59, no. 1 (2015): 1–18; John D. Griffin and Claudia Anewalt-Remsburg. "Legislator Wealth and the Effort to Repeal the Estate Tax." *American Politics Research* 41, no. 4 (2013): 599–622; Christian Grose, "Risk and Roll Calls: How Legislators' Personal Finances Shape Congressional Decisions," working paper (2013); Michael W. Kraus and Bennett Callaghan. "Noblesse Oblige? Social Status and Economic Inequality Maintenance among Politicians." *PLoS ONE* 9, no. 1 (2014): 1–6.

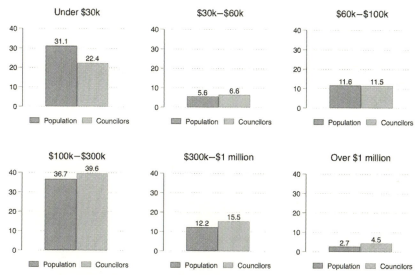

FIGURE 7.1 Share of community population and municipal council seats held by various wealth groups in communities in sample

held by each wealth group. The "bins" constituting each wealth group are those available to us through Catalist.

Figure 7.1 shows clear signs of inequality between the general population of a community and those who serve in local elected office. The gap that immediately jumps out from the figure appears in the top left panel. Across all communities, people in the lowest wealth bin (those with wealth under $30,000) make up about 31 percent of residents though, of course, the share of residents in this wealth bin varies alot community by community. However, people from this wealth group are much less likely to find their way into local elected office, as evidenced by the fact that just 22 percent of municipal councilors in the communities in our sample have a predicted wealth of less than $30,000. To be sure, the serious underrepresentation of the lowest wealth group is almost certainly attributable, at least in part, to the fact that lower wealth residents are least likely to have access to the leisure time and other supports needed to serve in what are frequently part-time and poorly paid (or even voluntary!) local elective offices.[20] Indeed, recall from Chapter 4 that people

[20] Kay Lehman Schlozman, Sidney Verba, and Henry E. Brady. *The Unheavenly Chorus: Unequal Political Voice and the Broken Promise of American Democracy.* Princeton, NJ: Princeton University Press, 2012.

who run for local office or attend local political meetings tend to be wealthier than those who do not. This is no accident: consider the likely effect of the famously low salaries of the offices held by local elected officials. Nearly one in five communities does not pay their councilors anything at all, and among those that do, the median community pays an annual salary of just $6,500. In fact, only one in ten communities offers councilors an annual salary in excess of $10,000 per year.[21] The effect is hardly surprising: The poorest citizens can ill afford to serve in local elected offices, even if they should somehow find the time to do so.

By contrast, the bottom three panels show that people in the middle and top of the wealth distribution tend to be overrepresented on municipal councils. For example, across all communities in our sample 36.7 percent of residents have an estimated wealth of between $100,000 and $300,000, and nearly 40 percent of municipal councilors are members of this group. And while 2.7 percent of all residents in the communities in our sample have an estimated wealth in excess of $1 million, millionaires account for 4.5 percent of all municipal councilors. This is a familiar story at all levels of government – serving in political office is a pursuit that some citizens can afford more than others.

Figure 7.1 summarized the picture of descriptive representation across all the communities in our sample. However, summarizing the data in this way hides some of the differences we find across American communities. That is to say, the aggregated figures do not tell us how these differences are expressed in individual communities. Figure 7.2 addresses this question, plotting for each community the percent of its population that falls into each of the six wealth bins against the share of the councilors from that community falling into the same wealth bin.

The plots in Figure 7.2 offer a more nuanced view of inequality in descriptive representation on municipal councils. There is substantial variation across communities in the extent to which wealth groups enjoy membership on municipal councils. Consider, for example, the plot for the least affluent group, those with less than $30,000 in wealth. On 42 percent of councils, members of this group are wholly unrepresented. The complete lack of representation of members of the least affluent group on many councils can be observed in the upper left plot of Figure 7.2, where a large number of circles representing communities cluster along the line on the y-axis indicating "0" representation of

---

[21] These figures come from the 2011 Form of Government survey conducted by the ICMA.

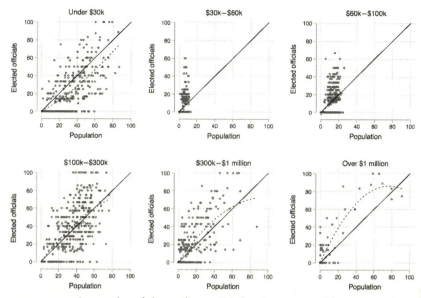

FIGURE 7.2 Scatterplot of share of council belonging to a wealth group against population share of the group in the community

members of this group. The solid reference line in each plot shows where a community would fall if the percent of that wealth group on their council perfectly matched the percent of that wealth group in the community's population. The broken line summarizes the actual relationship between the percent of the wealth group in the community and the share of the council comprised of members of that wealth group. Notably, the poorest citizens are consistently underrepresented in local government regardless of how much of the community's population they constitute. Even when more than half of a community's population is made up of people with an estimated wealth of less than $30,000, they are still underrepresented on the council by more than 10 percentage points. Of course, the plot also reveals that there are some communities where this group actually makes up a larger share of the council than they do of the population; but this situation is hardly the norm.

Contrast this with the $100,000–$300,000 wealth group. On only 18.9 percent of councils are members of this wealth group wholly unrepresented. Additionally, the broken line falls quite close to the solid line throughout the plot, indicating that, on average, councils represent this community at a level that is generally commensurate with their share of the population.

Meanwhile, as Figure 7.2 shows, while millionaires are not very common, they are vastly overrepresented on many councils, particularly when they compose a nontrivial share of the population. In one-fourth of our communities, there are no millionaires at all in the population, and where millionaires are not present they certainly cannot be overrepresented. But in communities where there are millionaires, there is a pretty good chance that the group will be significantly overrepresented in local government.

On the whole, our analysis of economic descriptive representation points to significant inequities, and in particular to the substantial descriptive underrepresentation of the least affluent on municipal councils. Our analysis also indicates that the wealthiest residents are, on the whole, overrepresented on municipal councils, even though they are absent from the great majority of councils.

IDEOLOGICAL CONGRUENCE REPRESENTATION ON MUNICIPAL COUNCILS

The patterns of inequality in descriptive representation that we have identified – and, in particular, the overrepresentation of the affluent and the extreme underrepresentation of the poor – raise concerns about inequality in the representation of the interests of different class groups. However, while economic descriptive representation may be an important ingredient of ideological representation, particularly for lower wealth groups, it is not identical to ideological representation. In practice, the relationship between economic descriptive representation and ideological representation can be quite complex. While some markers of economic class (particularly wealth and occupation) may significantly influence representatives' behavior in office on some issues,[22] others (such as economic circumstances during childhood or education level) seem not to have any consistent effect.[23] Additionally, existing research on the

[22] Nicholas Carnes. "Does the Numerical Underrepresentation of the Working Class in Congress Matter?" *Legislative Studies Quarterly* 3, no. 1 (2012): 5–34; Nicholas Carnes. *White-Collar Government: The Hidden Role of Class in Economic Policy Making.* Chicago: University of Chicago Press, 2013; John D. Griffin and Claudia Anewalt-Remsburg. "Legislator Wealth and the Effort to Repeal the Estate Tax." *American Politics Research* 41, no. 4 (2013): 599–622; Michael W. Kraus and Bennett Callaghan. "Noblesse Oblige? Social Status and Economic Inequality Maintenance among Politicians." *PLoS ONE* 9, no. 1 (2014): 1–6.

[23] Nicholas Carnes. "Does the Numerical Underrepresentation of the Working Class in Congress Matter?" *Legislative Studies Quarterly* 3, no. 1 (2012): 5–34; Nicholas Carnes and Meredith L. Sadin. "The 'Mill Worker's Son' Heuristic: How Voters Perceive

influence of class on representatives' behavior most commonly focuses on core economic issues like taxation, regulation of business, and government efforts to reduce economic inequality, while paying less attention to other high-profile issues such as civil rights, women's rights, and the environment.[24] Finally, while studies of inequalities in descriptive representation on municipal councils are common, it has not to date been possible, due to data limitations, to directly assess economic inequities in ideological congruence representation in local politics. As was the case for race, then, if we truly want to evaluate how well residents, particularly those at lower levels of wealth, are represented by elected officials, we need to move beyond economic descriptive representation to an assessment of ideological congruence representation.

For this analysis, we use the measure of ideological congruence representation that we applied in our analysis of ideological congruence representation by race – the distance between the ideology of the mean group member and the mean ideology of the municipal council. In the previous section, we examined wealth groups in terms of the amount of wealth held, but we now adopt a different strategy. Here, we assign individuals to one of three terciles (low wealth, middle wealth, and high wealth) based on their position in the wealth distribution within their local community. We assign individuals to a tercile based on their position within the *local* wealth distribution in order to account for substantial differences between communities in the standard of living.[25] Because communities vary dramatically in living standards, an amount of wealth that would qualify as affluence in one community might represent mere middle-class status in another (and vice versa). By assigning individuals to wealth terciles based on their position in the local wealth distribution,

Politicians from Working-Class Families—and How They Really Behave in Office." *The Journal of Politics* 77, no. 1 (2015): 285–298.

[24] Nicholas Carnes. "Adam Smith Would Be Spinning in His Grave." *The Forum* 15, no. 1 (2017): 151–165, though see for an exception, Nicholas Carnes. "Does the Numerical Underrepresentation of the Working Class in Congress Matter?" *Legislative Studies Quarterly* 3, no. 1 (2012): 5–34; Nicholas Carnes, *White-Collar Government: The Hidden Role of Class in Economic Policy Making*. Chicago: University of Chicago Press, 2013.

[25] A challenge that arises in creating this distribution is that the wealth bins are coarse and do not perfectly divide into terciles. When this happens, individuals are randomly assigned to the tercile that the wealth bins spanned. For example, if 40% of a community's population is in the bottom wealth bin (under \$30,000 in wealth) then the people in that bin are randomly ordered and the first 33% are assigned to the bottom tercile with the remaining people in that bin being assigned to the middle tercile.

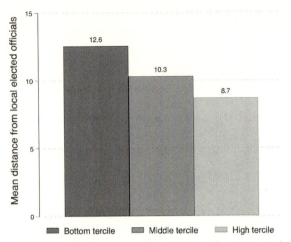

FIGURE 7.3 Mean ideological distance between wealth groups and municipal elected officials in communities in sample

Note: Wealth terciles are assigned based on an individual's location within the wealth distribution of their own community. Sampling weights applied.

therefore, we can more accurately represent different economic groups as they actually appear within communities (rather than as they appear in relation to a national distribution), and better evaluate inequities in the representation of these different groups. However, we also supplement this analysis by showing the results for each of the absolute wealth bins we analyzed.

Existing research on class inequalities in ideological representation at other levels of government consistently finds that less affluent residents receive less representation than do more affluent residents, particularly when the representative is a member of the Republican Party.[26] We thus have reason to anticipate that this may also be the case at the local level, though (due to the proximity of local governments to residents and to the constraints on local decision-making) we hold out the possibility that there are not important class differences in ideological congruence.

Figure 7.3 suggests that, within communities, there are indeed important differences in the ideological congruence representation enjoyed by

---

[26] See, e.g., Bartels, *Unequal Democracy*; Ellis, "Understanding Economic Biases in Representation"; Ellis, "Social Context an Economic Biases in Representation"; Jesse H. Rhodes and Brian F. Schaffner. "Testing Models of Unequal Representation: Democratic Populists and Republican Oligarchs?" *Quarterly Journal of Political Science* 12, no. 2 (2017): 185–204; Thomas J. Hayes. "Responsiveness in an Era of Inequality: The Case of the US Senate." *Political Research Quarterly* 66, no. 3 (2012): 585–599.

low, middle, and high wealth groups. The mean ideological distance of poorer residents from local elected officials is 12.6 points. This is about 45 percent larger than the mean ideological distance between the wealthiest residents and municipal elected officials (8.7 points), and about 23 percent larger than the distance between the middle wealth group and local elected officials (10.3 points). On average, when it comes to ideological congruence representation, members of the bottom wealth tercile are at a distinct disadvantage compared to those in the middle and high wealth groups. This finding is broadly consistent with the patterns presented in the previous section, which revealed the serious descriptive underrepresentation of poorer individuals on municipal councils.

To look at this dynamic from another angle, the mean ideological distance between the low wealth group and municipal councilors is similar to the mean distance between Latinos and their elected officials (13.96 points), though noticeably smaller than the mean distance between African Americans and municipal councilors (17.60 points). Poor residents are also more distant from councilors than are whites on average (the mean distance between whites and councilors is 9.83 points). These patterns reinforce the conclusion that economically disadvantaged individuals are on average poorly represented by local governments, compared to more advantaged groups (especially middle- and upper-class whites).

The gap in ideological congruence representation between the middle wealth group and the top wealth tercile is smaller, but still noticeable. The distance between the middle wealth group and local elected officials (10.3 points on average) is 18 percent larger than the distance between the wealthiest group and local elected officials (8.7 points on average). In other words, those in the middle of the wealth distribution in their communities suffer from a disadvantage in ideological congruence representation relative to the richest residents. Examined from another perspective, however, middle wealth residents enjoy ideological congruence representation on fairly favorable terms. This group is closer to their elected officials, on average, than are either African Americans or Latinos; and they are on average about the same distance from local councilors as are whites. All things considered, then, when it comes to ideological congruence representation, members of the middle class enjoy a comparatively enviable position.

Of course, the reference to our analysis of race and ideological congruence representation raises some concerns about the plot shown. After all, we know that racial and ethnic minorities tend to be less wealthy than their white neighbors; thus, it is possible that the differences we are

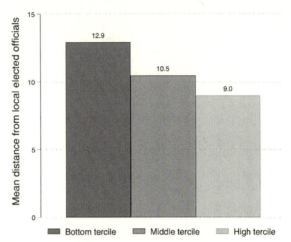

FIGURE 7.4 Mean ideological distance between wealth groups and municipal elected officials in predominantly white communities

Note: Wealth terciles are assigned based on an individual's location within the wealth distribution of their own community. Graph is limited to only communities where whites make up more than 95 percent of the population. Sampling weights applied.

illustrating are largely driven by the racial inequalities we detailed earlier in this book. To examine whether this might be the case, we reconstruct the same analysis, limiting our focus this time to only the 208 communities from our sample where whites make up more than 95 percent of the population. Figure 7.4 presents this analysis. The patterns are remarkably similar to what we found in Figure 7.3. Specifically, in these predominantly white communities, the wealthiest individuals are about 43 percent closer to the mean ideology of the municipal council than are the poorest individuals (9 points versus 12.9 points). Thus, the patterns of economic inequality in local representation that we document here are not attributable to the racial inequalities we explored earlier in this book.

Of course, our analysis thus far has focused on relative wealth, to account for the fact that standards of living can vary substantially across different communities. But one might naturally wonder what the results would look like if we simply plotted the ideological congruence measure by actual wealth. We do this in Figure 7.5. Recall that we have six wealth bins available to us, but several of them are relatively underpopulated. Thus, for this plot, we collapse the six bins into three – people with an estimated wealth under $30,000, those with an estimated wealth between $30,000 and $300,000, and those with an estimated wealth above $300,000. On

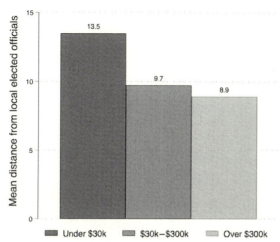

FIGURE 7.5 Mean ideological distance between municipal elected officials and wealth groups defined in absolute terms (actual wealth)
Note: Sampling weights applied.

average, in the communities in our sample, about 35 percent of the population falls into the bottom wealth group, 52 percent falls into the middle wealth group, and 13 percent into the top wealth category. Of course, there is substantial variance in these figures across communities.

Even when we define wealth groups in such absolute terms, the picture of inequality is fairly consistent. Specifically, the poorest Americans receive the worst ideological congruence representation. In fact, people with an estimated wealth under $30,000 find themselves 4.6 points farther away, on average, from their local elected officials than the group with an estimated wealth over $300,000. This significant advantage of the rich over the poor exists even though the poor have a population advantage over the rich in about four-fifths of the communities in our sample.

The analysis in Figure 7.5 does show a diminished gap in the ideological congruence representation of the middle and top wealth groups when we define them in this way. This is largely due to the fact that there is significant variance in what constitutes middle and upper class across the communities in our sample. In fact, in half of the communities in our sample, less than 3.5 percent of the population has an estimated wealth over $300,000. This is one benefit of our approach, which focuses on where people stand relative to others in their community: In this way, we are better able to differentiate the middle and upper wealth groups from each other.

TABLE 7.1 *Communities with greatest inequities in ideological congruence representation between low and high wealth residents*

	Distance between low wealth residents and council	Distance between high wealth residents and council	Difference
Greenville, NC	16.93	3.31	13.62
Brookhaven, MS	15.51	2.72	12.79
Childersburg, AL	14.66	3.17	11.49
Madison, NE	12.23	1.09	11.14
Abbeville, AL	18.73	7.60	11.13
Sealy, TX	26.79	16.13	10.66
Ennis, TX	13.52	3.15	10.37
Bluffton, IN	11.82	1.59	10.23

Note: Table shows only those communities where we matched all the local elected officials to the voter file.

Which communities are the worst offenders when we look at disparities in ideological congruence representation? To identify the communities with the largest differences favoring the rich, we calculate the difference between the distances between poor residents and councils, on the one hand, and the distances between wealthy residents and councils, on the other, for all of the communities in our sample. Eight communities with the greatest inequities favoring the wealthy are presented in Table 7.1.

As we can see, in each of these communities, the wealthiest citizens find themselves at least ten points closer to the members of the council than do the poorest residents. Indeed, in each of these communities the *difference* in ideological congruence representation favoring high wealth residents is larger than the *average* distance between low wealth residents and their councilors. In most cases, the wealthy have an advantage because they find themselves quite close ideologically to their councilors. However, Sealy, TX, is an exception. In that community, the wealthiest residents are about sixteen points away from the average councilor – not particularly good representation – but they still have an advantage since Sealy residents in the bottom wealth tercile find themselves twenty-six points away from the council.

To be sure, these communities represent extreme instances of class inequities in ideological congruence representation. It bears remembering, though, that significant inequities in ideological congruence representation between low and high wealth residents are not uncommon. In 50 percent of the communities in our sample, the wealthiest residents are at least five points closer to municipal councils than are the poorest residents, and in 25 percent of communities they are at least seven points closer. In contrast, low wealth residents are more than five points closer to their councils than are wealthy residents in only about 7 percent of communities. Put simply, the rich are closer to their elected officials than the poor in the overwhelming majority of American communities.

It is worth noting that the communities with the greatest differences in ideological representation between the low and high wealth residents tend to have city councils that are top-heavy with wealthy elected officials. In Greenville, for example, which has the largest gap between low and high wealth residents, we have wealth data for five of the seven elected officials, and all of them are in the top wealth tercile. This outcome contrasts significantly with the economic plight of many Greenville residents. Data from the US Census indicates that one neighborhood in Greenville had the largest recent increase in concentrated poverty (a poverty rate of 40 percent or greater) in North Carolina, rising 16.8 percentage points from 5.9 percent in 2010 to 23.3 percent in 2016.[27] To put this in perspective, during this same period, concentrated poverty in the United States actually declined from 14 percent to 11.6 percent as the economy improved. We are not claiming a one-to-one relationship between deepening poverty and wealthy local leaders; rather, we are suggesting that a poor community might have a better chance of seeing its concerns addressed in policy-making deliberations if more members of the council belonged to the lower third of the wealth distribution.

DOES DESCRIPTIVE REPRESENTATION TRANSLATE INTO IDEOLOGICAL CONGRUENCE REPRESENTATION?

As we noted at the beginning of this chapter, the dearth of working-class Americans who serve in public office has been cited as one potential explanation for the fact that the wealthy appear to exert more influence over the direction of public policy than the poor. We have also shown that the largest disparity in descriptive representation on local councils is among the group of Americans whose wealth is estimated to be less than $30,000. While this group made up 31 percent of the populations in the

---

[27] Evan Comen and Samuel Stebbins, "What City Is Hit Hardest by Extreme Poverty in Your State?" 24/7 Wall Street, *USA Today*, July 13, 2018, www.usatoday.com/story/money/economy/2018/07/13/city-hit-hardest-extreme-poverty/36658191.

communities in our sample, it accounted for just 22 percent of local elected officials. Thus, we are suggesting that the lack of descriptive representation for the poor in local elected office may explain at least partially why the least wealthy individuals tend to be further away ideologically from their local councils than the rich.

To investigate this possibility further, we plot the amount of ideological congruence representation received by each wealth group against the percentage of elected officials that come from that group. This will allow us to test, for example, whether a community where one-third of the council comes from the bottom wealth tercile is better at representing poor constituents than one where just 15 percent of the council is from the bottom wealth group. Figure 7.6 presents these plots for each of the wealth groups. If descriptive representation helps to facilitate ideological congruence representation, we would expect to see the line summarizing the data to decrease as the values on the x-axis increase. This would indicate that the citizens of a group find themselves ideologically closer to the mean elected official in communities where more of the council comes from that group.

Overall, the results in Figure 7.6 suggest a rather modest relationship between descriptive and ideological congruence representation with respect to wealth. For the middle and top wealth terciles, the line is almost exactly flat. This means that these groups enjoy about the same amount of ideological congruence representation regardless of how much of the council belongs to that group. In other words, middle-class and wealthy citizens do not need to rely on electing members of their own class into office in order to see their views represented by local government. These are important patterns that underscore the advantaged political position of more affluent residents.

By contrast, there is a small but significant downward slope to the line for the bottom wealth tercile. Based on the plot, the poorest citizens in a community can move about three points closer, ideologically, to the municipal council if their share of the council increases from 0 to 50 percent. This is certainly a modest increase in ideological congruence representation, but it would help to close the gap significantly between the poorest and wealthiest residents in a community. So, on average, a community like Greenville, NC, is unlikely to become dramatically more responsive to its poorest residents with elected officials having similar wealth, but there is evidence that increasing wealth diversity among those who hold office could shift the preferences of the council closer to those at the bottom tier of wealth in the community.

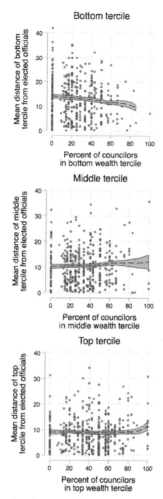

FIGURE 7.6 The relationship between descriptive and ideological congruence representation for each wealth tercile

Note: Sampling weights applied. Shaded areas are 95 percent confidence intervals.

POLICY RESPONSIVENESS

As we have noted in previous chapters, policy responsiveness is arguably the ultimate indicator of representation in democratic systems.[28] Policy outputs can have real consequences for the life chances of local

---

[28] Zoltan Hajnal and Jessica Trounstine. "Identifying and Understanding Perceived Inequities in Local Politics." *Political Research Quarterly* 67, no. 1 (2014): 56–70.

residents – especially those of lesser economic means – so it is essential that policy decisions reflect the demands of those affected by them. At the same time, in a fair democratic system no group should enjoy more policy representation than any other (after taking differences in group size into account).[29] The equitable weighting of resident preferences reflects the bedrock democratic principle that, at least when it comes to politics, all people are created equal.

But do municipalities actually provide equitable policy responsiveness to residents of different economic classes? In considering this question, it is important to keep in mind the overwhelming evidence from the federal and state levels that policymaking is *not* equitably responsive to residents of different economic classes.[30] Thus, in answering this question, we are also investigating whether patterns in local policy responsiveness are, in a broad sense, similar to or different from those at the federal and state levels.

To begin to assess whether there are class inequities in policy responsiveness at the local level, we construct bivariate plots of the relationship between the mean ideology of each economic group (low wealth, middle wealth, and high wealth) and policy liberalism in each community, along with a line fitted to the data describing the relationship between these two factors. Recall that our policy liberalism scale is focused especially on items that address inequality. These plots (which are similar to the bivariate plots of racial group ideology and policy liberalism presented in Chapter 5) appear in Figure 7.7.

The bivariate plots seem to provide good news. In each of the panels in Figure 7.7, there is a positive, moderately strong bivariate relationship between class group ideology and policy liberalism. In other words, as each wealth group's ideology becomes more liberal, the overall direction of local government policy also becomes more liberal (and as each group's ideology becomes more conservative, local government policy also becomes more conservative). What is especially notable is that there do not seem to be major differences across the three panels of Figure 7.7 in the respective slopes of the fitted lines. Indeed, if we estimate three separate naive bivariate regression models with policy liberalism as the

[29] Larry M. Bartels. *Unequal Democracy: The Political Economy of the New Gilded Age.* Princeton, NJ: Princeton University Press, 2008.

[30] Gilens, "Inequality and Democratic Responsiveness"; Gilens, *Affluence and Influence*; Gilens and Page, "Testing Theories of American Politics"; Page and Gilens, *Democracy in America?*; Flavin, "Income Inequality and Policy Representation in the American States"; Flavin, "Campaign Finance Laws, Policy Outcomes, and Political Equality in the American States."

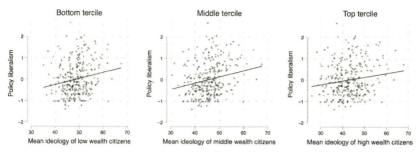

FIGURE 7.7 Responsiveness of municipality's policy to each class group's ideology

dependent variable in each model and the ideology of the bottom, middle, and top wealth tercile, respectively, as the sole predictor in each one of the three models, the coefficient estimate for each wealth group is similar in both magnitude (.03, .03, and .02, respectively) and statistical significance. The similarities among the three panels of Figure 7.7 imply that, at least at the bivariate level, there are no major differences in the policy responsiveness enjoyed by poor, middle-class, and wealthy populations. At a very general level, these findings are also consistent with recent research indicating that the ideological orientation of local policy is closely related to the ideology of community residents.[31]

Of course, the patterns presented in each panel in Figure 7.7 do not take into consideration the simultaneous influence of the ideology of each of the other wealth groups on policy liberalism, so the estimates of the relationship between each group's ideology and policy liberalism may conflate actual responsiveness with responsiveness emanating from coincidental representation. Accordingly, we could seek to sort out to which group policy outcomes are more responsive by including a measure of the mean ideology of each wealth group in the same regression model. This would be a reasonable way of determining how responsive policy outcomes are to each group's ideology, while accounting for the ideologies of the other two groups. Unfortunately, doing this is complicated by the fact that the ideologies of each of our wealth terciles are very highly correlated with one another (a circumstance called *multicollinearity*). To be clear, this does not mean that these groups necessarily have similar ideologies. Rather, it means that if the mean ideology of the wealthy is more

---

[31] Tausanovitch and Warshaw, "Representation in Municipal Government."

conservative in community A than it is in community B, then the mean ideology of the poor will also tend to be more conservative in community A than it is in community B. In other words, a high correlation does not imply that the wealthy and the poor have ideologies that are very close together, but rather that the distance between the ideologies of the rich and the poor tend to be fairly consistent across communities. Unfortunately, coefficient estimates for highly correlated variables in standard regression models may be unstable, and standard errors may be substantially inflated. For these reasons, both the coefficient estimates and the measures of statistical significance for highly correlated variables must be treated with a great deal of caution.

With this caution in mind, we construct a multivariate model of policy liberalism that simultaneously estimates the effects of the ideologies of the bottom, middle, and top wealth terciles. We use the same control variables as we did in Chapter 5 (population size, median income, and percent white). Shortly, we present coefficient plots showing policy responsiveness to each of these groups while accounting for the views of the other groups. The horizontal lines are 95 percent confidence intervals, showing the range of values that are plausible for capturing responsiveness to each group.

The results presented in Figure 7.8 seem to indicate that local policy is most responsive to the ideologies of middle-class residents. The model predicts that each one-unit increase in the liberalism of the ideology of the middle wealth group is associated with a .07 standard deviation increase in the liberalism of local government policy ($p < .01$). Put another way, a community where the middle wealth tercile has an ideology of 60 will adopt policies that are seven-tenths of a standard deviation more liberal than a community where the middle wealth tercile has an ideology of 50. This is fairly high responsiveness.

Interestingly, the model finds that the ideologies of both the poor and the rich are not significantly associated with the liberalism of local government policy. For both class groups, the coefficient estimates are actually negative, though small; but these estimates are also statistically indistinguishable from zero. As noted, however, because the ideologies of the bottom, middle, and top wealth terciles are so intercorrelated, great caution should be exercised in interpreting these results. In particular, we should not necessarily conclude that the bottom and top wealth groups have no influence over the ideological direction of local policy. At the same time, the finding that local policy is responsive to middle-class residents is notable, as research on policy responsiveness at

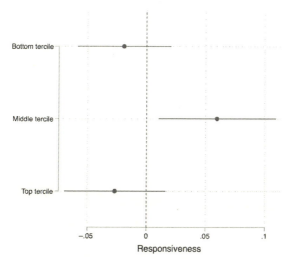

FIGURE 7.8 Responsiveness of municipality's policy to ideologies of
class groups
Note: Plot shows the responsiveness to each group after controlling for a community's
population size, median income, and proportion of the population that is white. N = 237.

higher levels of government suggests that the middle class has little or no
independent influence over policy, after accounting for the views of
the wealthy.[32]

We can speculate as to why there appears to be responsiveness to
middle wealth preferences (even if city councilors are, on average, closer
in ideology to high wealth residents). This group tends to comprise
homeowners who vote in larger absolute numbers than the very wealthy,
and in larger proportion than low wealth residents. And unlike policymaking at the federal or state level, local government decisions about
zoning, schools, or property taxes have an immediate and transparent
effect on this significant voting bloc. Under these circumstances it seems
rational that local officials would be attuned to the preferences of middle
wealth residents. The broader takeaway is that the influence (or lack
thereof) of the middle class on policymaking may not be a constant, but
instead may vary depending on level of government as well as other
moderating factors.

[32] Gilens, "Inequality and Democratic Responsiveness"; Gilens and Page, "Testing Theories
of American Politics."

CONCLUSION

Whether affluence is associated with influence[33] in politics is a question that has long preoccupied philosophers and social scientists. In recent years, researchers have given this question extensive attention, with the preponderance of evidence suggesting that wealthy people do indeed enjoy greater representation from government. So far, however, this work has focused almost entirely on the federal and state levels, to the exclusion of local government. This is primarily due to the brute fact that the evidence needed to study economic inequality in representation in local politics has been unavailable up to now, but it also reflects a prevailing assumption that, especially outside of large urban areas, class-based ideological disagreement in local politics is muted. Indeed, the conventional wisdom about local politics outside of metropolitan areas is that municipal politics revolve much more around personalities and managerial competence than class-based ideological differences.

Yet, as suggested by the story of Mount Pleasant that opened this chapter, we need to reconsider the assumption that class-based conflicts are largely absent from municipal politics. Indeed, given the dramatic increase in economic inequality in the United States over the last four decades – and the federal government's retreat from efforts to redress inequities – assessments of whether economic inequalities in representation in local government exist are needed now more than ever.

In this chapter we have used the unique evidence accumulated for this book to provide an unprecedented assessment of economic inequality in political representation in a diverse array of large cities, midsize communities, and small towns. Examining patterns in descriptive representation, ideological congruence representation, and policy responsiveness, our investigation has yielded considerable evidence of inequalities in representation on the basis of class. Perhaps most important, we uncover strong evidence that the poor are woefully underrepresented in local communities. The lowest wealth residents are severely underrepresented on municipal councils in relation to their share of community populations. They are also quite ideologically distant from their municipal councils, and they appear to have little if any influence on the ideological

---

[33] Martin Gilens. *Affluence and Influence: Economic Inequality and Political Power in America*. Princeton, NJ: Princeton University Press, 2012.

direction of local government policy. Our findings that the least affluent residents have little influence in local politics resonate with the predominant findings of research on class inequalities in representation at other levels of government. At least when it comes to the (lack of) representation of the poor, local governments do not seem very distinctive from the federal government or the states.

However, when it comes to representation in local government, middle wealth residents fare pretty well. Although middle wealth residents do not receive as much ideological congruence representation as do high wealth residents, they enjoy a generous share of economic descriptive representation, and they also appear to receive the greatest amount of policy responsiveness from local governments. Not only do middle wealth residents on average enjoy better representation than do low wealth residents, they experience much greater descriptive representation, ideological congruence representation, and policy responsiveness than do either African Americans or Latinos, and they enjoy about the same level of representation as whites in general.

Yet, though middle wealth residents enjoy significant representational advantages in municipal politics, the fact remains that high wealth residents fare even better. Although high wealth residents represent a small share of municipal populations, they are consistently overrepresented on municipal councils in relation to their proportion in local communities. Moreover, on average high wealth residents are much closer ideologically to municipal councils than are either middle wealth or low wealth residents. To be sure, high wealth residents do not appear to obtain much policy representation from local governments, but this inference should be treated with caution because the ideologies of high wealth residents are so closely correlated with the ideologies of middle wealth residents. Finally, across all measures of representation, high wealth residents do better than African Americans, Latinos, and whites on average.

All things considered, our findings point to considerable economic inequality in representation, although the class-based inequities we discovered are not quite as stark as those based on race revealed in Chapter 5 (largely due to the substantial representation enjoyed by middle wealth residents). What stands out most clearly is the severe underrepresentation of the least affluent residents of local communities. In line with research on economic inequality in representation at other levels of government, this finding highlights the unresponsiveness of officials to the demands of the least fortunate Americans. Coupled with the body of previous research, our findings present an extremely troubling picture, in which the least affluent find themselves largely excluded from real political influence at all levels of government. For the least affluent residents, the practice of municipal democracy seems to be largely failing to deliver on its promise.

8

Predictors of Economic Inequality in Representation

In the previous chapter, we examined patterns in descriptive representation, ideological congruence representation, and policy responsiveness across economic groups in communities throughout the United States, revealing the substantial underrepresentation of citizens with low wealth at the municipal level. Importantly, however, Chapter 7 focused largely, though not exclusively, on general patterns of (inequality in) representation. This emphasis, while vital, has the effect of minimizing the nontrivial number of instances in which less affluent residents receive considerable representation at the local level.

Indeed, low wealth residents are quite well represented in some communities in our sample. We find numerous communities, such as Florence, South Carolina, or Terrell, Texas, where low wealth residents actually appear *better* represented ideologically than their wealthier neighbors. At the same time, as we noted in Chapter 7, we found many localities where individuals with low wealth fare very poorly relative to the richest residents. These communities, like many across the nation, struggle to meet the needs of their least affluent residents and have tried a variety of strategies to accomplish this difficult task, many of which are influenced heavily by federal policies.

Take, for example, Aiken, South Carolina, a community of about 30,000 residents. Aiken sits in the western part of the state near the Savannah River at the border with Georgia. Tourists are attracted by its thoroughbred racing, fox hunts, polo games, and natural beauty.[1] At the

---

[1] "City of Aiken Tourism Division," City of Aiken, www.visitaikensc.com.

same time, however, many residents struggle to earn a living. Almost one in five residents lives below the poverty level. Nonprofits providing social support are experiencing major increases in the demand for services, while funding has been stable or even been subjected to cuts.[2] To spur investment, the city of Aiken has pursued a strategy of development through tax abatements to attract businesses, taking advantage most recently of tax reforms passed by Congress in 2017, which encourage the designation of opportunity zones.[3]

Simultaneously, though, the local housing authority has promoted what its CEO calls "de-concentration of poverty." Recently it demolished one of the largest public housing developments in the county, Hahn Village, built in 1978 and home to 500 individuals.[4] Residents who were interviewed by the local press appeared to support the demolition. One young woman, who recounted a recent double homicide in the complex, said, "Maybe there will be less fighting and guns if we move to a better place." However, few residents at the time appeared to know of the plan until it was announced, and most had no information about where they might live following the demolition of the public housing development. This episode can be viewed as emblematic of a more systematic problem of the underrepresentation of the interests of Aiken's least affluent residents: Aiken has one of the largest gaps between the amount of ideological congruence representation received by low wealth residents and high wealth residents (a difference of nearly fifteen points on the 100-point scale).

Indeed, it is a difficult truth that civic boosterism does not always raise all boats. Consider Perry, Georgia, a town of about 16,000 located 90 miles south of Atlanta. The mayor touts the municipality's proximity to "Robins Air Force base, excellent schools, unique downtown, high quality of life, and location in transforming from a small town to a

---

[2] These groups include the Aiken-Barnwell Community Action Commission, Inc., serving low-income residents, Aiken Area Council on Aging, and the Brothers and Sisters of Aiken County. See Amy Banton and Maayan Schechter, "Poverty Numbers Difficult to Track in Aiken," *The Aiken Standard*, January 26, 2014, www.aikenstandard.com/news/poverty-numbers-difficult-to-track-in-aiken/article_6402244f-d9e7-5303-8dfc-01e7baa59ff2.html.

[3] Colin Demarest, "City of Aiken Seeking Opportunity Zone Expert to Spur Investments, Development," *The Aiken Standard*, March 3, 2019, www.aikenstandard.com/news/city-of-aiken-seeking-opportunity-zone-expert-to-spurinvestments/article_ac637518-3c3b-11e9-bd39-d3c3346befo7.html.

[4] The CEO of the Housing Authority claimed it was too expensive to repair the complex, particularly because of budget cuts of $9 billion to the US Department of Housing and Urban Development, which previously subsidized maintenance work.

vibrant and growing community."[5] And, at least in some ways, Perry does seem to be a vibrant place. The community is home to numerous music and agricultural festivals. Town officials have focused on trying to maintain high-quality public services; they have, for example, created a new phone app enabling residents to report potholes and missed garbage pickup, and facilitating notifications from local agencies about events and billing.[6] And the town has also secured some small housing grants from the Community HOME Investment Program (CHIP) and Community Development Block Grant (CDBG) program to help revitalize neighborhoods by funding home repairs.[7]

Despite these positive signs, the town seems largely unresponsive to the needs of its least advantaged residents. Perry's responses to the 2015 Sustainability Survey administered by the ICMA reveal that the government does relatively little to help its low-income citizens. The community reports that it does not provide incentives for affordable housing and indicates that social equity is not a priority for the local government. In responding to the 2014 Economic Development Survey administered by ICMA, the respondent for Perry's municipal government noted that income inequality was only of "minimal motivation" when it came to developing the city's economic development policy. While Perry's local government did report providing job training for low-skilled workers, the overall picture gleaned from these reports is one of minimal attention to addressing economic inequality among residents. In a telling illustration of the town's apparent indifference to the needs of its least fortunate residents, town officials stood by as large rental complexes in a working-class neighborhood (which happens to be owned by Fox News celebrity Sean Hannity) took unusually aggressive measures to collect rents, seeking court-ordered evictions at twice the statewide rate.[8]

Given these observations, it is worth noting that Perry voters have not been offered many choices at the ballot box. The mayor and three city

[5] "Mayor's Office," City of Perry, Georgia, www.perry-ga.gov/government/mayors-office.

[6] "Your Perry App Is Live!," City of Perry, Georgia, www.perry-ga.gov/your-perry-app-is-live.

[7] "City of Perry Receives $300K for Neighborhood Revitalization," Fox24 (WGXA), March 13, 2019, https://wgxa.tv/news/local/city-of-perry-receives-300k-for-neighborhood-revitalization.

[8] Aaron C. Davis and Shawn Boburg, "At Sean Hannity Properties in Working-Class Areas, an Aggressive Approach to Rent Collection," *The Washington Post*, May 11, 2018, www.washingtonpost.com/investigations/at-hannitys-properties-in-low-income-areas-an-aggressive-approach-to-rent-collection/2018/05/10/964be4a2-4eea-11e8-84a0-458a1aa9acoa_story.html?utm_term=.26cc78193ca7.

council members ran unopposed twice in the past three election cycles (two-year terms).[9] The mayor took this as a sign that "for the majority of people in Perry, we are doing the right things and moving in the right direction." He also mentioned, apparently without irony, that canceling the election saved the city $30,000. Similarly, the city manager attributed the lack of opposition in the sixteen years he had been serving the city to a policy of "transparency and openness" with the public, while an eighteen-year veteran on the council, who has never faced opposition, averred, "I think that what the public realizes is that we as a group spend a lot of time doing what needs to be done for the whole city ... We have a very good working relationship with each other and that makes a big difference."[10] We do not doubt the efforts and sincerity of these elected officials, but our data indicate that low-income residents are not necessarily receiving good representation in these communities. Like Aiken, Perry has one of the largest gaps between the ideological congruence representation received by high wealth residents and that received by low wealth residents (a difference of thirteen points on the 100-point scale).

The cases of Florence, South Carolina; Terrell, Texas; Aiken, South Carolina; and Perry, Georgia, provide greatly contrasting examples of how well or poorly less affluent residents are represented by their local governments. What accounts for these differences? In recent years, scholars studying inequalities in national and state politics have sought to explain variation in the severity of economic biases across different contexts.[11] In this chapter, we extend this inquiry to the municipal level, using our three theoretical lenses to account for differences in the degree of economic inequality in representation across the communities in our sample.

Our findings in this chapter indicate both the possibilities and – more starkly – the limits of equal representation of less affluent residents in local communities. First, we find that the coincidental representation lens provides powerful insights on the representation received by the less

---

[9] Wayne Crenshaw, "Perry Leaders Can Relax on Election Day, Again," *The Telegraph*, August 31, 2017, www.macon.com/news/local/community/houston-peach/article170403727.html

[10] Ibid., Crenshaw August 31, 2017.

[11] Griffin, Hajnal, Newman, and Searle, "Political Inequality in America"; Ellis, "Social Context and Economic Biases in Representation"; Ellis, *Putting Inequality in Context*; Flavin, "Campaign Finance Laws, Policy Outcomes, and Political Equality in the American States"; Flavin, "Lobbying Regulations and Political Inequality in the American States"; Flavin, "Labor Union Strength and the Equality of Political Representation."

well-to-do. The most important determinants of the amount of ideological congruence representation received by low wealth residents are the degree of ideological overlap between low wealth residents and middle wealth residents, and the amount of ideological overlap between low wealth residents and high wealth residents. When the ideologies of low wealth residents overlap to a greater degree with those of more affluent residents, they receive more representation, but when they do not, low wealth residents receive less representation. As was the case for African Americans and Latinos, low wealth residents depend heavily on coincidental representation to obtain representation on municipal councils. In stark contrast, neither middle wealth residents nor high wealth residents are especially dependent on coincidental representation for their representation on municipal councils.

Meanwhile, the institutional lens does not provide much help in explaining variation in the severity of class bias in representation across communities. Indeed, most electoral institutions have little to no relationship with the ideological congruence representation received by low wealth residents. This finding suggests that most political "quick fixes" will have limited impact on economic inequality in representation. However, one ray of light in this picture is that the timing of elections does have an appreciable effect on the ideological congruence representation enjoyed by low wealth residents. Specifically, elections held in November (either on-cycle with federal contests or in off years) produce a noticeable increase in ideological congruence representation for the least affluent. But because these elections also increase ideological congruence representation for middle and high wealth residents, this reform does not decrease between-class inequality in ideological congruence representation in local government. Nonetheless, it seems important to point out that scheduling elections in November improves representation for all citizens, as previous research has indicated.[12]

Finally, the economic and racial inequality lens provides important, and nuanced, insights on the prospects for representation of the less affluent. On the one hand, communities with more economic inequality are characterized by somewhat greater ideological distance between low

---

[12] Sarah F. Anzia. *Timing and Turnout: How Off-Cycle Elections Favor Organized Groups.* Chicago: Chicago University Press, 2013; Zoltan L. Hajnal. *America's Uneven Democracy: Race, Turnout, and Representation in City Politics.* Cambridge: Cambridge University Press, 2009; Vladimir Kogan, Stephane Lavertu, and Zachary Peskowitz. "Election Timing, Electorate Composition, and Policy Outcomes: Evidence from School Districts." *American Journal of Political Science* 62 (2018): 637–651.

wealth residents and high wealth residents. Because greater distance between the least affluent and the well-to-do is associated with less representation on municipal councils for low wealth residents, this pattern suggests that increased economic inequality is associated with even worse representational outcomes for the least advantaged residents. On the other hand, increased economic inequality within a community is also associated with *increased* ideological overlap between low wealth residents and those of middle wealth, a strong predictor of increased representation on municipal councils for low wealth residents.

Together, these observations point to the varied role of context in moderating the representation available to residents of different economic classes at the municipal level. For low wealth residents, contextual factors like ideological overlap with other wealth groups and the economic inequality of the community matter a lot. But for more advantaged residents, such factors are less consequential. Put another way, when it comes to representation on municipal councils, low wealth residents are at the mercy of local context to a degree that more affluent residents are not.

VARIATION IN CLASS BIASES IN REPRESENTATION ACROSS COMMUNITIES

We begin our analysis by simply examining the range of experiences of ideological congruence representation of different economic groups across all the communities in our sample. Figure 8.1, which plots the distribution of distances between the mean ideology of municipal councils and the mean ideologies of people who are in the low, middle, and top terciles of wealth in their communities, provides an illustration of this range of experiences. (When examining the figure, recall that larger distances between the mean ideology of a group and the mean ideology of the council mean that there is less ideological congruence representation.)

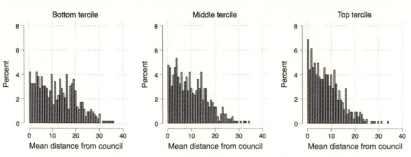

FIGURE 8.1 Distribution of mean ideological distance from municipal council

As the figure suggests, there is great variation in the degree of ideological congruence between each of the wealth groups and their municipal councils across communities. In some communities, the distances are very large, indicating that there is relatively little ideological congruence between these groups and their councils. And, generally speaking, these distributions again point to a major theme of Chapter 7, that low wealth residents are more likely to receive worse ideological congruence representation than are higher wealth residents. Indeed, in half of the communities in our sample, low wealth residents are eleven points or more from the mean elected official and in 10 percent of the communities the low wealth population is more than twenty-two points away from the council average. By comparison, in more than half of the communities we have sampled, the wealthiest people in the community are just seven points or fewer away from their local representatives. And in only about 5 percent of towns and cities do the wealthiest individuals find themselves more than twenty points from their elected officials.

At the same time, though, the various distributions also illustrate the opposite, and very important, point: In a nontrivial share of communities, low wealth residents receive considerable ideological congruence representation, while in some communities, middle wealth and even high wealth residents are relatively far from the average councilor. There is considerable variation across communities in the representation allocated to various wealth groups and – more pointedly – in some communities, low wealth residents enjoy much more representation than they do in others. The striking variation across communities in the ideological congruence representation afforded various wealth groups deserves explanation, because doing so may shed light on why inequities occur and point the way to reforms to improve local democracy.

WHAT PREDICTS IDEOLOGICAL CONGRUENCE REPRESENTATION ON MUNICIPAL COUNCILS?

Our objectives in examining the predictors of ideological congruence representation are both to assess the overall impact of each variable and to weigh the relative influence of each. As with our earlier analysis of racial disparities in ideological congruence representation, we use a random forest model to examine which factors are most important for predicting how close each wealth group finds itself to local elected officials. The dependent variable in each random forest model is our measure of ideological congruence representation – the distance between the mean

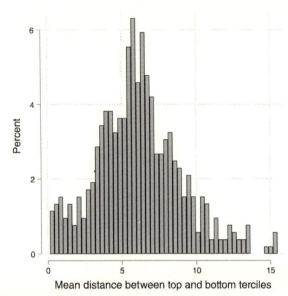

FIGURE 8.2 Distribution of ideological overlap between bottom and top wealth terciles

ideology of each wealth group and the mean ideology of the council in the same community.

Once again, we include a variety of contextual variables in the model, with a special focus on variables relating to each of our three theoretical lenses. First, to represent the coincidental representation lens, we account for how close each wealth group's views are to the views of the other two wealth groups in the same community. Figure 8.2, which shows the distribution of communities in our sample based on the distance between the mean ideologies of the bottom and top wealth terciles, provides insights on the prospects for the coincidental representation of low wealth residents. One thing to note is that there is generally more ideological overlap (and less ideological distance) between the poor and the rich than we found between whites and blacks in Chapter 5. On average, as we showed in Chapter 7, the bottom and top wealth terciles are just 5.9 points apart in our communities. By comparison, recall that the average distance between white and black citizens in our communities was greater than ten points. The fact that low and high wealth residents are relatively close ideologically in a large share of the communities in our sample suggests that the prospects for coincidental representation of low wealth residents are quite good in many places. At the same time, though, it is important to keep in mind that coincidental representation is inevitably a tentative and uncertain form of representation, because by definition it makes the beneficiary of coincidental representation dependent on the more influential group.[13] In the dynamic of coincidental representation, the disadvantaged group benefits solely by virtue of its fortuitous ideological proximity to the advantaged group – it does not exercise any real independent influence over elected officials.

In addition to ideological overlap, we also consider two additional contextual variables in our models: (1) the ideological diversity within each wealth group and (2) the gap in wealth between the top and bottom terciles. The first variable is one that we also included in our analysis of racial inequalities in representation. Again, the expectation is that when a wealth group's views are more diverse, it may be more difficult for elected officials to represent that group, simply because representing some members of an ideologically diverse group necessarily puts elected officials at odds with other members of that group. Thus, greater diversity in group ideology should be associated with less ideological congruence representation, while greater homogeneity in group ideology should be associated with more ideological congruence representation.[14]

More importantly, the second variable helps capture how much wealth inequality there is in a community, and thus relates to our racial and economic inequality lens. As we have suggested, overall wealth inequality likely influences the degree of economic-based inequality in representation within communities. After all, as the disparity in socioeconomic resources between the rich and the poor increases, the rich will likely exert relatively more influence over who is elected to local office and on the policies that those individuals pursue. In short, greater wealth inequality is likely to be associated with greater inequality in representation favoring the wealthy. In contrast, less affluent residents should receive more representation from local governments in communities with lower levels of wealth inequality.[15]

Finally, to represent the institutional lens, the models test for any effect of the main electoral institutions that we have focused on to this

---

[13] Martin Gilens. "The Insufficiency of 'Democracy by Coincidence': A Response to Peter K. Enns." *Perspectives on Politics* 13, no. 4 (2015): 1065–1071.

[14] Yosef Bhatti and Robert S. Erikson. "How Poorly Are the Poor Represented in the US Senate?" In *Who Gets Represented?*, eds. Peter K. Enns and Christopher Wlezien. New York: Russell Sage Foundation 2011. 223–246.

[15] Christopher Ellis. "Social Context and Economic Biases in Representation." *The Journal of Politics* 75, no. 3 (2013): 773–786.

point – ballot type (partisan versus nonpartisan), jurisdiction type (at-large, district, or mixed) and election timing (on-cycle in November, off-cycle in November, and off-cycle at some other time). Again, we anticipate that electoral institutions that increase the information available to voters and reduce the costs of political participation – that is, elections that are partisan in organization, based in geographically delimited districts, and scheduled to coincide with federal contests or in off-cycle November elections – may be associated with increased ideological congruence representation of less affluent residents. Previous research has cast doubt that the difference between Political and Professional models of electoral and governing institutions makes much difference, at least when it comes to the representation of the *average* resident.[16] We assess whether institutions matter for the degree of *class inequality* in representation using granular data on a broader set of municipalities. After all, it is plausible that institutions matter depending on different contexts.[17] Our data allow us to evaluate the potential impact of institutions in a variety of contexts, across towns with varying gaps in ideology, diversity, and wealth.

Finally, we note a difference between the models we estimate in this chapter and the parallel analysis of the determinants of *racial* inequalities in representation we undertook in Chapter 6. Recall from Chapter 7 that we assigned residents into one of three wealth groups based on their position in the *local* wealth distribution in order to provide the most meaningful economic groupings. Since our wealth groups are defined to be a constant size – each group constitutes one-third of the community's population – we do not include measures of the size of each group in the models in this chapter.

THE MOST IMPORTANT PREDICTORS
OF IDEOLOGICAL CONGRUENCE

Figure 8.3 shows a variable importance plot, similar to what we presented in Chapter 6. The size of each bar indicates how important that variable is

---

[16] Chris Tausanovitch and Christopher Warshaw. "Representation in Municipal Government." *American Political Science Review* 108, no. 3 (2014): 605–641.

[17] Vladimir Kogan, Stephane Lavertu, and Zachary Peskowitz. "Election Timing, Electorate Composition, and Policy Outcomes: Evidence from School Districts." *American Journal of Political Science* 62 (2018): 637–651. Melissa J. Marschall, Anirudh V. S. Ruhil, and Paru R. Shah. "The New Racial Calculus: Electoral Institutions and Black Representation in Local Legislatures." *American Journal of Political Science* 54, no. 1 (2010): 107–124.

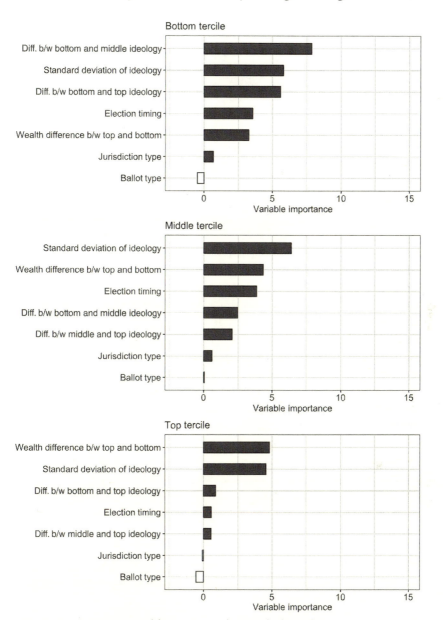

FIGURE 8.3 Importance of factors in predicting ideological congruence representation for wealth terciles

Note: Variable importance is measured as the change in the mean squared error when values of each variable are replaced with randomly assigned values.

for predicting the closeness of each wealth group to the average elected official in their local government. Note that, while we first discuss variable *importance*, we will also describe later in this chapter the predicted *effect* of these variables on the amount of ideological congruence representation received by wealth groups. The top plot in the figure shows the importance of the variables for predicting representation for people in the lowest tercile of wealth. Note that the two "difference" variables (distance of the group's ideology from the ideology of the middle wealth tercile and distance from the ideology of the top tercile) are the most important factors in predicting representation for low wealth individuals. These findings point to the power of the coincidental representation lens in accounting for variation in the ideological congruence representation received by low wealth residents. Indeed, as the figure indicates, disadvantaged citizens depend most heavily on coincidental representation as a means to achieving ideological congruence representation on municipal councils.

This pattern suggests that low-income residents are doubly disadvantaged. Not only are local governments frequently unresponsive to the ideologies of low wealth residents, as we showed in the previous chapter, but any responsiveness they show is in significant part due to the fortuitous similarity between the ideologies of low wealth residents and more affluent residents. In other words, low wealth residents seem to have little if any *independent* influence on the ideologies of municipal councils.

Another contextual factor that appears to be a strong predictor of representation for low wealth residents is the extent of ideological diversity among members of that group. For low wealth residents, it matters a lot for ideological congruence representation whether members of this wealth group have similar ideologies. When low wealth residents are relatively unified ideologically, they receive more ideological congruence representation on municipal councils. But when low wealth residents within a community have more diverse ideologies, they receive less ideological congruence representation.

When we turn to examination of the factors associated with the ideological congruence representation enjoyed by more affluent residents, however, different patterns emerge. First, the coincidental representation lens provides little insight into how much ideological congruence representation these groups receive. Indeed, for the high wealth group, ideological overlap with other groups hardly has any relationship at all to the ideological congruence representation this group enjoys. What this means is that, compared with the low wealth group, more affluent residents are much less dependent on the dynamic of coincidental representation as a means for obtaining ideological congruence representation on municipal councils.

At the same time, though, the size of the wealth gap between the bottom and top terciles appears to play an important role in predicting the ideological congruence representation received by middle and high wealth groups. Put another way, local economic inequality moderates how well the ideologies of these groups match up with those of municipal elected officials.

Finally, the institutional lens provides limited insight into the amount of ideological congruence representation enjoyed by residents of different economic classes. There is just one electoral institution that appears to be an important predictor of ideological congruence representation: election timing. This institutional factor is fairly important in predicting the ideological congruence representation received by low and middle wealth residents (though not high wealth residents). As we will see, when communities hold local elections on-cycle in November or off-cycle in November, low and middle wealth residents receive more ideological congruence representation on municipal councils than they do when elections are held off-cycle at another time of year. To the degree that November elections (on- or off-cycle with federal contests) raise turnout among middle and lower wealth residents (relative to high wealth residents), this relatively simple timing factor should plausibly give these groups a commensurately stronger voice in the selection of local representatives. We elaborate on this situation shortly.

To gain a better sense of how these variables matter, we examine how each factor affects the predicted distance between a group and local elected officials, while holding all other variables constant. Figure 8.4 produces this analysis for the influence of the three most important contextual factors for the low wealth tercile. The y-axis in these plots shows the predicted ideological distance between the average low wealth individual and the average councilor; thus, lower values mean better representation for the group. The left-hand plot in the figure shows the influence of ideological distance from the top wealth tercile. Low wealth citizens have a predicted distance of about 8.5 points from the elected officials in their community until their ideologies differ by more than seven points from the ideology of the top wealth tercile. Once this happens, their representation begins to suffer. Indeed, when the distance between the ideology of the average bottom and top wealth tercile citizen grows to eight points or more, low wealth citizens find themselves more than twelve points away from their elected officials.

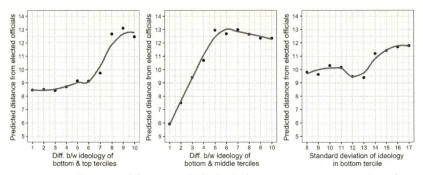

FIGURE 8.4 Contextual factors and ideological congruence representation of bottom wealth tercile
Note: Figure presents partial dependence plots, which account for the role of other variables in our random forest model.

Even more important is the distance between low wealth individuals and the middle wealth group. This relationship is depicted in the center plot. As the distance between low wealth individuals and middle wealth individuals moves from one point to six points, the predicted distance of the low wealth group from elected officials more than doubles (from six points to thirteen points). In short, the ideological congruence representation received by low wealth residents suffers greatly when low wealth residents have ideologies that are distinctive from those of middle wealth residents. Thus, from the perspective of ideological congruence representation, low wealth residents derive the greatest benefits from being close ideologically to middle wealth residents (and also suffer most when they are most distant from middle wealth residents).

Finally, ideological diversity among low wealth residents is somewhat less important than their degree of ideological overlap with either high wealth or middle wealth residents. However, as views among low wealth citizens become particularly diverse, they receive somewhat less representation from their local elected officials. This is shown in the right-hand plot.

Figure 8.5 uses plots that are similar to those in Figure 8.4 to show the ideological congruence representation of those in the middle wealth tercile. As noted in Chapter 7, the middle wealth tercile tends to be closer, on average, to elected officials than the bottom tercile, and this pattern is reflected in these charts. However, the distance between the ideological views of middle tercile residents and those of the other wealth terciles does matter for that group, but not as much as it does for members of the low wealth group. For example, the left-hand plot in the figure shows that as

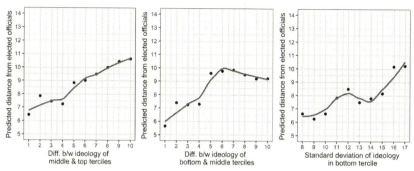

FIGURE 8.5 Contextual factors and ideological congruence representation of middle wealth tercile

Note: Figure presents partial dependence plots, which account for the role of other variables in our random forest model.

citizens in the middle of the wealth distribution move from one point to ten points away from those in the top wealth tercile, their distance from local elected officials increases by about four points. The middle plot shows that distance from the bottom wealth tercile also matters for predicted representation, though only up to about five points of distance between the groups. Finally, the pattern for ideological diversity is non-linear, but it does suggest that when there is a high level of ideological diversity among middle wealth citizens, they do receive somewhat less representation from the council.

An overarching goal of this book is to compare the relative severity of racial inequality in representation and class inequality in representation, respectively, in municipal politics. And one very important observation from the plots in this chapter is that – at least in comparison with the parallel plots for African Americans and Latinos shown in Chapter 6 – the impact of the contextual factors on the ideological congruence representation received by both low wealth and middle wealth residents is relatively modest. For example, while a ten-point increase in ideological difference between low wealth and high wealth residents is associated with an increase of about five points in ideological distance of low wealth residents from the municipal council, an identical increase in ideological difference between African Americans and whites is associated with an increase of *ten points* in ideological distance of African Americans from the council. Likewise, an increase of ten points in ideological difference between Latino and white residents is associated with an increase of *ten points* in ideological distance between Latinos and their council. Put simply, the penalty in ideological congruence representation inflicted on

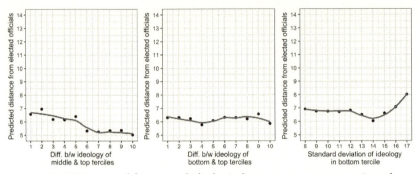

FIGURE 8.6 Contextual factors and ideological congruence representation of top wealth tercile

Note: Figure presents partial dependence plots, which account for the role of other variables in our random forest model.

residents of color for deviating from the ideological views of whites is twice as large as that imposed on less affluent residents for departing from the ideologies of affluent residents. This observation tends to reinforce the view, suggested throughout this book, that racial biases in representation in local government are much more severe than class biases.

Finally, Figure 8.6 examines the role of contextual factors in the ideological congruence representation of people at the top of the wealth distribution. Here we witness the development of a unique, and uniquely inequitable, story. Specifically, the predicted distance between high wealth citizens and elected officials tends to be small relative to the other groups – and contextual factors appear to make little difference. In fact, the left-hand plot in the figure shows that, as the distance between high and middle wealth groups increases, the wealthiest individuals may actually receive somewhat better representation (though the magnitude of this effect is small). The relationship is flat for distance between the top and bottom wealth terciles (the middle plot). The bottom line appears to be that high wealth constituents are well represented regardless of contextual factors. Readers should note that this pattern is very similar to that which we revealed for whites in Chapter 6. For both whites and high wealth residents, the amount of ideological congruence representation received appears to be relatively impervious to local context. This is a remarkable advantage, which both reflects and reinforces the political power of the most privileged residents.

Bringing all these disparate observations together, we conclude that the influence of contextual factors on ideological congruence representation appears to vary inversely with the affluence of residents. These factors

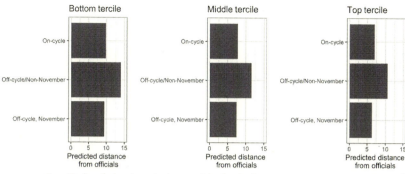

FIGURE 8.7 Role of election timing on ideological congruence representation of wealth groups
Note: Figure presents predicted effects, holding the other variables in our random forest model at their median values.

matter quite a bit for determining the amount of representation received by low wealth individuals, and they matter to some degree for those in the middle of the wealth distribution. But they matter very little for the richest individuals in a community. As we have suggested, this is a subtle – but important – mechanism by which inequality in representation is transmitted. Not only are the less affluent worse off on average in terms of representation on municipal councils, but they are also much more at the mercy of contextual factors that are largely beyond their control.

As the variable importance plot in Figure 8.3 showed, election timing may also play a role in determining how much representation the different groups receive. To see how this matters, Figure 8.7 plots the predicted distance of each wealth group from elected officials based on when elections are held, while holding all other factors constant. Notably, election timing seems to matter for ideological congruence representation, but it matters to a similar degree for all three wealth groups. Elected officials are predicted to be about five points closer to individuals in the lowest wealth tercile when elections are held in November of an on- or off-cycle year. Similar effects are evident for predicted distance from the middle and top tercile groups as well.

What this means is that scheduling elections in November (either on-cycle or in off years) can help the poorest citizens receive better representation, but this will also simultaneously improve representation for wealthier constituents. Moving to November elections will noticeably improve the *quality* of representation enjoyed by less affluent residents, but it will do little to increase *equality* of representation between less affluent residents and their more privileged peers.

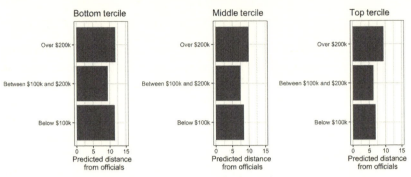

FIGURE 8.8 Role of wealth dispersion on ideological congruence representation of wealth groups
Note: Figure presents predicted effects, holding the other variables in our random forest model at their median values.

Finally, our random forest models indicate that the disparity in wealth between the bottom and top wealth terciles is also a modest predictor of ideological congruence representation for each group. In the vast majority of communities (63 percent), the discrepancy between the bottom and top wealth terciles is between $100,000 and $200,000. In 14 percent of the communities, the difference between the bottom and top wealth groups is less than $100,000, and in 23 percent it is greater than $200,000. In Figure 8.8, we plot the predicted ideological congruence representation for each wealth group based on whether the wealth gap between the bottom and top wealth terciles is relatively small (less than $100,000), more typical (between $100,000 and $200,000), or quite large (over $200,000).

Notably, each wealth group finds itself with the best ideological congruence representation when the wealth disparity between the poor and the rich is in the $100,000–$200,000 range. This is shown in each panel of Figure 8.8, where the predicted distance between the wealth group and its elected officials is *smallest* – thus indicating the best representation – when the wealth disparity between the least and most affluent is between $100,000 and $200,000. Interestingly, it is in communities with smaller absolute wealth gaps that we see more disparities between the representation of the poor and rich. The top wealth group finds itself a predicted 6.9 points from the municipal council in communities where the wealth gap between rich and poor is less than $100,000; in these same communities, the predicted distance between the poor and their local elected officials is 11.5 points.

SOCIOECONOMIC DISPARITIES AND IDEOLOGICAL OVERLAP

We have shown that the poorer residents in local communities are more likely to receive representation when their ideologies are closer to those in the middle and top wealth terciles. Recall that when we examined racial inequalities in representation in Chapter 6, we found that such overlap was least common in communities where socioeconomic disparities were the greatest. The implication was that African American residents were least likely to enjoy coincidental representation in precisely the communities in which they would benefit from this boost in representation the most.

Here, we examine whether a similarly troubling pattern holds for the poorest citizens in local communities. We have reason for concern that this is the case, as some existing research indicates that class inequalities in representation are exacerbated in the presence of greater economic inequality within communities.[18]

Figure 8.9 plots the Gini index from each community against the degree of ideological distance between people in the bottom and top wealth terciles. The Gini index is a commonly used measure to make comparisons in the level of economic inequality between communities (or between other political units such as states or nations). A value of zero on the index would indicate that everyone in the community earns the same income; however, as the Gini value increases, it indicates that more of the income in a community is earned by a smaller share of the population. Arguably, the communities where the poor are likely to be most in need of representation are those places where economic inequality is greatest.

Figure 8.9 plots the ideological distance between people in the low wealth tercile with those in the middle tercile and then the top wealth tercile, based on the Gini coefficient in each community. The most important point to emerge from these plots is that there is tremendous variance in the distance between the views of low wealth individuals and those in the other terciles. This can be seen in the broad spread of values along the y-axis. Nevertheless, despite substantial variance, some modest trends are still observable and, interestingly, those trends move in disparate directions. In particular, increasing economic inequality is associated with the slightly increasing distance of low wealth individuals from those in the top

---

[18] E.g., Ellis, "Social Context and Economic Biases in Representation."

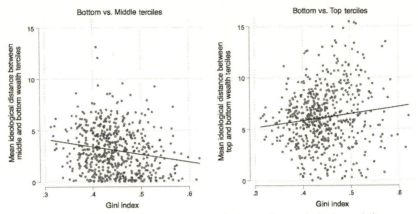

FIGURE 8.9 Relationship between economic inequality and ideological distance between wealth terciles

wealth tercile, while the distance between low and middle wealth individuals actually declines as economic inequality increases.

One interesting implication of these relationships is that, as inequality increases, people at the bottom and middle of the wealth distribution may be more likely to share views that are distinctive from those of the wealthiest citizens. Such a pattern may help to amplify the voices of the poorest citizens in such communities. At the same time, though, it is important to remember that there is substantial variance in how close or distant poor citizens find themselves from people in the other wealth terciles, and that there are many communities in which a high level of inequality is combined with a large gap between the ideologies of low wealth residents and the ideologies of affluent residents. It is in these communities that representation of the poor is likely to suffer.

Comparing these results with the parallel results presented in Chapter 6, we can conclude that community-level inequality has more complex and cross-cutting effects for *economic* inequality in representation than it does for *racial* inequality in representation. Whereas an increase in racial inequality in socioeconomic outcomes consistently reinforces racial inequality in representation, increasing community-level economic inequality appears to have more mixed implications for economic inequality in representation. Yet again, the general impression is that racial inequality in representation – particularly between African Americans and whites – is more deep-rooted and intractable than is economic inequality in representation between less and more affluent residents.

CONCLUSION

Economic inequality in representation is a reality in local communities throughout the United States. But the magnitude of this inequity varies a great deal across municipalities. In this chapter, we have sought to identify the factors that contribute the most to the amount of ideological congruence representation received by economic groups in local communities, with a particular focus on understanding the circumstances that mitigate or reinforce the substantial inequities in representation experienced, on average, by low wealth residents. In so doing, we have highlighted the respective roles of coincidental representation, patterns of local economic inequality, and institutional characteristics in moderating the representation received by different class groups, and particularly the least affluent. We have also looked at how ideological diversity within groups affects the representation they receive.

The overarching theme of this chapter is that the representation on municipal councils enjoyed by low wealth residents is affected by contextual factors to a much greater degree than is the representation experienced by more affluent residents. Most importantly, the ideological congruence representation experienced by low wealth residents is highly sensitive to the amount of ideological overlap that exists between low wealth residents and more affluent residents. But the ideological congruence representation experienced by the more affluent is much less affected by ideological overlap with other wealth groups. In a similar vein, within-group ideological diversity is much more consequential for the ideological congruence representation of low wealth residents than it is for the ideological representation of more privileged residents. That is to say, when the preferences among low wealth residents vary considerably, it is harder for them to achieve more equitable representation relative to other wealth groups.

While contextual factors predominate in explaining the ideological congruence representation received by wealth groups, institutional factors, particularly election timing, have a notable, if limited, role to play. All wealth groups enjoy more ideological congruence representation on municipal councils when councilors are elected in contests held in November (either on-cycle with federal elections or in off years). Thus, while this policy will not reduce economic inequalities in representation, it does enhance the quality of representation received by all residents. At the same time, other electoral institutions had negligible impacts on the amount of ideological representation received by low, middle, and high wealth groups. Our findings thus support previous research about the impact of election timing and the otherwise limited impact of electoral institutions. We should point out, however, that it is quite possible that institutions do not matter because, as we noted in Chapter 4, rates of voting are abysmally low in local elections, so political structures that (in theory) increase representation cannot do the work of translating citizens' preferences into action.

Overall, then, our analysis of economic inequality and representation in local governments delivers mixed news. On one hand, we have found that poor residents do not, generally speaking, suffer nearly the same representational inequalities as racial and ethnic minority groups. On the other hand, we have shown that this pattern is largely reliant on the extent to which poor citizens share the views of their wealthier neighbors. When the ideologies of these groups do in fact diverge, it is more common for elected officials to share the views of those at the top of the wealth distribution than of those at the bottom. Furthermore, as we showed in Chapter 6, it is the ideologies of local elected officials (rather than the community's citizens) that matter most when it comes to predicting whether local governments will adopt policies that address inequalities. This helps us to understand why communities like Aiken, South Carolina, or Perry, Georgia, where elected officials take on ideologies quite distant from the poorest citizens, appear to be doing little to ease the problems of their least fortunate citizens.

9

Race, Class, and Representation in Local Politics

On August 9, 2014, Michael Brown, an unarmed eighteen-year-old African American man, was fatally shot by Darren Wilson, a white police officer, following a violent altercation on the streets of Ferguson, Missouri.[1] With many of the crucial facts surrounding Brown's death under dispute – in particular, whether Wilson's stop of Brown was justified, whether Wilson or Brown initiated the confrontation, whether Brown surrendered or resisted arrest – many residents in the majority African American community took to the streets to protest what they viewed as an emblematic instance of police brutality, as well as general indifference among community leaders toward the concerns of black and brown residents.[2] In response, Ferguson police – and eventually the Missouri National Guard – mustered an intimidating show of force in an effort to contain the protests. The presence of large numbers of heavily armed police and guardsmen exacerbated an already tense situation, leading to charged and sometimes violent encounters between protestors and law enforcement officials.[3] Wilson's killing of Brown, the heated and sometimes violent protests, and the extraordinary heavy-handedness of the police response made the events in Ferguson national news, riveting public attention and forcing conversations about police brutality and the over-policing of communities of color.

---

[1] Sandhya Somashekhar and Kimbrell Kelly. "Was Michael Brown Surrendering or Advancing to Attack Officer Darren Wilson?," *The Washington Post*, November 29, 2014.
[2] German Lopez. "What Were the Ferguson Protests About?," *Vox*, January 27, 2016.
[3] German Lopez, "The 2014 Ferguson Protests over the Michael Brown Police Shooting, Explained," *Vox*, January 27, 2016.

The situation in Ferguson deteriorated in November 2014 following the announcement that a grand jury had declined to indict Wilson for the murder of Brown. Although many residents continued to protest peacefully, others reacted violently to the news, looting local businesses and clashing with police and guardsmen. Dozens of businesses were destroyed and more than 100 people were arrested in the week following the announcement.[4] In the months and years that followed, African American residents continued to protest serious racial disparities in the community and the state at large. Meanwhile, many white residents in the state complained that the Ferguson protests – and other similar demonstrations within the state, including at the University of Missouri – had gone too far, challenging respect for "law and order" and tarnishing the reputation of Missouri residents.[5]

The severity of the crisis, along with serious allegations of civil rights violations by Wilson and other Ferguson officials, brought the sustained scrutiny of then–Attorney General Eric Holder and the US Department of Justice. A thorough March 2015 investigation by the department ultimately cleared Wilson of civil violations in the shooting of Brown.[6] But the department also found that the Ferguson Police Department and city administrators had engaged in a systematic pattern of discrimination against the city's black residents. While African Americans composed two-thirds of the city's population, they accounted for 85 percent of traffic stops, 90 percent of tickets, 93 percent of arrests, and 88 percent of cases involving the use of police force.[7] Meanwhile, city officials regularly imposed substantial fines on black residents for minor violations, largely to pad the city's coffers; and routinely circulated racist jokes on government email accounts.[8]

These tragic events unfolded in a political context in which whites dominated an overwhelmingly African American community. While African Americans constituted a supermajority of Ferguson's population, they made up only 47 percent of the city's voters in the 2013 municipal

---

[4] James Queally, "Ferguson: What You Need to Know," *Los Angeles Times*, March 17, 2015.

[5] Maggie Severns, "In Missouri, Ferguson Is Still Burning," *Politico*, July 31, 2016.

[6] Erik Eckholm and Matt Apuzzo, "Darren Wilson Is Cleared of Rights Violations in Ferguson Shooting," *The New York Times*, March 4, 2015.

[7] Matt Apuzzo, "Ferguson Police Routinely Violate Rights of Blacks, Justice Dept. Finds," *The New York Times*, March 3, 2015.

[8] Jamelle Bouie, "Ferguson's True Criminals," *Slate*, March 5, 2015.

elections.[9] Five of the six city council members, and the mayor, were white. And perhaps most significantly, virtually all the city's police officers were also white.[10]

These events exposed a rot at the core of local democracy in Ferguson. Far from serving the community's African American residents, Ferguson's elected officials and the bureaucrats they supervised all too frequently victimized them. Sadly, in the years following the clashes of 2014, the city made only halting and uneven efforts to address the serious problems that Brown's death brought to light. To be sure, there were some indications of progress. By late 2018, the number of black representatives on the city council had increased from one to three; the number of black police officers on the Ferguson force had grown from four to ten; and the community had installed an African American chief of police.[11] On the economic front, numerous new businesses moved to Ferguson, and the community partnered with the Urban League to establish a Community Empowerment Center for job training and employment placement.[12]

Yet, beneath the surface, many of the problems plaguing Ferguson that had been highlighted in the Department of Justice's report remained. A 2018 report by the Missouri Attorney General's office found that African Americans continued to bear the brunt of police scrutiny in the city. The previous year, blacks accounted for 88 percent of drivers stopped by Ferguson police and 85 percent of those arrested – numbers very close to those previously identified by the Department of Justice as indicative of a pattern of racial discrimination.[13] Furthermore, relatively little of the city's new economic development benefited the neighborhoods most affected by the discrimination identified in the Department of Justice's report. According to a 2018 *Washington Post* analysis, "Of the more than $36 million in bricks-and-mortar development that poured into the city [of Ferguson] after 2014, only $2.4 million – for a job

---

[9] Schaffner, Van Erve, and La Raja, "How Ferguson Exposes the Racial Bias in Elections."

[10] Dylan Matthews, "Black Underrepresentation Is a National Problem – But It's Way Worse in Ferguson," *Vox*, August 18, 2014.

[11] Clark Mindock, "Ferguson Shooting: Four Years after Michael Brown's Death, How Have Things Changed?," *The Independent*, August 8, 2018.

[12] Ellen McGirt, "Three Years after Michael Brown's Death Ferguson Has New Leadership, Contentious Debates and Hope," *Fortune*, August 9, 2017; Ron Mott, "Three Years after Michael Brown's Death, Has Ferguson Changed?," NBC News, August 9, 2017.

[13] Jim Salter, "Missouri Report: Blacks 85 Percent More Likely to Be Stopped," Associated Press, June 1, 2018.

training center – has directly benefited [the predominantly African American southeast neighborhood where Michael Brown was fatally shot]"; instead, "nearly all of the new development is concentrated in the more prosperous – and whiter – parts of town."[14]

Perhaps most worrisome of all, African American activists reported relentless harassment in the form of anonymous death threats, attempted assaults, and vandalism and break-ins of property, putting "everybody ... on pins and needles," according to one local leader.[15] At least six men closely associated with the Ferguson protests died under mysterious circumstances between 2015 and 2019, raising anxieties among community activists about possible targeting by white supremacists or pro-police vigilantes.[16]

Ferguson represents a particularly extreme example of racial inequality and local government indifference to the needs of a community's African American residents. Yet the unresponsiveness of the city's municipal government is typical of a much broader problem that touches communities across the United States. In this book, we have arrived at the following key findings about the nature of inequality in representation in the cities and towns in America:

- It is the norm, not the exception, for local governments to be minimally responsive to the ideologies of residents of color and the poor. The disparities in representation are largely consistent with findings from studies of federal and state government.
- Less advantaged residents are less likely to be descriptively represented on municipal councils, less likely to share the ideological preferences of these town leaders (what we call "ideological congruence"), and less likely to have their preferences reflected in local government policy.
- Local voters and officeholders tend to be more conservative, older, wealthier, and white compared to the communities they represent.
- Racial inequalities in representation are much more severe and pervasive than are economic-based inequalities in representation.

[14] Tracy Jan, "Four Years after Michael Brown Was Killed, Ferguson Neighborhood Still Feels Left Behind," *The Washington Post*, June 23, 2018.
[15] Jim Salter, "A Puzzling Number of Men Tied to the Ferguson Protests Have Since Died," Associated Press, March 18, 2019.
[16] Joe Penny, "The Fight for Justice Takes Its Toll on Ferguson Activists," *New York Review of Books*, February 12, 2019; E. J. Dickson, "Mysterious Deaths Leave Ferguson Activists 'On Pins and Needles.'" *Rolling Stone*, March 18, 2019.

We have also reached several conclusions about the relationship between social, economic, and political contexts and inequalities in local democracy:

- To the degree that less advantaged residents receive representation, it is largely due to the fortuitous circumstances of coincidental representation.
- Political institutions have a limited impact on the representation enjoyed by residents of color and those of modest wealth. The only institution that appears to make a difference in improving representation is holding local elections to coincide with major state or federal elections in November.
- Electing council members from less advantaged groups (descriptive representation) helps improve ideological congruence representation, but this effect is quite attenuated until leaders from disadvantaged groups make up a majority of the council. In contrast, levels of descriptive representation do not appear to affect the high degree of substantive representation received by whites, middle-class, and wealthy residents.
- Inequalities in representation tend to be worse when racial and economic inequalities within communities are more severe.
- Inequalities in representation tend to be worse in small town and rural local governments (as we show shortly).

Together, our findings point to severe democratic deficits at the local level. We can give some sense of the magnitude of the problem of inequality in local democracy by describing just what share of communities in the United States provide "very inequitable" ideological congruence representation to disadvantaged residents. For the purposes of this discussion, we define "very inequitable" as circumstances in which the disadvantaged group is at least ten points further away from the municipal council on the 100-point ideological scale than is the advantaged group. Since ten points represents 10 percent of the full ideological scale, we believe a difference in ideological congruence representation of ten points or more is quite substantial.

First, we assess the pervasiveness of very racially inequitable ideological congruence representation. In conducting this exercise, we excluded any communities where nonwhites were less than 25 percent of the population, in order to focus on communities in which nonwhites *should* receive substantial representation. Even when we took this step, we found that a troubling percentage of America's communities provided especially unequal representation. In fact, in fully 45 percent of these communities, nonwhites were at least ten points further away than whites from the municipal council. Moreover, in 11 percent of these communities, the distance between nonwhites and local elected officials was more than twenty points further away than the distance between whites and municipal councilors. It is important to note that these estimates were calculated using our sampling weights, meaning that they were representative of all communities across the United States (and not just of our sample). By this definition, conditions of "very inequitable" ideological congruence representation of nonwhite residents were astonishingly common – indeed, *they were present in nearly half of those communities in the United States containing at least 25 percent residents of color.*

Things were not quite as bad with respect to the ideological representation of low wealth residents. In 8 percent of communities, people in the bottom wealth tercile found themselves more than ten points farther away from municipal councils than those in the top tercile; and in 3 percent of communities residents in the bottom tercile were more than twenty points farther away from elected officials than those in the top wealth tercile. Nonetheless, because these estimates are nationally representative, these patterns imply that local government officials must seem very distant to tens, if not hundreds, of thousands of low wealth residents living in communities all across the United States.

These comparisons point to a broader theme in this book: While both racial inequality in representation and economic inequality in representation are serious issues in municipal democracy, the analyses in this book point to the conclusion that racial inequality is a much more severe and intractable problem. As we have shown, the magnitude of racial inequality in representation is significantly larger, on average, and it is also much more pervasive. Remarkably, the pervasiveness of racial inequality in representation is starkest, as we suggest in the next section, in the thousands of smaller cities and towns that dot suburban and rural America. Thus, while many scholars have focused on racial inequality in large metro areas, our research suggests that it is precisely in small, racially diverse communities like Ferguson that the problem of racial inequality in representation is greatest.

INEQUALITY FLOURISHES IN RURAL AMERICA

Our study is the first to systematically measure inequality in representation across a representative sample of small towns and cities across the United States. The unprecedented scope of our analysis allows us to detect a pattern that simply focusing on large and medium-sized cities would

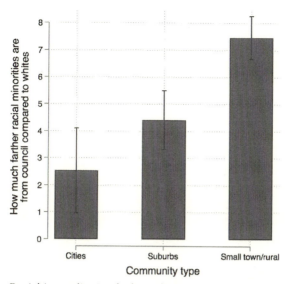

FIGURE 9.1 Racial inequality in ideological congruence representation across community types

Note: Plot shows predicted relative distance by community type while holding the community's population size and percent white at their mean values. Vertical lines represent 95 percent confidence intervals.

miss: Racial inequality is most pronounced in America's small towns and rural communities. To demonstrate this, Figure 9.1 shows the difference in the ideological distance between minorities (blacks and Latinos) and local elected officials on the one hand, and the difference between whites and local elected officials on the other. For example, a value of 5 on the y-axis would indicate that minority groups find themselves five points further away from local elected officials, on average, than do whites. This measure of inequality in representation is plotted separately for cities, suburbs, and small towns/rural communities. Importantly, this graphic also controls for the population and the racial composition of a community. Thus, the differences documented in Figure 9.1 account for the proportion of the community's population that is made up of whites versus minority groups.

Overall, Figure 9.1 shows that minorities are the least disadvantaged in cities. Indeed, in the 109 communities defined as cities in our sample, blacks and Hispanics were only about two points further way from local elected officials compared to whites, after controlling for community size and racial composition. By contrast, in suburbs, racial minorities were on average about four points further away compared to whites, and in small towns they were over seven points further away. Put another way, the racial inequality in ideological congruence representation is more than three times worse in America's small towns and rural communities than it is in its cities.

Why do blacks and Latinos fare so much worse in small towns and rural communities? The answer has to do with one of the most powerful patterns we documented in this book – coincidental representation. As we have noted, whites who live in cities tend to be significantly more liberal than whites who live in suburbs, and even more liberal than whites who live in small towns and rural communities. In fact, according to the Catalist data that we have used extensively in our research, the average ideology for whites living in cities is 48.8, compared to 45.6 for whites living in suburbs and 40.2 for whites living in small towns and rural areas. By contrast, the ideologies of blacks and Latinos vary much less across community types – urban minorities have an average ideology of 53.4 whereas rural minorities have an ideology of 49.1. Simply put, blacks and Latinos are at a much smaller disadvantage in cities and suburbs because these communities are populated with whites whose ideologies are closer to their own. In rural communities, however, whites are much more conservative than their black and Latino neighbors, making it less likely that racial minorities will benefit from coincidental representation.

Figure 9.2 mirrors the comparison from Figure 9.1, this time comparing the inequality in representation for low versus high wealth individuals. As in Figure 9.1, we control for population size and the racial composition of each community. Again, we see a divide between America's small towns and rural communities compared to its cities and suburban areas. Specifically, in cities and suburbs, people in the bottom wealth tercile are, on average, about two points further away from their local elected officials than are people in the top wealth tercile. However, in small towns and rural communities, the relative distance doubles, with low wealth individuals finding themselves more than four points farther away from their local elected officials than their wealthier neighbors.

In contrast to the racial inequality across community types that we document in Figure 9.1, we offer no straightforward explanation for the patterns we see in Figure 9.2. After all, the difference between the ideologies of individuals in the bottom and top wealth terciles is not particularly larger in small towns and rural communities than it is in cities and suburbs. Still, there is something particular to how politics works in small towns and rural communities that appears to put poorer individuals at a greater disadvantage than their counterparts in cities and suburbs. We can

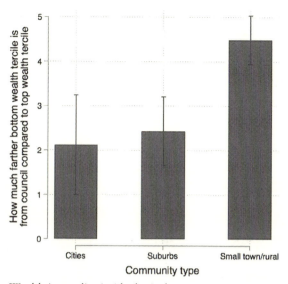

FIGURE 9.2 Wealth inequality in ideological congruence representation across community types
Note: Plot shows predicted relative distance by community type while holding the community's population size and percent white at their mean values. Vertical lines represent 95 percent confidence intervals.

only speculate as to why this is so. Some of the difference may be attributable to the difficulty of mobilizing poorer residents in rural towns to take action or perhaps to the more limited amounts of political information that is available in these areas. At the same time, however, the disadvantages faced by low wealth individuals in small towns are less than half as large as those experienced by nonwhites in small towns, so, again, it appears that patterns of economic inequality in representation are relatively muted compared with those relating to racial inequality.

RECONSIDERING LOCAL POLITICS IN VISIONS OF AMERICAN DEMOCRACY

The overwhelming evidence that local governments – especially small town and rural local governments – are much less responsive to disadvantaged residents than to advantaged community members represents a serious challenge to common tropes about the role of local democracy in American life. Municipalities have traditionally been celebrated as especially "close to the people" – as accessible spaces where ordinary Americans can practice civic skills, participate in the workings of government, and enjoy faithful representation of their needs and values. Moreover, in an increasingly fractious and polarized political climate, local governments have often been portrayed as the last bastions of political sanity, moderation, and reasoned compromise. Our research suggests that these common perceptions – while comforting – are overly optimistic and highly romanticized. As we have seen, in many communities throughout the United States, there are significant ideology-based differences between different groups of residents, and when such differences occur, the ideologies of advantaged residents are much more likely to receive a hearing in the local halls of power than are those of disadvantaged residents. By painting a misleadingly pleasant portrait of the state of local democracy, these common tropes about local government may stand in the way of difficult, but necessary, critical conversations about how to transform municipalities to make them more responsive to the needs of all their residents.

The prevalence of racially and economically inequitable representation in local government is especially problematic today, in an era of increasing diversity, rising economic inequality, and the devolution of more and more responsibilities to municipalities. As communities in many parts of the country grow more diverse and more economically unequal, the need for local governments that are responsive to all their residents grows ever more pressing. Our research indicates that local governments are not prepared *politically* to deal with the challenges posed by the twin dynamics of diversity and inequality. It's not just that local governments face more – and more difficult – tasks today than they did in the past. Rather, it's that many local governments are unlikely to be politically responsive to the increased needs and demands of racially and economically disadvantaged residents. To make matters worse, as we have shown, local government unresponsiveness is most likely to be manifest in precisely those communities where inequality – particularly racial inequality – is most severe.

All of these observations point to the pressing need to reconnect the study of inequality in representation at the municipal level with parallel examinations of national and state politics. In recent years, scholars and activists have sounded the alarm that the federal government and the states do not provide representation on an equitable basis to people of color and those of lesser means. These concerns are warranted, of course. But the lack of attention to inequalities in representation in municipal politics (due in no small part to the absence of adequate data) contributed, if unintentionally, to the impression that things were much better at the local level, and particularly in suburban and rural communities. Our findings firmly reject this view. Racial and class biases in representation appear at all levels of American government; and the story at the local level is part of a much broader narrative about how American democracy is, at present, failing to fulfill its promise to all of its citizens.

THE LIMITED PROMISE OF INSTITUTIONAL REFORMS

An especially sobering conclusion of this book is that reforming local institutions – often the go-to strategy among municipal activists interested in strengthening democracy – is unlikely to bring about a significant improvement in racial or economic equality of representation in local politics. As political scientists, we were astounded to find that the organization of local institutions has a limited impact on the representation enjoyed by residents of color and those of modest wealth. Even scheduling local elections to coincide with federal and state contests – frequently viewed as an especially promising measure for increasing equality of representation at the municipal level – has only a modest influence on equality of representation in comparison with contextual factors such as the degree of ideological overlap between less advantaged and more advantaged residents or the diversity of ideology among less advantaged groups.

How can it be that institutional reforms seem relatively ineffectual in addressing local inequalities in representation? For starters, it is important to remember that many of these inequalities exist at every level of American government; no institutional panacea has been found to eliminate political inequality in American politics. But there is good reason to expect that local institutions may especially struggle to address this issue because local government is most commonly designed to foster deep but not broad participation. What this means is that many local governments boast that they provide citizens with a myriad of ways to make their voices heard, including through frequent elections and through open meetings with time devoted to public comments. But the likely outcome of these measures is that a small group of highly engaged citizens account for most of the participation while the rest of the community's citizens sit on the sidelines. And, as we demonstrated in Chapter 4, the group that actually participates in local government largely comprises older, wealthier, and white individuals.

In some ways, the institutional factors we examined may have mattered less than we expected because very few communities adopt institutional structures that would aggressively expand the breadth of participation. For example, while there is some variance in when local communities hold their elections, almost no local elections are held when America enjoys its most diverse turnout – during a presidential election. In fact, less than 4 percent of the communities in our sample held their local elections concurrent with a presidential election. The incidence of local elections being held in conjunction with a presidential election was so rare that we could not even study the potential outcomes from that possibility.

Given our findings about the relationship between the timing of election dates and improved representation, we want to underscore the point that significant increases in turnout for local elections has the potential to improve equality. We encourage reformers to focus on the abysmal levels of turnout in towns throughout America and ways to expand it. There may be good arguments for cordoning off the timing of local elections from state and federal elections, but advancing representational equality is not one of them. We also believe that low turnout may attenuate the impact of other political institutions. One possible reason why the configuration of political institutions (e.g. mayor or manager, partisan or nonpartisan, at-large vs. district election) does not appear to matter might be because turnout is too low to effectively exploit the institutional mechanisms that might spur better representation. For example, partisan elections may help disadvantaged citizens hold their elected officials more accountable than in elections held on nonpartisan ballots, but only if they actually turn out to vote.

It is also possible that institutional factors may have mattered less than we expected because some communities may be so captured by a group of political elites that the institutional arrangements themselves are not respected. Consider, for example, communities like Brookhaven, Mississippi, and Mount Pleasant, Wisconsin, where elected officials seemed to skirt open meeting rules in order to advance their favored policies. Or the case of Perry, Georgia, where there was so little competition for local office that the incumbent politicians felt justified in canceling an election altogether. In places where elections are rarely contested, it would hardly be surprising that changing when they occur or whether they are held on partisan ballots or not would matter very little.[17] What

---

[17] Melissa Marschall and John Lappie. "Turnout in Local Elections: Is Timing Really Everything?" *Election Law Journal* 17, no. 3 (2018): 221–233.

this suggests is that scholars, reformers, and elected officials interested in revitalizing local democracy must consider additional extra-institutional initiatives to promote this essential goal.

So what should be done? We wish we had an easy answer to this question. Unfortunately, our sustained analysis of the state of local democracy in communities throughout the United States suggests that things are not so simple. Racial and economic inequality of representation in local government is widespread, entrenched, and resistant to easy resolution. And the obstacles to equitable representation are greatest in the communities where inequality is most severe. Recognition of the magnitude of the problem suggests humility about the prospects of initiatives to solve it.

Nonetheless, as citizens of a nation committed to the ideals of democracy and equality under the law, we have the obligation to try. The values that constitute the bedrock of our polity call us to the work of making local governments live up to those principles. In a country with a history like that of the United States – glorious and horrifying in turn – inaction is not an option.

And while we don't pretend that there are panaceas for the problems we have identified in this book, we do believe that concerned citizens and organizations can take concrete steps to increase the odds that less advantaged community residents will enjoy more equitable representation from local governments. In practice, these steps require new partnerships between researchers, activists, foundations, and government, as well as significant investments of energy and resources.

With these considerations in mind, we briefly lay out some ideas for strengthening local democracy and increasing the influence of residents of color and less affluent residents.

INCREASING RESIDENTS' ACCESS TO GOOD INFORMATION ABOUT LOCAL POLITICS

As a first observation, local residents need more – and better – information about how well or poorly local governments are serving their interests and meeting their needs. When it comes to politics, information about what candidates stand for, what politicians are doing (or not doing), and how well or poorly local governments are performing their responsibilities is a vital source of power. With such information in hand, individuals are better able to make reasonable choices in the voting booth, hold elected officials accountable for their campaign promises, and evaluate the performance of government agencies.[18] Putting relevant information about official and government behavior in the hands of citizens is an essential ingredient of a well-functioning democracy.

Unfortunately, and perhaps surprisingly, when it comes to news about local politics, many Americans are faced with an information desert. Even as the media options available to Americans have exploded over the past few decades, the availability of good information about *local politics* has suffered a large decline. The local newspaper industry has faced severe challenges due to declining circulation and advertising revenues, which has led to widespread newspaper closures, deep staff cuts, and significant reductions in coverage of local politics in many areas throughout the country.[19] Meanwhile, even as viewership of local television news remains strong, changes in the industry – particularly consolidation of ownership of local news stations by national conglomerates such as Sinclair Broadcast Group – have resulted in a significant decline in television coverage of local *political* news.[20] And while many people seek out news about politics online, the proliferation of highly partisan information or "fake news," especially on social media, as well as the dearth of online content about specifically local political issues, are serious obstacles to informed understanding of municipal politics.[21]

We know that the dearth of information about local politics can have serious deleterious consequences for the quality of local democracy. The loss of news sources focusing on local politics is associated with reductions in residents' political knowledge, declining civic engagement, and

---

[18] Christopher R. Berry and William G. Howell. "Accountability and Local Elections: Rethinking Retrospective Voting." *The Journal of Politics* 69, no. 3 (2007): 844–858; Oliver James and Alice Moseley. "Does Performance Information about Public Services Affect Citizens' Perceptions, Satisfaction, and Voice Behavior? Field Experiments with Absolute and Relative Performance Information." *Public Administration* 92, no. 2 (2014): 493–511; Étienne Charbonneau and Gregg G. Van Ryzin. "Benchmarks and Citizen Judgments of Local Government Performance: Findings from a Survey Experiment." *Public Management Review* 17, no. 2 (2015): 288–304; Joshua D. Clinton and Jason A. Grissom. "Public Information, Public Learning and Public Opinion: Democratic Accountability in Education Policy." *Journal of Public Policy* 35, no. 3 (2015): 355–385.

[19] Hayes and Lawless, "As Local News Goes, So Goes Citizen Engagement"; Hayes and Lawless, "The Decline of Local News and Its Effects"; Rubado and Jennings, "Political Consequences of the Endangered Local Watchdog."

[20] Martin and McCrain, "Local News and National Politics."

[21] Allcott and Gentzkow, "Social Media and Fake News in the 2016 Election"; Guess, Nyhan, and Reifler, "Selective Exposure to Misinformation."

falling voter turnout.[22] Declining news coverage of the performance of local government is also associated with a decreased capacity of residents to hold local officials accountable for government outcomes.[23]

We thus have every reason to believe that the availability, or lack of availability, of information about local politics is consequential, and that the decline of coverage of local politics has undesirable implications for local democracy. Given that less advantaged residents are on average least likely to possess the knowledge and resources to be effective players in politics, it is a virtual certainty that the decline of coverage of local politics has the most serious negative impact on members of these groups. The absence of good information about local politics therefore magnifies the obstacles to equitable representation that less advantaged community members already face.

What can be done to increase the availability of information about local politics for residents within communities – particularly nonwhite and less affluent residents? Given that the decline of media coverage of local politics is likely to continue, academics, advocacy organizations, foundations, and state governments need to think creatively about alternative means for getting pithy, accurate, and attention-grabbing information about local elected officials and municipal government performance into the hands of residents in communities throughout the nation. To be sure, some work in this area is being done, but existing efforts are inadequate to the task at hand. Organizations such as Project VoteSmart (votesmart.org) and Vote411 (vote411.org) attempt to provide information about candidates and elections across the nation, but much of their research is focused on national and state contests, offering little if any information about local government performance. Meanwhile, relatively few local governments collect, let alone publicize, systematic information about the performance of municipal agencies (with the exception of local schools).[24] In fact, we had students code the local government websites of each of the communities in our sample, and

---

[22] Hayes and Lawless, "The Decline of Local News and Its Effects"; Lee Shaker. "Dead Newspapers and Citizens' Civic Engagement." *Political Communication* 31, no. 1 (2014): 131–148; Sam Schulhofer-Wohl and Miguel Garrido. "Do Newspapers Matter? Short-Run and Long-Run Evidence from the Closure of The Cincinnati Post." *Journal of Media Economics* 26, no. 2 (2013): 60–81.

[23] Berry and Howell, "Accountability and Local Elections."

[24] Kevin C. Desouza, Gregory S. Dawson, Alfred Ho, and Rashmi Krishnamurthy. "Using Performance Analytics in Local Government." Brookings Institution, November 30, 2017.

20 percent of communities did not post agendas for upcoming meetings, 17 percent did not post minutes from previous meetings, and 38 percent posted no information whatsoever about the municipal budget. Few people will actually take the time to look for this information, but even if they should want to, they may very well live in a community where it is impossible to find such information online.

We believe that academics, activists, foundations, and engaged citizens need to work together to build on existing efforts to (1) provide more coverage of local candidates, elected officials, and government agencies; and (2) more directly deliver to community residents information about the promises of candidates, the actions of local elected officials, and the performance of municipal government agencies. Ideally, such efforts would be coordinated across local governments – perhaps organized at the state level, with support from state governments – so that residents of communities could make informed comparisons both over time within communities and across similar communities in different parts of a given state. Additionally, since not all citizens enjoy politics or follow it closely, it is especially important to find venues where citizens will glean information about local politics, even as a by-product of other activities they pursue.[25] These could be via kiosks while they are waiting to order food, at sporting events, or in any other place where they might have the opportunity to peruse local news. The point is to think imaginatively about ways of conveying important political information to citizens with diverse backgrounds and interests.

INCREASING ELECTED OFFICIALS' INFORMATION ABOUT RESIDENTS' PREFERENCES

Providing better information to residents about local candidates, elected officials, and government activities is an important first step in improving equity in representation in local politics. But, if less advantaged residents are to enjoy better representation from municipal elected officials, we also need to ensure that local elected officials acquire a much better understanding of the needs and preferences of their constituents.

At first blush, this might seem a strange recommendation. After all, finding out what constituents prefer and then representing those views in

[25] Markus Prior. *Post-Broadcast Democracy: How Media Choice Increases Inequality in Political Involvement and Polarizes Elections.* Cambridge: Cambridge University Press, 2007.

government is supposed to be what being an elected official is all about. But it turns out that elected officials are often quite misinformed about the real preferences of their constituents. Of special note, given our findings in this book, recent research suggests that elected officials tend to over-weight the preferences of wealthier and more conservative constituents in imagining the demands of their constituencies.[26]

Elected officials' misperceptions about what their constituents want stem from several sources. First, because elected officials tend to come from a relatively privileged stratum of society – an observation that our research findings certainly corroborate – they tend to bring unrepresentative information, opinions, and beliefs with them to their jobs.[27] Second, once in office, elected officials tend to hear most frequently from a biased sample of their constituents. In particular, they tend to learn most about the political views of those with political views and demographic characteristics that are similar to their own. Moreover, they tend to rely most heavily for political support on the same group of political and demographic look-alikes.[28] Because the people who have the means and motivation to reach out to representatives also tend to be from the wealthier and whiter side of society, elected officials naturally tend to give short shrift to the needs of other important groups, particularly the less advantaged, within their constituencies.[29] Finally, rather than equit-ably weighing diverging perspectives, elected officials are inclined to discount as uninformed or unrepresentative the views of constituents with whom they disagree.[30]

Although biases in representation are real, there is some good news to consider. Existing evidence suggests that politicians typically *want* to be congruent with the opinions of their constituents, and that they change their behavior when they learn more about what their constituents

---

[26] David E. Broockman and Christopher Skovron. "Bias in Perceptions of Public Opinion among Political Elites." *American Political Science Review* 112, no. 3 (2018): 542–563; Alexander Hertel-Fernandez, Matto Mildenberger, and Leah C. Stokes. "Legislative Staff and Representation in Congress." *American Political Science Review* 113, no. 1 (2019): 1–18.

[27] Carnes, *White-Collar Government*; Butler, *Representing the Advantaged*.

[28] Broockman, "Black Politicians"; Broockman and Ryan, "Preaching to the Choir"; Joshua L. Kalla and David E. Broockman. "Campaign Contributions Facilitate Access to Congressional Officials: A Randomized Field Experiment." *American Journal of Political Science* 60, no. 3 (2016): 545–558.

[29] Schlozman, Verba, and Brady, *The Unheavenly Chorus*.

[30] Butler and Dynes, "How Politicians Discount the Opinions of Constituents with Whom They Disagree."

truly want.[31] Moreover, recent research, including field experiments on elected officials, suggests that officials are responsive in meaningful ways to coordinated campaigns that mobilize ordinary citizens to contact officials about their demands.[32] Put simply, there are reasons to believe that, when properly informed about what their constituents want, elected officials will take concrete steps to better represent those demands.

These observations suggest that scholars, data analysts, activists, and concerned citizens need to develop new ways to get accurate information about what constituents (particularly less advantaged constituents) want into the hands of local elected officials. Eitan Hersh argues that one approach to making local governments responsive to the needs of their citizens is for people to spend less time treating politics like a hobby and more time treating it as a legitimate way to pursue and exercise political power.[33] Hersh highlights the successes of local grassroots organizations that emerged after the 2016 election in places where local politics had previously seemed to be off-limits to all but incumbent politicians. In some cases, these groups were able to wield influence by reviving long-moribund party precinct committees. In Davidson, North Carolina, a small group of locals and students who organized the local Democratic Party witnessed immediate success not just in winning local elections, but also in building bridges with the African American community that had traditionally been shut out of town politics. In Haverhill, Massachusetts, a Latino Coalition formed in 2018 to provide a voice for the Latino community, which makes up about 20 percent of the town's population. When the mayor heard about this organization, he immediately requested a meeting with the group, heard their concerns, and acted on many of them in short order.

What's remarkable about Hersh's stories of successful local organizing is how quickly a few dozen residents were able to make a significant impact on local politics. In Davidson, it took just forty supporters showing up at the first party committee meeting to ensure that the old guard in the town was unable to derail the organization. In Haverhill, only a week after a meeting with sixty-four members of the Latino Coalition, the

---

[31] Bergan, "Does Grassroots Lobbying Work?"; Butler and Nickerson, "Can Constituency Learning Affect How Legislators Vote?"

[32] Daniel E. Bergan and Richard T. Cole. "Call Your Legislator: A Field Experimental Study of the Impact of a Constituency Mobilization Campaign on Legislative Voting." *Political Behavior* 37, no. 1 (2015): 27–42.

[33] Eitan Hersh. *Politics Is for Power: How to Move beyond Political Hobbyism, Take Action, and Make Real Change.* New York: Simon & Schuster, 2020.

town's previously English-only website began to appear in Spanish for the first time. These stories suggest that it doesn't take a massive movement of hundreds or thousands to influence local government; in fact, the problem of extremely low levels of participation in local politics may also be an opening. After all, when local government is dominated by a small cadre of local elites, even a modest number of individuals organizing themselves can have a major impact.

One promising possibility for helping these groups form and grow is to encourage new collaborations between scholars and data analysts, on the one hand, and activists and concerned citizens, on the other, geared toward transmitting more accurate and representative information about constituent preferences to municipal representatives. As suggested by this book and by other recent research on representation in local government, researchers are developing a range of new techniques for estimating constituency opinions at the local level and for investigating relationships between constituents' demands and the behaviors of local officials and municipal governments. If such researchers and concerned activists collaborate with local citizens' groups and earn the support of foundations (and possibly government agencies), there is no reason why such information could not be conveyed to local elected officials – and, as an accountability measure, circulated publicly for review by interested residents. We think that such efforts could be a powerful mechanism both for helping local elected officials understand what their constituents want and for holding them accountable for delivering on those demands.

A very different – though equally effective – means for increasing the availability of information about constituent preferences to municipal elected officials might be to make it easier for residents of color and those with less wealth to run for and win local elective office.[34] This approach would address the information problem facing local elected leaders simply by empowering people who already have good information about the preferences of disadvantaged constituencies to serve in local government. At present – and as we and many others have shown – people from less advantaged circumstances are systematically underrepresented on elective bodies, and this most likely translates into inequitable representation of the demands of less privileged groups.

We have an increasingly clear understanding of why people from less advantaged circumstances are much less likely to serve in elective office.

---

[34] Nicholas Carnes. *The Cash Ceiling: Why Only the Rich Run for Office –And What We Can Do about It*. Princeton, NJ: Princeton University Press, 2018.

As recent research has documented, the primary obstacles to service in elective office by disadvantaged groups are (1) the high costs (in terms of money, time, and energy) associated with running for office and (2) the disinclination of party leaders and political power brokers to recruit and mobilize less privileged people into elective politics.[35] However, candidates of color may face the additional challenge of (3) racial bias on the part of white voters.[36]

Although addressing the racial biases of white voters is a difficult challenge, there are concrete ways of encouraging disadvantaged groups to run and of lowering the costs of running for and serving in office. For example, state governments could provide public funding for municipal campaigns or help to subsidize the salaries of local elected officials as a way to relieve some of the financial burdens associated with running for and serving in elective office at the local level. Meanwhile, nonprofit and activist organizations can and should allocate more resources to recruiting, training, and supporting candidates from disadvantaged backgrounds. Such initiatives could learn from the example of the New Jersey AFL-CIO affiliate, which has a well-established "labor candidates school" to prepare working-class candidates for campaigns for state and local offices. The labor candidates school has a model that seems to work – graduates of this school have won 75 percent of the contests in which they have run.[37] We urge scholars and activists to work with foundations and state governments to help make running for and holding local office more accessible to less advantaged residents.

INCREASING STATE MONITORING OF THE QUALITY OF DEMOCRACY IN MUNICIPALITIES

Because municipalities are creatures of states with no independent sovereignty or constitutional status, the success or failure of democracy at the local level is ultimately the responsibility of the state government. The widespread racial and class inequities in representation that we reveal in

---

[35] Carnes, *The Cash Ceiling*.

[36] See, e.g., Spencer Piston. "How Explicit Racial Prejudice Hurt Obama in the 2008 Election." *Political Behavior* 32, no. 4 (2010): 431–451; Vesla M. Weaver. "The Electoral Consequences of Skin Color: The 'Hidden' Side of Race in Politics." *Political Behavior* 34, no. 1 (2012): 159–192; Michael Tesler. *Post-Racial or Most-Racial? Race and Politics in the Obama Era*. Chicago: University of Chicago Press, 2016.

[37] Nicholas Carnes, "Working Class People Are Underrepresented in Politics. The Problem Isn't Voters," *Vox*, October 24, 2018.

this book are, properly understood, an indictment of state governments as much as, if not more than, of the localities themselves. State governments should be much more involved in assessing how well local governments are meeting their democratic responsibilities to all their residents. Taking this reasoning a step further, state governments have a responsibility to take remedial action if and when municipalities fail to meet those obligations.

Many states already monitor some areas of local government performance, especially educational achievement and local government finance. However, it would be a startling innovation if states began monitoring the effectiveness of local democracy in equitably serving all their residents because such an approach is basically unheard of in the United States. At the same time, the idea is not completely outlandish. International organizations such as the Institute for Democracy and Electoral Assistance (IDEA) provide tools to help governments, universities, and citizens' groups to conduct evaluations of the "State of Local Democracy" within various nations. But let us be clear: We are not advocating that American state governments adopt in whole or in part IDEA's approach. Given the limited state of knowledge in this area, we leave open both the specific content of such policies and the precise process by which they might be developed.

To be sure, developing appropriate tools to help state governments assess the quality of municipal democracy in communities within their borders is a big task that would require the involvement of a wide range of stakeholders – most importantly residents, but also government officials, citizens' groups, and technical experts. Remediation is an even more fraught subject that would even more strongly necessitate engagement by a wide array of participants, simply because there is no guarantee that remedial interventions by state governments would not perversely make the situation worse. Even so, given the circumstances we have described in this book, states have an obligation to develop means for assessing local democracy and helping to improve matters in instances of democratic failure.

At the very least, the states could work more diligently at improving turnout in local elections. We demonstrated that having local elections on the same day as federal and state elections tends to increase representation for all groups in a community. But this institutional change does not appear to diminish the inequalities in representation among marginal groups because such groups still vote at rates substantially lower than better represented citizens. In Chapter 4, we showed that major increases in turnout would change the ideological composition of voters participating in elections. As things stand now, the overall composition of actual voters and of the citizens elected to office is of a much more conservative bent than is the eligible electorate. Having less bias in the turnout population should affect both the type of candidates who win office and the responsiveness of officeholders.

For this reason, policymakers at the state level should consider imaginative ways to boost turnout in elections. We know that turnout depends considerably on political interest and the availability of personal resources, such as time, money, and civic skills.[38] But it also depends on the mobilization of voters by local campaigns, news media, and various social networks.[39] For this reason, reforms at the state level should focus not simply on making voting easier, but on activating potential voters. Holding local elections simultaneously with state and federal elections would have the effect of those higher-level campaigns drawing attention to the fact that a local election is also taking place.[40] States might also ensure that localities make it as easy as possible for candidates to run for office, because contestation for office generates political campaigns and drives interest.[41] More creatively, states might make it more attractive to attend the polls by encouraging festive atmospheres on Election Day or offering lotteries or other extrinsic rewards to those who vote.[42] Compulsory voting should be considered as well, just as it is in many democratic nations as diverse as Argentina, Australia, Belgium, and Brazil. Reformers will meet fierce resistance from groups that tend to benefit from low-turnout elections, but if we truly want to advance democratic principles of equality this resistance should be challenged forthrightly.

---

[38] Verba, Schlozman, and Brady, *Voice and Equality*.

[39] Matt A. Barretto. "¡Sí Se Puede! Latino Candidates and the Mobilization of Latino Voters." *American Political Science Review* 101, no. 3 (2007): 425–441; Thomas M. Holbrook and Aaron C. Weinschenk. "Campaigns, Mobilization, and Turnout in Mayoral Elections." *Political Research Quarterly* 67, no. 1 (2014): 42–55; David Niven. "The Mobilization Solution? Face-to-Face Contact and Voter Turnout in a Municipal Election." *The Journal of Politics* 66, no. 3 (2004): 868–884.

[40] Anzia, *Timing and Turnout*; Hajnal and Lewis, "Municipal Institutions and Voter Turnout in Local Elections."

[41] Marschall and Lappie, "Turnout in Local Elections."

[42] Elizabeth M. Addonizio, Donald P. Green, and James M. Glaser. "Putting the Party Back into Politics: An Experiment Testing Whether Election Day Festivals Increase Voter Turnout." *PS: Political Science & Politics* 40, no. 4 (2007): 721–727; Costas Panagopoulos. "Positive Social Pressure and Prosocial Motivation: Evidence from a Large-Scale Field Experiment on Voter Mobilization." *Political Psychology* 34, no. 2 (2013): 265–275.

LOOKING FORWARD: ADVANCING EQUALITY IN REPRESENTATION IN MUNICIPAL POLITICS

We forthrightly acknowledge that our proposals to advance racial and economic equality in representation in local politics are not the only possible strategies, and that they may not even be the best ones. In the end, the focus of this chapter – and of this book more generally – has been on describing the nature and severity of the problem rather than on prescribing particular solutions. This may strike readers as a little dissatisfying.

However, we insist that there is tremendous value in clarifying the failures of local democracy as it is currently practiced in the United States. This book has been written in the spirit of an observation made by Abraham Lincoln in his famous "House Divided" speech, delivered on the eve of the American Civil War: "If we could first know *where* we are, and *whither* we are tending, we could then better judge *what* to do, and *how* to do it."[43] We believe that we have clearly delineated where we are with respect to the democratic performance of municipal governments, as well as whither we are tending. The situation is bad, and without focused and sustained action, the outlook is equally grim. While we have made initial observations about what to do, and how to do it, the responsibility for further developing these and other solutions to the problems that we have highlighted ultimately rests in the hands of all Americans.

Establishing equality in representation in local government may seem like a daunting – if not insurmountable – task. Yet we must somehow find the political will, economic resources, and democratic faith to achieve it. In contemplating this necessary labor, we might take some solace in other lines from Lincoln's stirring address:

Did we brave all *then* to falter *now?* ... The result is not doubtful. We shall not fail – if we stand firm, we shall not fail. Wise councils may accelerate or mistakes delay it, but sooner or later the victory is sure to come.[44]

With a sense of tempered optimism, let us begin the essential task of renewing municipal democracy in the United States.

---

[43] Abraham Lincoln, "A House Divided," Springfield, Illinois, June 16, 1858, www .abrahamlincolnonline.org/lincoln/speeches/house.htm.
[44] Lincoln, "A House Divided."

Bibliography

Achen, Christopher H. "Measuring Representation." *American Journal of Political Science* 22, no. 3 (1978): 475–510.

Addonizio, Elizabeth M., Donald P. Green, and James M. Glaser. "Putting the Party Back into Politics: An Experiment Testing Whether Election Day Festivals Increase Voter Turnout." *PS: Political Science & Politics* 40, no. 4 (2007): 721–727.

Adrian, Charles R. "Some General Characteristics of Nonpartisan Elections." *American Political Science Review* 46, no. 3 (1952): 766–776.

Alesina, Alberto and Edward Glaeser. *Fighting Poverty in the US and Europe: A World of Difference.* New York: Oxford University Press, 2004.

Alesina, Alberto and Eliana La Ferrara. "Participation in Heterogeneous Communities." *The Quarterly Journal of Economics* 115, no. 3 (2000): 847–904.

Alesina, Alberto, Reza Baqir, and William Easterly. "Public Goods and Ethnic Divisions." *The Quarterly Journal of Economics* 114, no. 4 (1999): 1243–1284.

An, Brian, Morris Levy, and Rodney Hero. "It's Not Just Welfare: Racial Inequality and the Local Provision of Public Goods in the United States." *Urban Affairs Review* 54, no. 5 (2018): 833–865.

Anderson, Lisa R., Jennifer M. Mellor, and Jeffrey Milyo. "Inequality and Public Good Provision: An Experimental Analysis." *The Journal of Socio-Economics* 37, no. 3 (2008): 1010–1028.

Ansolabehere, Stephen and Eitan Hersh. "Validation: What Big Data Reveal about Survey Misreporting and the Real Electorate." *Political Analysis* 20, no. 4 (2012): 437–459.

Anzia, Sarah F. "Election Timing and the Electoral Influence of Interest Groups." *The Journal of Politics* 73, no. 2 (2011): 412–427.

Timing and Turnout: How Off-Cycle Elections Favor Organized Groups. Chicago: University of Chicago Press, 2013.

Apergis, Nicholas, Oguzhan C. Dincer, and James E. Payne. "The Relationship between Corruption and Income Inequality in US States: Evidence from a

Panel Cointegration and Error Correction Model." *Public Choice* 145, no. 1–2 (2010): 125–135.

Arceneaux, Kevin. "Does Federalism Weaken Democratic Representation in the United States?" *Publius: The Journal of Federalism* 35, no. 2 (2005): 297–311.

Avery, James M. and Jeffrey A. Fine. "Racial Composition, White Racial Attitudes, and Black Representation: Testing the Racial Threat Hypothesis in the United States Senate." *Political Behavior* 34, no. 3 (2012): 391–410.

Bailey, Michael A. and Mark Carl Rom. "A Wider Race? Interstate Competition across Health and Welfare Programs." *The Journal of Politics* 66, no. 2 (2004): 326–347.

Banducci, Susan A., Todd Donovan, and Jeffrey A. Karp. "Minority Representation, Empowerment, and Participation." *The Journal of Politics* 66, no. 2 (2004): 534–556.

Baqir, Reza. "Districting and Government Overspending." *Journal of Political Economy* 110 (2002): 1318–1354.

Barretto, Matt A. "Sí Se Puede! Latino Candidates and the Mobilization of Latino Voters." *American Political Science Review* 101, no. 3 (2007): 425–441.

Bartels, Larry M. "Constituency Opinion and Congressional Policy Making: The Reagan Defense Buildup." *American Political Science Review* 85, no. 2 (1991): 457–474.

"Where the Ducks Are: Voting Power in a Party System." In *Politicians and Party Politics*, ed. John Geer. Baltimore: Johns Hopkins University Press, 1998. 43–79.

Unequal Democracy: The Political Economy of the New Gilded Age. Princeton, NJ: Princeton University Press, 2008.

Beach, Brian and Daniel B. Jones. "Gridlock: Ethnic Diversity in Government and the Provision of Public Goods." *American Economic Journal: Economic Policy* 9, no. 1 (2017): 112–136.

Benabou, Roland. "Inequality and Growth." *NBER Macroeconomics Annual* 11 (1996): 11–74.

Bergan, Daniel E. "Does Grassroots Lobbying Work? A Field Experiment Measuring the Effects of an E-mail Lobbying Campaign on Legislative Behavior." *American Politics Research* 37, no. 2 (2009): 327–352.

Bergan, Daniel E. and Richard T. Cole. "Call Your Legislator: A Field Experimental Study of the Impact of a Constituency Mobilization Campaign on Legislative Voting." *Political Behavior* 37, no. 1 (2015): 27–42.

Berman, David R. *Local Government and the States: Autonomy, Politics, and Policy.* Armonk, NY: ME Sharp Incorporated, 2003.

Berry, Christopher R. and William G. Howell. "Accountability and Local Elections: Rethinking Retrospective Voting." *The Journal of Politics* 69, no. 3 (2007): 844–858.

Bhatti, Yosef and Robert S. Erikson. "How Poorly Are the Poor Represented in the US Senate?" In *Who Gets Represented?*, eds. Peter K. Enns and Christopher Wlezien. New York: Russell Sage Foundation 2011. 223–246.

Bobo, Lawrence and Franklin D. Gilliam. "Race, Sociopolitical Participation, and Black Empowerment." *American Political Science Review* 84, no. 2 (1990): 377–393.

Bonica, Adam, Nolan McCarty, Keith T. Poole, and Howard Rosenthal. "Why Hasn't Democracy Slowed Rising Inequality?" *Journal of Economic Perspectives* 27, no. 3 (2013): 103–124.

Bonilla-Silva, Eduardo. *Racism without Racists: Color-Blind Racism and the Persistence of Racial Inequality in the United States.* New York: Rowman & Littlefield Publishers, 2006.

Boudreau, Cheryl, Christopher S. Elmendorf, and Scott A. MacKenzie. "Lost in Space? Information Shortcuts, Spatial Voting, and Local Government Representation." *Political Research Quarterly* 68, no. 4 (2015): 843–855.

Boustan, Leah, Fernando Ferreira, Hernan Winkler, and Eric M. Zolt. "The Effect of Rising Income Inequality on Taxation and Public Expenditures: Evidence from US Municipalities and School Districts, 1970–2000." *Review of Economics and Statistics* 95, no. 4 (2013): 1291–1302.

Branham, J. Alexander, Stuart N. Soroka, and Christopher Wlezien. "When Do the Rich Win?" *Political Science Quarterly* 132, no. 1 (2017): 43–62.

Brazil, Noli. "The Unequal Spatial Distribution of City Government Fines: The Case of Parking Tickets in Los Angeles." *Urban Affairs Review* (2018): DOI: 1078087418783609.

Bridges, Amy. "Textbook Municipal Reform." *Urban Affairs Review* 33, no. 1 (1997): 97–119.

Broockman, David E. "Black Politicians Are More Intrinsically Motivated to Advance Blacks' Interests: A Field Experiment Manipulating Political Incentives." *American Journal of Political Science* 57, no. 3 (2013): 521–536.

"Distorted Communication, Unequal Representation: Constituents Communicate Less to Representatives Not of Their Race." *American Journal of Political Science* 58, no. 2 (2014): 307–321.

Broockman, David E. and Timothy J. Ryan. "Preaching to the Choir: Americans Prefer Communicating to Copartisan Elected Officials." *American Journal of Political Science* 60, no. 4 (2016): 1093–1107.

Broockman, David E. and Christopher Skovron. "Bias in Perceptions of Public Opinion among Political Elites." *American Political Science Review* 112, no. 3 (2018): 542–563.

Browning, Rufus, Dale R. Marshall, and David Tabb. *Protest Is Not Enough: The Struggle of Blacks and Hispanics for Equality in Urban Politics.* Los Angeles: University of California Press, 1984.

Bullock III, Charles S. and Bruce A. Campbell. "Racist or Racial Voting in the 1981 Atlanta Municipal Elections." *Urban Affairs Quarterly* 20, no. 2 (1984): 149–164.

Bullock III, Charles S. and Susan A. MacManus. "Staggered Terms and Black Representation." *The Journal of Politics* 49, no. 2 (1987): 543–552.

Butler, Daniel M. *Representing the Advantaged: How Politicians Reinforce Inequality.* Cambridge: Cambridge University Press, 2014.

Butler, Daniel M. and David E. Broockman. "Do Politicians Racially Discriminate against Constituents? A Field Experiment on State Legislators." *American Journal of Political Science* 55, no. 3 (2011): 463–477.

Butler, Daniel M. and Adam M. Dynes. "How Politicians Discount the Opinions of Constituents with Whom They Disagree." *American Journal of Political Science* 60, no. 4 (2016): 975–989.

Butler, Daniel M. and David W. Nickerson. "Can Learning Constituency Opinion Affect How Legislators Vote? Results from a Field Experiment." *Quarterly Journal of Political Science* 6, no. 1 (2011): 55–83.

Campbell, Angus, Philip E. Converse, Warren E. Miller, and Donald E. Stokes. *The American Voter*. Ann Arbor: University of Michigan Press, 1960.

Campbell, David E. and Christina Wolbrecht. "See Jane Run: Women Politicians as Role Models for Adolescents." *The Journal of Politics* 68, no. 2 (2006): 233–247.

Canes-Wrone, Brandice, David W. Brady, and John F. Cogan. "Out of Step, Out of Office: Electoral Accountability and House Members' Voting." *American Political Science Review* 96, no. 1 (2002): 127–140.

Cann, Damon M. "The Structure of Municipal Political Ideology." *State and Local Government Review* 50, no. 1 (2018): 37–45.

Carmines, Edward G., Michael J. Ensley, and Michael W. Wagner. "Political Ideology in American Politics: One, Two, or None?" *The Forum*, vol. 10, no. 3 (2012): https://doi.org/10.1515/1540-8884.1526.

Carnes, Nicholas. "Does the Numerical Underrepresentation of the Working Class in Congress Matter?" *Legislative Studies Quarterly* 37, no. 1 (2012): 5–34.

  White-Collar Government: The Hidden Role of Class in Economic Policy Making. Chicago: University of Chicago Press, 2013.

  "Why Are There So Few Working-Class People in Political Office? Evidence from State Legislatures." *Politics, Groups, and Identities* 4, no. 1 (2016): 85.

  "Adam Smith Would Be Spinning in His Grave." *The Forum* 15, no. 1 (2017): https://doi.org/10.1515/for-2017-0009.

  The Cash Ceiling: Why Only the Rich Run for Office – And What We Can Do about It. Princeton, NJ: Princeton University Press, 2018.

Carnes, Nicholas and Noam Lupu. "Rethinking the Comparative Perspective on Class and Representation: Evidence from Latin America." *American Journal of Political Science* 59, no. 1 (2015): 1–18.

  "What Good Is a College Degree? Education and Leader Quality Reconsidered." *Journal of Politics* 78, no. 1 (2016): 35–49.

Carnes, Nicholas and Meredith L. Sadin. "The 'Mill Worker's Son' Heuristic: How Voters Perceive Politicians from Working-Class Families—And How They Really Behave in Office." *The Journal of Politics* 77, no. 1 (2015): 285–298.

Caughey, Devin and Christopher Warshaw. "Public Opinion in Subnational Politics." *The Journal of Politics* 81, no. 1 (2019): 352–363.

Charbonneau, Étienne and Gregg G. Van Ryzin. "Benchmarks and Citizen Judgments of Local Government Performance: Findings from a Survey Experiment." *Public Management Review* 17, no. 2 (2015): 288–304.

Choi, Sang Ok, Sang-Seok Bae, Sung-Wook Kwon, and Richard Feiock. "County Limits: Policy Types and Expenditure Priorities." *The American Review of Public Administration* 40, no. 1 (2010): 29–45.

Chong, Alberto and Mark Gradstein. "Inequality and Institutions." *The Review of Economics and Statistics* 89, no. 3 (2007): 454–465.

Cingano, Federico. "Trends in Income Inequality and Its Impact on Economic Growth." OECD Social, Employment, and Migration Working Papers, no. 163, OEC Publishing: http://englishbulletin.adapt.it/wp-content/uploads/2014/12/oecd_9_12_2014.pdf.

Clinton, Joshua D. and Jason A. Grissom. "Public Information, Public Learning and Public Opinion: Democratic Accountability in Education Policy." *Journal of Public Policy* 35, no. 3 (2015): 355–385

Converse, Philip E. "The Nature of Belief Systems in Mass Publics." In *Ideology and Discontent*, ed. David E. Aptor. New York: Free Press of Glencoe, 1964.

Corcoran, Sean and William N. Evans. *Income Inequality, the Median Voter, and the Support for Public Education*, no. 16097, National Bureau of Economic Research, 2010.

Craw, Michael. "Deciding to Provide: Local Decisions on Providing Social Welfare." *American Journal of Political Science* 54, no. 4 (2010): 906–920.

"Overcoming City Limits: Vertical and Horizontal Models of Local Redistributive Policy Making." *Social Science Quarterly* 87, no. 2 (2006): 361–379.

Dahl, Robert A. *Who Governs? Democracy and Power in an American City*. New Haven, CT: Yale University Press, 2005.

Davidson, Chandler and George Korbel. "At-Large Elections and Minority-Group Representation: A Re-examination of Historical and Contemporary Evidence." *Journal of Politics* 43, no. 4 (1981): 982–1005.

DeHoog, Ruth Hoogland, David Lowery, and William E. Lyons. "Citizen Satisfaction with Local Governance: A Test of Individual, Jurisdictional, and City-Specific Explanations." *The Journal of Politics* 52, no. 3 (1990): 807–837.

Derthick, Martha. *Keeping the Compound Republic: Essays on American Federalism*. Washington, DC: Brookings Institution Press, 2004.

DeSantis, Victor and Tari Renner. "Minority and Gender Representation in American County Legislatures: The Effect of Election Systems." In *United States Electoral Systems*, eds. Wilma Rule and Joseph F. Zimmerman. New York: Greenwood Press, 1992.

Desouza, Kevin C., Gregory S. Dawson, Alfred Ho, and Rashmi Krishnamurthy. "Using Performance Analytics in Local Government." Brookings Institution, November 30, 2017.

Dovi, Suzanne. "Preferable Descriptive Representatives: Will Just Any Woman, Black, or Latino Do?" *American Political Science Review* 96, no. 4 (2002): 729–743.

"In Praise of Exclusion." *The Journal of Politics* 71, no. 3 (2009): 1172–1186.

Dowding, Keith, Peter John, and Stephen Biggs. "Tiebout: A Survey of the Empirical Literature." *Urban Studies* 31, no. 4–5 (1994): 767–797.

Durlauf, Steven N. "A Theory of Persistent Income Inequality." *Journal of Economic Growth* 1, no. 1 (1996): 75–93.

Einstein, Katherine Levine and Vladimir Kogan. "Pushing the City Limits: Policy Responsiveness in Municipal Government." *Urban Affairs Review* 52, no. 1 (2016): 3–32.

Einstein, Katherine Levine, David Glick, and Conor LeBlanc. "2016 Menino Survey of Mayors." (2017), www.bu.edu/ioc/files/2017/01/2016-Menino-Survey-of-Mayors-Final-Report.pdf.

Einstein, Katherine Levine, Maxwell Palmer, and David M. Glick. "Who Participates in Local Government? Evidence from Meeting Minutes." *Perspectives on Politics* 17, no. 1 (2019): 28–46.

Eisinger, Peter K. *The Politics of Displacement: Racial and Ethnic Transition in Three American Cities*. New York: Academic Press, 1980.

Ellis, Christopher. "Social Context and Economic Biases in Representation." *The Journal of Politics* 75, no. 3 (2013): 773–786.

Enamorado, Ted and Kosuke Imai. "Validating Self-Reported Turnout by Linking Public Opinion Surveys with Administrative Records." SSRN working paper (2018), https://papers.ssrn.com/sol3/papers.cfm?abstract_id=3217884.

Engstrom, Richard L. and Michael D. McDonald. "The Election of Blacks to City Councils: Clarifying the Impact of Electoral Arrangements on the Seats/Population Relationship." *American Political Science Review* 75, no. 2 (1981): 344–354.

Enns, Peter K. "Relative Policy Support and Coincidental Representation." *Perspectives on Politics* 13, no. 4 (2015): 1053–1064.

Erikson, Robert S., Gerald C. Wright, and John P. McIver. *Statehouse Democracy: Public Opinion and Policy in the American States*. Cambridge: Cambridge University Press, 1993.

Ezcurra, Roberto and Andrés Rodríguez-Pose. "Can the Economic Impact of Political Decentralisation Be Measured?" Centre for Economic Policy Research (2011): https://ideas.repec.org/p/imd/wpaper/wp2011-02.html.

Fajnzylber, Pablo, Daniel Lederman, and Norman Loayza. "What Causes Violent Crime?" *European Economic Review* 46, no. 7 (2002): 1323–1357.

Ferreira, Fernando and Joseph Gyourko. "Do Political Parties Matter? Evidence from US Cities." *The Quarterly Journal of Economics* 124, no. 1 (2009): 399–422.

Fiorina, Morris P. *Representatives, Roll Calls, and Constituencies*. Lanham, MD: Lexington Books, 1974.

Fischel, William A. *The Homevoter Hypothesis: How Home Values Influence Local Government Taxation, School Finance, and Land-Use Policies*. Cambridge, MA: Harvard University Press, 2001.

Flavin, Patrick. "Income Inequality and Policy Representation in the American States." *American Politics Research* 40, no. 1 (2012): 29–59.

Fox, Richard L. and Jennifer L. Lawless. "To Run or Not to Run for Office: Explaining Nascent Political Ambition." *American Journal of Political Science* 49, no. 3 (2005): 642–659.

Fraga, Bernard L. "Candidates or Districts? Reevaluating the Role of Race in Voter Turnout." *American Journal of Political Science* 60, no. 1 (2016): 97–122.

  The Turnout Gap: Race, Ethnicity, and Political Inequality in a Diversifying America. Cambridge: Cambridge University Press, 2018.

Gerber, Elisabeth R. and Daniel J. Hopkins. "When Mayors Matter: Estimating the Impact of Mayoral Partisanship on City Policy." *American Journal of Political Science* 55, no. 2 (2011): 326–339.

Geronimus, Arline T. and J. Phillip Thompson. "To Denigrate, Ignore, or Disrupt: Racial Inequality in Health and the Impact of a Policy-Induced Breakdown of African American Communities." *Du Bois Review: Social Science Research on Race* 1, no. 2 (2004): 247–279.

Gilens, Martin. *Why Americans Hate Welfare: Race, Media, and the Politics of Antipoverty Policy*. Chicago: University of Chicago Press, 1999.

"Inequality and Democratic Responsiveness." *Public Opinion Quarterly* 69, no. 5 (2005): 778–796.

Affluence and Influence: Economic Inequality and Political Power in America. Princeton, NJ: Princeton University Press, 2012.

"The Insufficiency of 'Democracy by Coincidence': A Response to Peter K. Enns." *Perspectives on Politics* 13, no. 4 (2015): 1065–1071.

Gilens, Martin and Benjamin I. Page. "Testing Theories of American Politics: Elites, Interest Groups, and Average Citizens." *Perspectives on Politics* 12, no. 3 (2014): 564–581.

Gillion, Daniel Q. "Protest and Congressional Behavior: Assessing Racial and Ethnic Minority Protests in the District." *The Journal of Politics* 74, no. 4 (2012): 950–962.

Golder, Matt and Gabriella Lloyd. "Re-evaluating the Relationship between Electoral Rules and Ideological Congruence." *European Journal of Political Research* 53, no. 1 (2014): 200–212.

Golder, Matt and Jacek Stramski. "Ideological Congruence and Electoral Institutions." *American Journal of Political Science* 54, no. 1 (2010): 90–106.

Goldin, Claudia and Lawrence F. Katz. "The Origins of State-Level Differences in the Public Provision of Higher Education: 1890–1940." *The American Economic Review* 88, no. 2 (1998): 303–308.

Griffin, John D. and Claudia Anewalt-Remsburg. "Legislator Wealth and the Effort to Repeal the Estate Tax." *American Politics Research* 41, no. 4 (2013): 599–622.

Griffin, John D. and Brian Newman. "Are Voters Better Represented?" *The Journal of Politics* 67, no. 4 (2005): 1206–1227.

"The Unequal Representation of Latinos and Whites." *The Journal of Politics* 69, no. 4 (2007): 1032–1046.

Minority Report: Evaluating Political Equality in America. Chicago: University of Chicago Press, 2008.

Grofman, Bernard and Chandler Davidson. "The Effect of Municipal Election Structure on Black Representation in Eight Southern States." In *Quiet Revolution in the South*, eds. Chandler Davidson and Bernard Grofman. Princeton, NJ: Princeton University Press, 1994. 301–334.

Grose, Christian. "Risk and Roll Calls: How Legislators' Personal Finances Shape Congressional Decisions," working paper (2013).

Guinier, Lani. "The Supreme Court, 1993 Term: [E]Racing Democracy: The Voting Rights Cases." 108 *Harvard Law Review* 109 (1994): 109.

Hacker, Jacob S. and Paul Pierson. *Winner-Take-All Politics: How Washington Made the Rich Richer – And Turned Its Back on the Middle Class*. New York: Simon and Schuster, 2010.

Hajnal, Zoltan L. *America's Uneven Democracy: Race, Turnout, and Representation in City Politics*. Cambridge: Cambridge University Press, 2009.

Hajnal, Zoltan L. and Jeremy D. Horowitz. "Racial Winners and Losers in American Party Politics." *Perspectives on Politics* 12, no. 1 (2014): 100–118.

Hajnal, Zoltan L. and Paul G. Lewis. "Municipal Institutions and Voter Turnout in Local Elections." *Urban Affairs Review* 38, no. 5 (2003): 645–668.

Hajnal, Zoltan L. and Jessica Trounstine. "Where Turnout Matters: The Consequences of Uneven Turnout in City Politics." *The Journal of Politics* 67, no. 2 (2005): 515–535.

"Identifying and Understanding Perceived Inequities in Local Politics." *Political Research Quarterly* 67, no. 1 (2014): 56–70.

"What Underlies Urban Politics? Race, Class, Ideology, Partisanship, and the Urban Vote." *Urban Affairs Review* 50, no. 1 (2014): 63–99.

"Race and Class Inequality in Local Politics." In *The Double Bind: The Politics of Racial and Class Inequalities in the Americas*, eds. Rodney Hero, Juliet Hooker, and Alvin B. Tillery, Jr. Washington, DC: American Political Science Association, 2016.

Hayes, Danny and Jennifer L. Lawless. "As Local News Goes, So Goes Citizen Engagement: Media, Knowledge, and Participation in US House Elections." *The Journal of Politics* 77, no. 2 (2015): 447–462.

"The Decline of Local News and Its Effects: New Evidence from Longitudinal Data." *The Journal of Politics* 80, no. 1 (2018): 332–336.

Heilig, Peggy and Robert J. Mundt. *Your Voice at City Hall*. New York: SUNY Press, 1984.

Hero, Rodney E. and Morris E. Levy. "The Racial Structure of Inequality: Consequences for Welfare Policy in the United States." *Social Science Quarterly* 99, no. 2 (2018): 459–472.

Hersh, Eitan D. *Hacking the Electorate: How Campaigns Perceive Voters*. Cambridge: Cambridge University Press, 2015.

Hersh, Eitan D. *Politics Is for Power: How to Move beyond Political Hobbyism, Take Action, and Make Real Change*. New York: Simon and Schuster, 2020.

Hertel-Fernandez, Alexander, Matto Mildenberger, and Leah C. Stokes. "Legislative Staff and Representation in Congress." *American Political Science Review* 113, no. 1 (2019): 1–18.

Hill, Kim Quaile and Jan E. Leighley. "The Policy Consequences of Class Bias in State Electorates." *American Journal of Political Science* 36, no. 2 (1992): 351–365.

Hill, Kim Quaile and Tetsuya Matsubayashi. "Civic Engagement and Mass–Elite Policy Agenda Agreement in American Communities." *American Political Science Review* 99, no. 2 (2005): 215–224.

Holbrook, Thomas M. and Aaron C. Weinschenk. "Campaigns, Mobilization, and Turnout in Mayoral Elections." *Political Research Quarterly* 67, no. 1 (2014): 42–55.

Hopkins, Daniel J. and Lindsay M. Pettingill. "Retrospective Voting in Big-City US Mayoral Elections." *Political Science Research and Methods* 6, no. 4 (2018): 697–714.

Howell, Susan E. and Huey L. Perry. "Black Mayors/White Mayors: Explaining Their Approval." *Public Opinion Quarterly* 68, no. 1 (2004): 32–56.

Jackman, Simon and Bradley Spahn. "Why Does the American National Election Study Overestimate Voter Turnout?" *Political Analysis* 27, no. 2 (2019): 193–207.

Jacobs, Lawrence R. and Benjamin I. Page. "Who Influences US Foreign Policy?" *American Political Science Review* 99, no. 1 (2005): 107–123.

Jacoby, William G. "Ideological Identification and Issue Attitudes." *American Journal of Political Science* 35, no. 1 (1991): 178–205.

James, Oliver and Alice Moseley. "Does Performance Information about Public Services Affect Citizens' Perceptions, Satisfaction, and Voice Behavior? Field Experiments with Absolute and Relative Performance Information." *Public Administration* 92, no. 2 (2014): 493–511.

Jensen, Amalie, William Marble, Kenneth Scheve, and Mathew J. Slaughter. "City Limits to Partisan Polarization in the American Public," working paper, March 2019, https://williammarble.co/docs/CityLimits-Mar2019.pdf.

Jong-Sung, You and Sanjeev Khagram. "A Comparative Study of Inequality and Corruption." *American Sociological Review* 70, no. 1 (2005): 136–157.

Jost, John T. "The End of the End of Ideology." *American Psychologist* 61, no. 7 (2006): 651–670.

Jost, John T., Christopher M. Federico, and Jaime L. Napier. "Political Ideology: Its Structure, Functions, and Elective Affinities." *Annual Review of Psychology* 60 (2009): 307–337.

Kalla, Joshua L. and David E. Broockman. "Campaign Contributions Facilitate Access to Congressional Officials: A Randomized Field Experiment." *American Journal of Political Science* 60, no. 3 (2016): 545–558.

Kang, Naewon and Nojin Kwak. "A Multilevel Approach to Civic Participation: Individual Length of Residence, Neighborhood Residential Stability, and Their Interactive Effects with Media Use." *Communication Research* 30, no. 1 (2003): 80–106.

Karnig, Albert K. "Black Representation on City Councils: The Impact of District Elections and Socioeconomic Factors." *Urban Affairs Quarterly* 12, no. 2 (1976): 223–242.

"Black Resources and City Council Representation." *Journal of Politics* 41 (1979): 134–149.

Karnig, Albert K. and B. Oliver Walter. "Decline in Municipal Voter Turnout: A Function of Changing Structure." *American Politics Quarterly* 11, no. 4 (1983): 491–505.

Karnig, Albert K. and Susan Welch. *Black Representation and Urban Policy.* Chicago: University of Chicago Press, 1980.

Karp, Jeffrey A. and Susan A. Banducci. "When Politics Is Not Just a Man's Game: Women's Representation and Political Engagement." *Electoral Studies* 27, no. 1 (2008): 105–115.

Kawachi, Ichiro and Bruce P. Kennedy. "Socioeconomic Determinants of Health: Health and Social Cohesion: Why Care about Income Inequality?" *British Medical Journal* no. 314 (1997): 1037.

Kelleher Palus, Christine. "Responsiveness in American Local Governments." *State and Local Government Review* 42, no. 2 (2010): 133–150.

Key, V. O. *Southern Politics.* New York: Random House, 1949.

Klineberg, Stephen L. "Public Perceptions in Remarkable Times: Tracking Change through 24 Years of Houston Surveys." Rice University Kinder Institute for Urban Research, March 1, 2005, https://kinder.rice.edu/research/public-percep tions-remarkable-times-tracking-change-through-24-years-houston-surveys.

Kraus, Michael W. and Bennett Callaghan. "Noblesse Oblige? Social Status and Economic Inequality Maintenance among Politicians." *PLoS ONE* 9, no. 1 (2014): 1–6.

La Raja, Raymond and Brian F. Schaffner. *Campaign Finance and Political Polarization: When Purists Prevail*. Ann Arbor: University of Michigan Press, 2015.

Ladd, Helen F. and John Yinger. *Ailing Cities: Fiscal Health and the Design of Urban Policy*. Baltimore: Johns Hopkins University Press, 1989.

Lawless, Jennifer L. *Becoming a Candidate: Political Ambition and the Decision to Run for Office*. Cambridge: Cambridge University Press, 2012.

Lawless, Jennifer L. and Richard L. Fox. *It Still Takes a Candidate: Why Women Don't Run for Office*. Cambridge: Cambridge University Press, 2010.

Leal, David L., Valerie Martinez-Ebers, and Kenneth J. Meier. "The Politics of Latino Education: The Biases of At-Large Elections." *The Journal of Politics* 66, no. 4 (2004): 1224–1244.

Leighley, Jan E. and Jonathan Nagler. *Who Votes Now? Demographics, Issues, Inequality, and Turnout in the United States*. Princeton, NJ: Princeton University Press, 2013.

Lijphart, Arend. "Unequal Participation: Democracy's Unresolved Dilemma: Presidential Address, American Political Science Association, 1996." *American Political Science Review* 91, no. 1 (1997): 1–14.

Lineberry, Robert L. and Edmund P. Fowler. "Reformism and Public Policies in American Cities." *American Political Science Review* 61, no. 3 (1967): 701–716.

Lobao, Linda. "The Rising Importance of Local Government in the United States: Recent Research and Challenges for Sociology." *Sociology Compass* 10, no. 10 (2016): 893–905.

Lublin, David. "Racial Redistricting and African-American Representation: A Critique of 'Do Majority-Minority Districts Maximize Substantive Black Representation in Congress?'" *The American Political Science Review* 93, no. 1 (1999): 183–186.

Luttmer, Erso F. P. "Group Loyalty and the Taste of Redistribution." *Journal of Political Economy* 109, no. 5 (2001): 500–528.

MacKuen, Michael B., Robert S. Erikson, James A. Stimson, and Kathleen Knight. "Elections and the Dynamics of Ideological Representation." In *Electoral Democracy*, eds. Michael B. MacKuen and George Rabinowitz. Ann Arbor: University of Michigan Press, 2003. 200.

MacManus, Susan A. "City Council Election Procedures and Minority Representation: Are They Related?" *Social Science Quarterly* 59 (1978): 153–161.

Mansbridge, Jane. "Should Blacks Represent Blacks and Women Represent Women? A Contingent 'Yes.'" *The Journal of Politics* 61, no. 3 (1999): 628–657.

Marschall, Melissa and John Lappie. "Turnout in Local Elections: Is Timing Really Everything?" *Election Law Journal* 17, no. 3 (2018): 221–233.

Marschall, Melissa J. and Anirudh V. S. Ruhil. "Substantive Symbols: The Attitudinal Dimension of Black Political Incorporation in Local Government." *American Journal of Political Science* 51, no. 1 (2007): 17–33.

Marschall, Melissa J., Anirudh V. S. Ruhil, and Paru R. Shah. "The New Racial Calculus: Electoral Institutions and Black Representation in Local Legislatures." *American Journal of Political Science* 54, no. 1 (2010): 107–124.

Martin, Gregory J. and Joshua McCrain. "Local News and National Politics." *American Political Science Review* 113, no. 2 (2019): 372–384.

Martin, Paul S. and Michele P. Claibourn. "Citizen Participation and Congressional Responsiveness: New Evidence that Participation Matters." *Legislative Studies Quarterly* 38, no. 1 (2013): 59–81.

Mason, Liliana. *Uncivil Agreement: How Politics Became Our Identity*. Chicago: University of Chicago Press, 2018.

Matsubayashi, Tetsuya and Rene R. Rocha. "Racial Diversity and Public Policy in the States." *Political Research Quarterly* 65, no. 3 (2012): 600–614.

Mayhew, David. *Congress: The Electoral Connection*. New Haven, CT: Yale University Press, 1974.

Mill, John Stuart. "*On Liberty.*" In *Collected Works of John Stuart Mill*, ed. J. Robson. Toronto: University of Toronto Press, 1997. 213–310.

Miller, Warren E. and Donald E. Stokes. "Constituency Influence in Congress." *American Political Science Review* 57, no. 1 (1963): 45–56.

Mladenka, Kenneth R. "Blacks and Hispanics in Urban Politics." *American Political Science Review* 83, no. 1 (1989): 165–191.

Mundt, Robert J. and Peggy Heilig. "District Representation: Demands and Effects in the Urban South." *Journal of Politics* 44, no. 4 (1982): 1035–1048.

Nazroo, James Y. "The Structuring of Ethnic Inequalities in Health: Economic Position, Racial Discrimination, and Racism." *American Journal of Public Health* 93, no. 2 (2003): 277–284.

Niven, David. "The Mobilization Solution? Face-to-Face Contact and Voter Turnout in a Municipal Election." *The Journal of Politics* 66, no. 3 (2004): 868–884.

Nivola, Pietro S. *Tense Commandments: Federal Prescriptions and City Problems*. Washington, DC: Brookings Institution Press, 2002.

Oliver, J. Eric. *Democracy in Suburbia*. Princeton, NJ: Princeton University Press, 2001.

Oliver, J. Eric, Shang E. Ha, and Zachary Callen. *Local Elections and the Politics of Small-Scale Democracy*. Princeton, NJ: Princeton University Press, 2012.

Page, Benjamin I., Larry M. Bartels, and Jason Seawright. "Democracy and the Policy Preferences of Wealthy Americans." *Perspectives on Politics* 11, no. 1 (2013): 51–73.

Panagopoulos, Costas. "Positive Social Pressure and Prosocial Motivation: Evidence from a Large-Scale Field Experiment on Voter Mobilization." *Political Psychology* 34, no. 2 (2013): 265–275.

Pantoja, Adrian D. and Gary M. Segura. "Does Ethnicity Matter? Descriptive Representation in Legislatures and Political Alienation among Latinos." *Social Science Quarterly* 84, no. 2 (2003): 441–460.

Paolino, Phillip. "Group-Salient Issues and Group Representation: Support for Women Candidates in the 1992 Senate Elections." *American Journal of Political Science* no. 2 (1995): 294–313.

Peterson, Paul E. *City Limits*. Chicago: University of Chicago Press, 1981.

   The Price of Federalism. Washington, DC: Brookings Institution Press, 1995.

Phillips, Anne. *The Politics of Presence*. Oxford: Clarendon Press, 1995.

   "Democracy and Representation: Or, Why Should It Matter Who Our Representatives are?" In *Feminism and Politics*, ed. Anne Phillips. Oxford: Oxford University Press, 1998. 224–241.

Piston, Spencer. "How Explicit Racial Prejudice Hurt Obama in the 2008 Election." *Political Behavior* 32, no. 4 (2010): 431–451.

Pitkin, Hanna F. *The Concept of Representation*. Berkeley: University of California Press, 1967.

Polinard, Jerry, Robert Wrinkle, and Tomas Longoria. "The Impact of District Elections on the Mexican American Community: The Electoral Perspective." *Social Science Quarterly* 72, no. 3 (1991): 608–614.

Poterba James M. "Demographic Structure and the Political Economy of Public Education." *Journal of Policy Analysis and Management* 16, no. 1 (1997): 48–66.

Powell Jr., G. Bingham. "The Ideological Congruence Controversy: The Impact of Alternative Measures, Data, and Time Periods on the Effects of Election Rules." *Comparative Political Studies* 42, no. 12 (2009): 1475–1497.

   "Representation in Context: Election Laws and Ideological Congruence between Citizens and Governments." *Perspectives on Politics* 11, no. 1 (2013): 9–21.

Preuhs, Robert R. "The Conditional Effects of Minority Descriptive Representation: Black Legislators and Policy Influence in the American States." *The Journal of Politics* 68, no. 3 (2006): 585–599.

   "Descriptive Representation as a Mechanism to Mitigate Policy Backlash: Latino Incorporation and Welfare Policy in the American States." *Political Research Quarterly* 60, no. 2 (2007): 277–292.

Preuhs, Robert R. and Rodney E. Hero. "A Different Kind of Representation: Black and Latino Descriptive Representation and the Role of Ideological Cuing." *Political Research Quarterly* 64, no. 1 (2011): 157–171.

Prior, Markus. *Post-Broadcast Democracy: How Media Choice Increases Inequality in Political Involvement and Polarizes Elections*. Cambridge: Cambridge University Press, 2007.

Putnam, Robert D. "E Pluribus Unum: Diversity and Community in the Twenty-First Century: The 2006 Johan Skytte Prize Lecture." *Scandinavian Political Studies* 30, no. 2 (2007): 137–174.

Rae, Douglas W. *City: Urbanism and Its End*. New Haven, CT: Yale University Press, 2003.

Rahn, Wendy M. and Thomas J. Rudolph. "A Tale of Political Trust in American Cities." *Public Opinion Quarterly* 69, no. 4 (2005): 530–560.

Rhodes, Jesse H. "Learning Citizenship? How State Education Reforms Affect Parents' Political Attitudes and Behavior." *Political Behavior* 37, no. 1 (2015): 181–220.

Rhodes, Jesse H. and Brian F. Schaffner. 2017. "Testing Models of Unequal Representation: Democratic Populists and Republican Oligarchs?" *Quarterly Journal of Political Science* 12, no. 2 (2017): 185–204.

Rhodes, Jesse H., Brian F. Schaffner, and Sean McElwee. "Is America More Divided by Race or Class? Race, Income, and Attitudes among Whites, African Americans, and Latinos." *The Forum* 15, no. 1 (2017): 71–91.

Rigby, Elizabeth and Gerald C. Wright. "Political Parties and Representation of the Poor in the American States." *American Journal of Political Science* 57, no. 3 (2013): 552–565.

Rocha, Rene R., Caroline J. Tolbert, Daniel C. Bowen, and Christopher J. Clark. "Race and Turnout: Does Descriptive Representation in State Legislatures Increase Minority Voting?" *Political Research Quarterly* 63, no. 4 (2010): 890–907.

Rosenstone, Steven J. and John Mark Hansen. *Mobilization, Participation, and Democracy in America.* New York: Macmillan Publishing Company, 1993.

Rubado, Meghan E. and Jay T. Jennings. "Political Consequences of the Endangered Local Watchdog: Newspaper Decline and Mayoral Elections in the United States," *Urban Affairs Review* (2019), https://doi.org/10.1177/1078087419838058.

Sances, Michael W. "When Voters Matter: The Growth and Limits of Local Government Responsiveness," working paper, August 2, 2017, https://astro.temple.edu/~tul67793/papers/polarization.pdf.

Sances, Michael W. and Hye Young You. "Who Pays for Government? Descriptive Representation and Exploitative Revenue Sources." *The Journal of Politics* 79, no. 3 (2017): 1090–1094.

Sapiro, Virginia. "When Are Interests Interesting? The Problem of Political Representation of Women." *American Political Science Review* 75, no. 3 (1981): 701–716.

Sass, Tim R. and Stephen L. Mehay. "The Voting Rights Act, District Elections, and the Success of Black Candidates in Municipal Elections." *The Journal of Law & Economics* 38, no. 2 (1995): 367–392.

"Minority Representation, Election Method, and Policy Influence." *Economics & Politics* 15, no. 3 (2003): 323–339.

Sass, Tim R. and Bobby J. Pittman. "The Changing Impact of Electoral Structure on Black Representation in the South, 1970–1996." *Public Choice* 104, nos. 3–4 (2000): 369–388.

Schaffner, Brian F. and Matthew J. Streb. "The Partisan Heuristic in Low-Information Elections." *Public Opinion Quarterly* 66, no. 4 (2002): 559–581.

Schaffner, Brian F., Matthew Streb, and Gerald Wright. "Teams without Uniforms: the Nonpartisan Ballot in State and Local Elections." *Political Research Quarterly* 54, no. 1 (2001): 7–30.

Schlozman, Kay Lehman, Sidney Verba, and Henry E. Brady. *The Unheavenly Chorus: Unequal Political Voice and the Broken Promise of American Democracy.* Princeton, NJ: Princeton University Press, 2013.

Schulhofer-Wohl, Sam and Miguel Garrido. "Do Newspapers Matter? Short-Run and Long-Run Evidence from the Closure of The Cincinnati Post." *Journal of Media Economics* 26, no. 2 (2013): 60–81.

Scrugg, Lyle and Thomas J. Hayes. "The Influence of Inequality on Welfare Generosity: Evidence from the US States." *Politics & Society* 45, no. 1 (2017): 35–66.

Shah, Paru. "Racing toward Representation: A Hurdle Model of Latino Incorporation." *American Politics Research* 38, no. 1 (2010): 84–109.

Shah, Paru R., Melissa J. Marschall, and Anirudh V. S. Ruhil. "Are We There Yet? The Voting Rights Act and Black Representation on City Councils, 1981–2006." *Journal of Politics* 75, no. 4 (2013): 993–1008.

Shaker, Lee. "Dead Newspapers and Citizens' Civic Engagement." *Political Communication* 31, no. 1 (2014): 131–148.

Shor, Boris and Nolan McCarty. "The Ideological Mapping of American Legislatures." *American Political Science Review* 105, no. 3 (2011): 530–551.

Solt, Frederick. "Economic Inequality and Democratic Political Engagement." *American Journal of Political Science* 52, no. 1 (2008): 48–60.

"Does Economic Inequality Depress Electoral Participation? Testing the Schattschneider Hypothesis." *Political Behavior* 32, no. 2 (2010): 285–301.

Soroka, Stuart N. and Christopher Wlezien. "On the Limits to Inequality in Representation." *PS: Political Science & Politics* 41, no. 2 (2008): 319–327.

Stiglitz, Joseph E. "Inequality and Economic Growth." In *Rethinking Capitalism*, eds. Michael Jacobs and Mariana Mazzucato. Chichester: Wiley, 2016. 134–155.

Stimson, James A., Michael B. MacKuen, and Robert S. Erikson. "Dynamic Representation." *American Political Science Review* 89, no. 3 (1995): 543–565.

Straayer, John A., Robert D. Wrinkle, and Jerry L. Polinard. *State and Local Politics*. New York: St. Martin's Press, 1994.

Taebel, Delbert. "Minority Representation on City Councils: The Impact of Structure on Blacks and Hispanics." *Social Science Quarterly* 59, no. 1 (1978): 142–152.

Tausanovitch, Chris and Christopher Warshaw. "Measuring Constituent Policy Preferences in Congress, State Legislatures, and Cities." *The Journal of Politics* 75, no. 2 (2013): 330–342.

"Representation in Municipal Government." *American Political Science Review* 108, no. 3 (2014): 605–641.

Tesler, Michael. *Post-Racial or Most-Racial? Race and Politics in the Obama Era*. Chicago: University of Chicago Press, 2016.

Tiebout, Charles M. "A Pure Theory of Local Expenditures." *Journal of Political Economy* 64, no. 5 (1956): 416–424.

de Tocqueville, Alexis. *Democracy in America*. New York: Regnery Publishing, 2003.

Trebbi, Francesco, Philippe Aghion, and Alberto Alesina. "Electoral Rules and Minority Representation in US Cities." *The Quarterly Journal of Economics* 123, no. 1 (2008): 325–357.

Trounstine, Jessica. "Representation and Accountability in Cities." *Annual Review of Political Science* 13 (2010): 407–423.

"Segregation and Inequality in Public Goods." *American Journal of Political Science* 60, no. 3 (2016): 709–725.

Trounstine, Jessica and Melody E. Valdini. "The Context Matters: The Effects of Single-Member versus At-Large Districts on City Council Diversity." *American Journal of Political Science* 52, no. 3 (2008): 554–569.

Ura, Joseph Daniel and Christopher R. Ellis. "Income, Preferences, and the Dynamics of Policy Responsiveness." *PS: Political Science & Politics* 41, no. 4 (2008): 785–794.

Uslaner, Eric M. and Bo Rothstein. "The Historical Roots of Corruption: State Building, Economic Inequality, and Mass Education." *Comparative Politics* 48, no. 2 (2016): 227–248.

van Holm, Eric Joseph. "Unequal Cities, Unequal Participation: The Effect of Income Inequality on Civic Engagement." *The American Review of Public Administration* 49, no. 2 (2019): 135–144.

Van Ryzin, Gregg G., Douglas Muzzio, and Stephen Immerwahr. "Explaining the Race Gap in Satisfaction with Urban Services." *Urban Affairs Review* 39, no. 5 (2004): 613–632.

Verba, Sidney. "Would the Dream of Political Equality Turn Out to Be a Nightmare?" *Perspectives on Politics* 1, no. 4 (2003): 663–679.

Verba, Sidney, Kay Lehman Schlozman, and Henry E. Brady. *Voice and Equality: Civic Voluntarism in American Politics*. Cambridge, MA: Harvard University Press, 1995.

Voorheis, John, Nolan McCarty, and Boris Shor. "Unequal Incomes, Ideology and Gridlock: How Rising Inequality Increases Political Polarization," SSRN paper, August 21, 2015, https://papers.ssrn.com/sol3/papers.cfm?abstract_id=2649215.

Warshaw, Christopher. "Local Elections and Representation in the United States." *Annual Review of Political Science* (2019), https://doi.org/10.1146/annurev-polisci-050317-071108.

Weaver, Vesla M. "The Electoral Consequences of Skin Color: The 'Hidden' Side of Race in Politics." *Political Behavior* 34, no. 1 (2012): 159–192.

Welch, Susan. "The Impact of At-Large Elections on the Representation of Blacks and Hispanics." *The Journal of Politics* 52, no. 4 (1990): 1050–1076.

Welch, Susan and Timothy Bledsoe. *Urban Reform and Its Consequences: A Study in Representation*. Chicago: University of Chicago Press, 1988.

Whitby, Kenny J. "The Effect of Black Descriptive Representation on Black Electoral Turnout in the 2004 Elections." *Social Science Quarterly* 88, no. 4 (2007): 1010–1023.

Wilkinson, Richard G. and Kate E. Pickett. "Income Inequality and Population Health: A Review and Explanation of the Evidence." *Social Science & Medicine* 62, no. 7 (2006): 1768–1784.

Winters, Jeffrey A. and Benjamin I. Page. "Oligarchy in the United States?" *Perspectives on Politics* 7, no. 4 (2009): 731–751.

Wright, Gerald C. and Brian F. Schaffner. "The Influence of Party: Evidence from the State Legislatures." *American Political Science Review* 96, no. 2 (2002): 367–379.

Wrinkle, Robert D. and Jerry L. Polinard. "Structural Choices and Representational Biases: The Post-Election Color of Representation." *American Journal of Political Science* 49, no. 4 (2005): 758–768.

Index

absolute value
  as ideological measure, 71
Achen, Christopher, 113
African American
  representation, ideological congruence,
    209
African Americans
  descriptive representation, 150–151
  descriptive representation, districting
    effects on, 151
  ideological congruence, 118
  ideology of, 69–70, 72, 91, 145, 161
  ideology, socioeconomic effects on, 157
  representation, ideological, 136
  representation, ideological congruence,
    38, 132, 144, 151–152, 160
  representation, ideological congrunce,
    158
  representation, policy, 162
Aiken, South Carolina, 191–192, 194, 212
Ashburn, Georgia, 131, 135
Atlanta, Georgia, 62
audit experiments, 8

Baldwin, Louisiana, 131–132, 135
Bartels, Larry, 113
bias
  class, 13, 19
  demographic, municipal candidates, 97
  economic, 18, 83
  gender, municipal candidates, 98
  ideological, against African Americans
    and Latinos, 137

  racial, 13, 18–19, 83, 232
  socioeconomic, municipal candidates, 97
Blackburn, Maryline, 111
blacks
  ideology of, 220
  representation, coincidental, 144, 153,
    158
  representation, descriptive, 153
  representation, ideological, 151
  representation, ideological congruence,
    119, 142, 153
  representation, public policy, 150
Bolivar, Tennessee, 161
Boston, Massachusetts, 26–27, 46
Brookhaven, Mississippi, 103, 129, 224
Brown, Michael, 213

Carnes, Nicholas, 169–170
Carson, Ben, 3
Catalist, 12, 41–51, 55, 59, 64, 82, 88–90,
  99, 108, 123, 171, 220
CCES. *See* Cooperative Congressional
  Election Study
Chicago, Illinois, 89
Coincidental Representation Lens,
  24–27
Community Development Block Grant
  (CDBG), 193
Community HOME Investment Program
  (CHIP), 193
compound republic, 4
congruence
  ideological, 145, 197

Made in the USA
Middletown, DE
11 January 2022

58431879R00165